gilbert
LAW SUMMARIES

DICTIONARY OF LEGAL TERMS

First Edition

HARCOURT BRACE LEGAL AND PROFESSIONAL PUBLICATIONS, INC.
EDITORIAL OFFICES: 176 W. Adams, Suite 2100, Chicago, IL 60603

gilbert
LAW SUMMARIES

REGIONAL OFFICES: New York, Chicago, Los Angeles, Washington, D.C.
Distributed by: **Harcourt Brace & Company** 6277 Sea Harbor Drive, Orlando, FL 32887 (800)787-8717

[redacted]

PROJECT EDITOR
Elizabeth L. Snyder, B.A., J.D.
Attorney at Law

QUALITY CONTROL EDITOR
Ann R. Kerns, B.A.

SUMMARY OF CONTENTS

Preface

To someone first encountering the terminology of American law and the legal profession, "legalese" may seem somewhat like a foreign language. Indeed, the Latin phrases, complicated definitions of unfamiliar terms, and the specialized meanings of common words do give the legal field a language all its own. The purpose of the Gilbert Dictionary of Legal Terms is to provide the beginning law student (or any person encountering legal jargon) with a convenient, easy-to-understand reference guide.

The Gilbert Dictionary of Legal Terms defines over 3500 words and phrases in straightforward, layperson's language, without sacrificing the substantial legal meanings and applications. But defining these terms is only part of learning a new vocabulary. To aid the law student in the considerable task of learning to ***use*** the legal vocabulary, the Dictionary includes the following features:

1) Examples to clarify and apply the defining terms;
2) Clear distinctions between shades of meanings;
3) Cross-referencing between related entries; and
4) Notations as to specific areas of law to which the terms apply.

Also included as reference materials are the Declaration of Independence, the Constitution of the United States, a Table of Periodical Abbreviations, and a Table of Federal Governmental Agencies and Departments.

The entries in the Gilbert Dictionary of Legal Terms encompass the most common words and definitions in the legal vocabulary. The Dictionary is designed as a portable reference guide, abridged for convenience and facility. With this book in hand, the law student should soon come to understand the language of the law.

A

A.B.A.: *See* American Bar Association.
abandonment: Knowing relinquishment of one's right or claim to property without passing rights to another and with no intention to reclaim possession. Desertion of one's spouse or child.
ab ante: Lat. Before; in advance.
abatement: A decrease or termination of something—*e.g.*, abatement of taxes: a rebate of taxes previously paid or a decrease in an assessed valuation; abatement of action: ending or dismissal of lawsuit; abatement of legacy: reduction or extinction of a bequest due to insufficient funds or payment of debt.
abdicate: To give up completely; to renounce.
abduction: The criminal taking of a person by fraud, persuasion, or violence. Common law: taking of females for purpose of marriage, cohabitation, or prostitution. Civil law: taking of another's wife.
abet: To encourage, incite, or assist another in the commission of a crime with knowledge of its wrongfulness.
abettor: Person who incites, encourages, or commands another to commit a crime. Abettor must share criminal intent.
abeyance: State of being in waiting, expectation, or suspension; an undetermined or unsettled state of affairs. Property held "in abeyance" means there is a lapse in succession of ownership, and title is held in expectation of rightful owner.
abide: To comply with a decision; to accept the consequences of; to await a result.
ab initio: Lat. From the beginning. *E.g.*, a contract, deed, or marriage is said to be either lawful or void ab initio.
abjuration: The act of taking an oath to renounce or abandon an allegiance or right. *E.g.*, a citizen of a foreign country abjures allegiance to that country upon becoming a citizen of the United States.
abortion: The premature termination of a pregnancy. It may be spontaneous (*i.e.*, taking place unexpectedly) or induced (*i.e.*, intentionally removing a fetus from the womb thereby terminating its life).
abrogation: The annulment or cancellation of a law by legislative act, constitutional authority, or usage.
abscond: To hide or secretly travel out of a court's jurisdiction in order to avoid the legal process.
absolute: Final, complete, unconditional. *E.g.*, an absolute bond is perfect in itself and has no restrictions upon it.
absque hoc: Lat. Without this. Words of denial used to introduce the negative part of a plea.
abstention: Doctrine whereby a federal court relinquishes its jurisdiction to a state court; it is often used to avoid conflict between federal and state affairs.
abstract of title: A condensed history of the title to a piece of land listing all conveyances, liens, and liabilities on it.
abuse: Misuse; mistreat physically or mentally.
abuse of discretion: Failure to exercise sound legal discretion. The term is used as a rationale by an appellate court when it is of the opinion that a lower court made an error of law by ruling contrary to evidence, logic, or reason.
abuse of process: The improper use of the legal process, after it has been issued, for a reason other than that intended by law, *e.g.*, prosecuting a person in order to intimidate him.
abut: To touch; to border on, as where a lot touches another.
abuttals: The boundaries to a piece of property. Also has been used to express the end (as distinguished from side) boundary lines of a property.
acceleration: A shortening of the time required before an event will take place, such as the enjoyment of property rights.
acceleration clause: A provision in a credit agreement which allows a lender of money to call a debt due for failure of borrower to meet some obligation, such as to pay taxes or special assessment on mortgaged property.
acceptance: Consenting to specific terms of an offer thereby forming a binding contract. Act of receiving goods with the intention of keeping them. Act by which a buyer takes title to property. Act of a bank

promising to pay person named on a negotiable instrument.

access: The means or right to approach, as in the unobstructed ability to get to and from one's property, the ability to get from street to a place of business, a spouse's opportunity to have sexual intercourse with his or her partner.

accession: Acquiring a right to the thing that becomes part of something else already owned, *e.g.*, the vegetation that grows on one's property.

accessory: One who, in a secondary role, knowingly aids or contributes to the commission of a crime. An "accessory before the fact" counsels, encourages, or commands another to commit a crime, but is not present during its actual commission. An "accessory after the fact" knows of the crime yet still aids criminal afterwards, such as by comforting or hiding him.

accident: An unexpected, unforeseen event happening by chance. Term does not eliminate consideration of negligence on part of person who caused accident.

accommodation paper (note): A bill or note signed, without consideration, by one person to help another get a loan. The person who signed note freely lends his credit to the accommodated party, and is called the "accommodation maker."

accomplice: One who knowingly, voluntarily and with common criminal intent aids another in the commission or attempted commission of a crime; one who is guilty of complicity in a crime.

accord: Agreement to settle differences; agreement that a debt obligation be settled for less than the person owed the debt is entitled. It constitutes a contract and, after performance, bars further action.

accord and satisfaction: Payment of a disputed debt, often for less than debtor is entitled, which satisfactorily settles obligation for all concerned.

account: A written record of money received or paid. An unsettled claim between a debtor and creditor. Money deposited in a bank, such as a savings or checking account.

accountant: Person skilled in keeping financial records. A Certified Public Accountant (C.P.A.) is one who has met certain requirements and is licensed to practice as a public accountant.

accounts receivable: List of money owed to a person or entity; a debt.

accredit: To give official recognition or approval, especially to approve of a school for having met academic standards, or to recognize an envoy to a foreign country.

accretion: The act of adding to something, especially small bits of land added by action of water. The right of an heir to add to his estate the inheritance of a co-heir who is unable or refuses to take his inheritance.

accrual basis: Method of accounting which shows expenses incurred and income earned during a tax year; expenses need not have been paid to be deductible nor income received to be taxed.

accrue: To increase; to grow, as accrued interest is added to principal, and accrued profits on an investment are those due and payable.

accumulative sentence (judgment): An additional sentence imposed on a person already convicted of and sentenced for another offense. Second sentence begins when previous one expires.

accusation: A formal charge, made in court, that a person or corporation is guilty of a punishable offense.

accused: Person charged with the commission of a crime; the defendant. He is not called "the accused" until after an indictment or information is returned against him, or until he is restrained after an arrest.

acknowledgment: An admission or declaration that a thing is genuine. It is used in: "acknowledgment of paternity" where an individual admits his parental relationship; "acknowledgment of debt" where debtor admits his obligation to creditor; and in "acknowledgment instrument" which is a formal document attested to before a proper public officer.

acquiescence: Quiet approval or compliance; lack of disapproval. When questioned about a crime, for example, a person's acquiescence may imply guilt or consent.

acquit: To set free or discharge from accusation or obligation; to declare an accused innocent.

act: A law passed by a legislative body. A deed performed voluntarily.

action: A judicial proceeding in which a person demands the protection of his or her rights, or in which he or she prosecutes another for a wrong done. The term covers all the formal court proceedings including its decision and the enforcement of penalties. "Action" is used with various words to designate a particular area of lawsuit, *e.g.*, class action, civil action, criminal action. Conduct; behavior.

actionable: An act or occurrence that provides grounds for a lawsuit.

act of God: An event caused solely by the forces of nature, *e.g.*, an earthquake.

actual cash value: The fair and reasonable price for which an item or piece of property would sell on the open market. Also "fair market price."

actual notice: Express information of facts or circumstances from which it can be reasonably inferred that a party was notified of those facts and circumstances; the notice actually given to convey such information.

actuary: Statistician who calculates insurance and pension rates and premiums, and the value of annuities based on known risk and probability factors.
actus reus: At common law, the requisite criminal act accompanying the mens rea resulting in criminal culpability.
ad damnum: Lat. To the damages. The clause in a complaint which states the amount of damages or money loss being claimed.
addict: Person whose habitual use of narcotics, alcohol, or tobacco has become out of his or her control, and who may endanger the public morals, health, safety, or welfare.
additur: Lat. It is increased. The power of the court to increase the amount of damages awarded to a plaintiff by a jury as a condition for denying a new trial to a plaintiff if the defendant agrees to pay the plaintiff extra money. *Compare* remittitur.
adduce: To present, introduce, or state; used especially with reference to proof or evidence.
ademption: Revocation or taking away of a legacy by an act of the testator. It occurrs when a testator, while living, gives the bequest to the legatee or substitutes another bequest for that mentioned in the will. It also can occur when the testator does something to make it impossible for his or her will to be carried out, *e.g.*, if testator disposed of property before he or she died.
adequate: Sufficient; suitable; enough. "Adequate consideration" is a fair and reasonable consideration (or thing of value) under the circumstances. "Adequate compensation" is the fair market value of property.
adhesion contract: A one-sided contract, unilaterally written by a party who offers it to another on a "take it or leave it" basis. The accepting party has virtually no choice or bargaining power in reference to the contract's terms.
ad hoc: Lat. For this, for a particular purpose. Ad hoc committees are set up to handle special problems.
ad hominem: Lat. To the person. Most often used with argument. Ad hominem arguments are personal attacks directed not at an opponent's position but at his person.
ad idem: Lat. To the same thing, result, or idea, as in when two pieces of evidence prove the same thing.
ad infinitum: Lat. Infinitely, without end.
adjective law: The body of law that governs the procedure of the courts as opposed to the law that the courts administer (substantive law). It prescribes the method by which the courts operate.
adjourn: To postpone, put off or suspend business until a later time.
adjudicate: To act as a judge; to settle.
adjudication: The formal rendering of a final judgment in court.
adjuration: An oath.
adjuster: Person who settles or adjusts a matter as an insurance adjuster settles a claim against the insurance company by an insured person.
adjustment: The process of settling a claim; the actual settlement. An insurance adjustment ascertains the value of a property loss and the liability of the parties involved.
ad litem: Lat. For the suit. A guardian ad litem, for example, may be appointed by the court to handle a suit of an infant.
administration: The management of the estate of a deceased person. The management of a business or country. The body of people who work in the executive branch of government.
administrative law: Body of law that governs the running of administrative agencies. The rules and regulations created by administrative agencies, *e.g.*, the income tax laws.
administrator/administratrix (female): A person appointed by the court to manage an estate, as compared to an "executor" who is named by the person in the will.
admiralty law: Maritime law; body of law relating to activities at sea such as commerce, navigation, contracts, or torts.
admissible evidence: Evidence which may be introduced in court and considered by a jury; evidence which the court is bound to allow to be introduced. Note, though, that evidence which is otherwise admissible may be withheld from consideration if a judge determines its probative value is outweighed by other factors, such as if it misleads or prejudices the jury.
admission: A voluntary acknowledgment of the existence of facts which are usually favorable to an adversary. An admission is not limited to statements, but may be inferred from a person's conduct. An admission is not the same as a confession and does not imply guilt.
admonition: A judge's statement of advice, warning, or reprimand given to a jury, counsel, or an accused person.
adoption: The act of accepting a child born to another person as one's own with all the rights and responsibilities of parenthood. Passage of a bill into law. The acceptance or appropriation of a thing, such as property, as one's own.
adulteration: The act of mixing an inferior substance into the superior or pure product. It occurs with reference to drugs, cosmetics, foods, and drinks, and produces an inferior or even harmful product.

adultery: Voluntary sexual intercourse between a married person and someone not his or her spouse. It is grounds for divorce.
ad valorem: Lat. According to value. An ad valorem tax varies according to the value of the thing taxed, *e.g.*, property tax or sales tax.
adversary: An opponent in a lawsuit.
adversary proceeding: Legal proceeding involving opposing parties.
adverse interest: Interest opposed to one's own interest. Having adverse interest sometimes disqualifies a person from being a witness.
adverse party: The party whose interests are opposed to another party in a lawsuit.
adverse possession: Method of acquiring title to real property by openly occupying land for a continuous period of time set by statute. Occupancy must be hostile, that is, occupying party does not recognize title of actual holder, and he uses property without permission of the title holder. Occupant should visibly display his intent to claim and hold property.
advice: Opinion given by counsel to a client.
advisement: Consideration; deliberation. A case "under advisement" means the judge postpones a decision until after a period of consideration of evidence and arguments.
advisory opinion: Formal opinion given by a judge about a matter of law which has no binding effect. It is often given in response to questions of law asked by a legislative body or government official.
advocate: (Noun) One who speaks in favor of a cause or another person. A lawyer. (Verb) To speak in favor of; to support.
affiance: To promise to marry.
affiant: Person who makes and swears to the truth of a written statement or affidavit.
affidavit: A written statement sworn to or affirmed before a person with authority to witness the oath.
affiliate: Something allied, connected, or closely associated with a larger group. To join or closely associate with.
affiliation: A close association; used legally to mean the act of determining the parentage of a child.
affinity: Close attraction or relationship between persons, especially the relationship a person has to his or her spouse's blood relatives.
affirm: To confirm, reassert, or agree with, especially when a higher court supports a lower court's decision. To make a formal declaration about the truth of something in place of an oath.
affirmative action: Action taken to remedy a situation, especially discriminatory practices against minorities, the handicapped, or women. Action may involve hiring, promotion, or testing practices, and can be court-ordered, voluntary, or result from the organization's status as a federal contractor.
affirmative defense: A defendant's answer to a complaint which is more than a denial of the plaintiff's charge, and which presents evidence or arguments in favor of the defendant. *E.g.*, insanity, self-defense, and duress are pleas used in criminal cases which are affirmative defenses.
affirmative relief: Compensation or benefit owed to a defendant. It may come from an independent action by the defendant in which he proves his right to compensation.
affix: To attach, fasten to, or add on, as when a building is affixed to property. To inscribe or impress upon, as when a seal is affixed to a document.
affray: A fight in a public place which disturbs others.
affreightment: Contract made with a shipowner in which owner agrees to carry goods.
aforesaid: Already mentioned.
aforethought: Planned; premeditated; thought of beforehand.
a fortiori: Lat. With greater reason. Term is used in logic to mean if one thing is true then a thing which it encompasses or is less than it is also true; *e.g.*, if a person is dead, then a fortiori, he is not breathing.
against the weight of the evidence: Contrary to the evidence presented. A trial judge may set aside a verdict and order a new trial if he or she feels the verdict is clearly contrary to the evidence of the case. It is not proper for a judge to do this unless it can be clearly seen that the jury made a mistake or acted under a bias or with an improper motive, any of which would result in a miscarriage of justice.
agency: A fiduciary relationship in which one party represents another by the latter's authority. The relationship can be between an agent and a principal, in which case the agent acts for the principal by, for example, handling his finances; between a master and a servant, that is, between an employer and an employee; or between an employer and an independent contractor. The place where an agent operates. A branch of government, *e.g.*, a police department.
agent: A person who is authorized to act on behalf of another.
aggravated assault: Purposely causing or attempting to cause serious bodily injury to another. Definition varies according to statute, sometimes referring to an assault with intent to commit murder, rape, or robbery, and other times to the degree of fear inflicted by an assault. *See* assault.
aggravation: Circumstances tending to increase the seriousness or add to the injury of a crime, but which are not part of the actual crime itself, *e.g.*, malicious threats to inflict bodily harm on a kidnap victim.

aggrieved party: One whose personal or property rights have been violated or threatened. One who suffered a loss, which may have resulted from a judgment or decree operated against him.
agreement: A meeting of minds; a consensus between two or more parties which affects their legal rights and duties. Term is broader than "contract," as it may lack some requirement of a contract.
aid and abet: To knowingly, purposefully, and actively help in the commission of a crime. It can be by words, acts, or presence so long as person assisted in perpetration of a crime. One who aids and abets is liable as a principal.
air rights: Right to use the air space above a piece of real estate, *e.g.*, the right to build a bridge over a road.
alderman: Person elected to a city council; councilman.
aleatory contract: A contract in which performance by one party depends on the occurrence of an uncertain or contingent event; *e.g.*, life insurance is aleatory.
alia enormia: Lat. Other wrongs. Term used to claim additional injuries for a plaintiff.
alias: Short for Latin "alias dictus," meaning otherwise called, or another name by which a person is known. Abbreviation is a.k.a. for "also known as."
alibi: Account of a person's activities and whereabouts at the time a crime was committed which is used as a defense to show it was impossible for him to commit the crime.
alien: A foreigner; a person who is not a citizen of the country in which he is living. An alien does have the right to protection of life, liberty, and property afforded under the due process clause of the Constitution. A "resident alien" has permanent resident status but is not a citizen.
alienate: To transfer or convey title to property.
alienation: The voluntary and complete transfer of title and possession of real property. "Alienation clause" is a provision in an insurance policy which voids the policy when a transfer of ownership occurs.
alienation of affection: A malicious and willful interference with a marital relationship by a third party. It deprives a person of the affection of his or her spouse, and can result from embarrassing, disgracing, humiliating, or inflicting mental anguish on one of the spouses. *Note*: Many states have abolished this as a cause of action.
alimony: Payments made by a divorced or separated husband to his ex-wife (or vice versa) for her support. The amount is court-ordered. Alimony is based on the common law duty a husband has for the support of his wife.
aliquot: Lat. Literally means contained an exact number or times in something else. As applied to trusts it means a fractional interest.
aliunde: Lat. From another source. Term is used with "evidence," meaning evidence is from another source. An ambiguous will, for example, is clarified by evidence aliunde, *i.e.*, a source other than the will.
allegation: An assertion of fact, made in a pleading, stating what a person intends to prove.
allege: To charge; assert; to make an allegation. "Alleged" means only charged or asserted and not proven.
allegiance: Loyalty and obedience to a country and its government in return for the protection it affords. Allegiance can be natural: that owed to one's native country; acquired: that which applies to a naturalized citizen; or local and actual: that obedience owed to a foreign government in whose territory one is temporarily present.
all fours: Two cases alike in all legally relevant respects are said to be on "all fours."
allocation: Placement or assignment of something in or to a particular place, such as the allocation of cash dividends to income or principal.
allocution: A court formality of the sentencing procedure in which a trial judge asks the defendant if he has any legal reason why judgment should not be passed against him and a sentence imposed.
allograph: A signature made for another person.
allotment: A portion or share of something, usually property, *e.g.*, an allotment of land, or an allotment of shares in a company.
alternative pleading: A form of pleading in which a person presents two or more separate, and possibly inconsistent, sets of facts which may form the basis for a claim or defense.
alternative writ: A court order commanding a person to do something or show reason why he should not.
amalgamation: A union of two or more different entities, usually corporations, which forms a single concern. Term is also used when referring to the consolidation of unions, associations, organizations, and stock.
ambiguity: An uncertainty, doubtfulness, something that lacks specific meaning. Term is used in referring to an uncertainty in written documents, such as wills or contracts. There are two kinds of ambiguity: latent and patent. Latent ambiguity is when the document itself is clear but some extrinsic factor makes the document's execution unclear. Patent ambiguity is when the language of the document itself is obscure.

ambit: A boundary line marking the limit of something, such as the bounds of a district, jurisdiction, or sphere of influence.

ambulance chaser: A person who pursues accidents for the purpose of representing the injured party in the ensuing litigation or for the purpose of soliciting such a case for a lawyer.

ambulatory: Movable, changeable, revocable. An ambulatory will is one which can be changed or revoked. An ambulatory disposition is a changeable judgment or sentence. Ambulatory jurisdiction is not limited to one location.

amend: To correct, to change for the better.

amendment: A change or modification. An amendment of a pleading is any change (such as a correction of an error) in a pleading already made. An amendment of a bill is a change in the bill, and can be made while the bill is being debated in the legislative body or by the governor or president before signing it. An amendment to the Constitution is one of the changes made in or added to the original document.

amenity: An attractive feature of a piece of real property which makes the property more pleasant to live on, *e.g.*, a scenic view, an easily accessible location, or a swimming pool.

American Bar Association (A.B.A.): Organization of members of the United States bar, the primary function of which is the improvement of the legal profession.

amicus curiae: Lat. Friend of the court. A person who is not party to the law suit but who is permitted, upon petition, to submit information or arguments for the court's consideration.

amnesty: An act by a sovereign power by which a general pardon is granted to a class of persons who have been guilty of some offense, usually political in nature. Amnesty differs from a pardon in that a pardon excuses an individual for an offense against the peace of the nation.

amortization: The payment of a debt by equal, periodic payments over a course of time, *e.g.*, a mortgage on a house is amortized by making monthly payments on the loan for the number of years the mortgage runs.

ancestor: A person from whom another is descended, *e.g.*, a parent or grandparent. A former possessor.

ancillary: Something that acts to assist or is subordinate to something else. Ancillary jurisdiction is the power of a court to rule on a matter not normally within its primary jurisdiction, such as the power of a federal district court to handle actions from a circuit court. An ancillary proceeding is one which grows out of, aids, or is subordinate to another action.

animus: Lat. Will, intention, being of the mind. Term is used in conjunction with other terms—*e.g.*, animus cancellandi: with the intention of destroying or cancelling; animus furandi: with intent to steal; animus testandi: with intent to make a will.

annex: To attach to, to bind, to add to or join, as a piece of personal property is annexed to real property and so becomes a fixture (*see* fixture) or as a piece of land is annexed to a city.

annotation: Note on a passage in a book intended to explain the meaning of the passage. A legal annotation is an explanation that follows the text of the decision on a case. History of cases construing a statute.

annuity: A fixed periodic payment for life or a specified number of years usually from an insurance company. The payments are a partial return of a capital investment (insurance policy) plus interest. The person receiving the payments (annuitant) does not have an interest in the principal from which this money arises, but only in the periodic payments themselves.

annul: To cancel, void, to do away with, as a marriage or judicial proceeding can be annulled.

annulment: Act of making something void. A marriage annulment differs from a divorce in that a divorce ends a marriage in existence; an annulment voids the marriage from the beginning, as if it never existed.

answer: A reply, response. The first response or pleading made by a defendant to the charges leveled against him in a lawsuit. It must contain a denial of the allegations, and may also contain affirmative defenses, and any permissive or compulsory counterclaims.

antenuptial agreement: A contract made before marriage by the future spouses, usually to settle questions of support and distribution of wealth should one spouse die or should the planned marriage end in separation or divorce.

anticipation: Doing or taking something before its proper time, such as paying off a mortgage before it comes due. Expectation; knowledge of the probability that something will occur; principal by which negligence is determined if a prudent person could have reasonably expected a thing to happen.

anticipatory breach: The breaking of a contract after it has been entered into but before the actual time of performance arrives. In some jurisdictions, the aggrieved party has a right to sue for breach once the repudiating party states his intention not to perform.

antitrust acts: Federal and state statutes enacted to protect trade and commerce from unlawful restraint and monopolies. *See* the Sherman Antitrust Act of 1890 and the Clayton Act of 1914.

a posteriori: Lat. From effect to cause. In logic, term means that first one observes effects then ascertains their causes.
apparent authority: In law of agency, authority a principal permits an agent to have, or holds agent out as having; *e.g.*, an employer permits an employee to have a certain amount of authority in the performance of his job. It includes authority a prudent person would reasonably assume the agent to have.
appeal: To ask a superior court (*i.e.*, an appellate court) to review a decision of a lower court. The process is called "an appeal."
appearance: A coming before the court either as a plaintiff or defendant and thereby submitting oneself to the court's jurisdiction. It can be in person or through an attorney, the latter being the case in most civil suits.
appellant: The party who appeals a decision of one court to a higher court.
appellate court: A court with jurisdiction to review cases from a lower court. The U.S. Supreme Court is the highest appellate court in the country. *See* appeal.
appellee: The party against whom an appeal is made, usually the winner of a case in a lower court.
appoint: To assign to a position or office. To give "power of appointment" in a will or deed is the authority to determine who gets one's property and how it is to be used.
apportionment: A fair and proportionate division and distribution of something, such as property, corporate shares, or estate taxes. Process of determining the number of representatives to a legislative body an area is entitled to, *i.e.*, their proportionate distribution throughout the state based on population.
appraisal: An estimation of the value of a property by a qualified, disinterested person.
appreciation: The increase in the value of property for reasons other than improvements, *e.g.*, due to inflation or greater demand for property.
apprehend: To seize, capture, take hold of bodily. To grasp in the mind, as in to understand, conceive or fear.
appropriate: To set something apart for a particular use, such as land for a public park or funds for highway repair. Appropriation is the governmental act of taking private property and setting it aside for public use. (*See* eminent domain.) To take something as one's own. To set apart money or goods for a particular purpose.
appurtenance: Something that is attached or belongs to something else of greater value, such as a barn or a fence to the land it is on. In property law, term refers to a burden attached to land which restricts the use or enhances the enjoyment of the land, *e.g.*, easement, covenant, or servitude (*see* easement, covenant, and servitude).
arbiter: Person chosen to decide a controversy according to the rules of equity and law; a referee; arbitrator.
arbitrage: The purchase of stock or other security in one market and its sale in another market for the profit made in the exchange.
arbitrary: By mere opinion; by will alone; not according to reasoned judgment, rules, or determining principles; nonrational. Legally, without substantial legal cause.
arbitration: The submission of a dispute between two parties to a third, impartial party (arbitrator) with the agreement that the decision of the arbitrator will be binding and final. It is a quasi-judicial procedure that avoids the formality, delay, and expense of a normal trial.
arguendo: Lat. In the course of an argument. A hypothetical statement made and assumed to be true for the sake of argument. A judge may make a statement arguendo, *e.g.*, to illustrate a point.
argument: An attempt to persuade through a course of reasoning which sets forth facts and laws. Legally, statements made by counsel to a judge or jury in an attempt to further her cause.
arm's length: Relationship which exists between parties who are unrelated, and have no duty or obligation to each other. An arm's length transaction is one in which parties act entirely for their own interest. Term is often used in transactions which determine the fair market value of property.
arraignment: The initial step of a criminal proceeding in which an accused person is brought before a judge to be informed of the charges against him, and during which time defendant enters a plea.
array: The body of persons summoned from which a jury is selected. Also, the list of persons impaneled on a jury. (Verb) To select jurors.
arrears, arrearages: Debts unpaid and overdue.
arrest: The taking of a person into custody for the purpose of bringing him before a court. The arresting person must have legal authority, must adequately communicate his intent to arrest, and must actually restrain the arrested person for the act to be called an arrest. He must have probable cause to seize and detain; *i.e.*, suspicion is not enough.
arrest of judgment: Act of withholding judgment on legal action because of some error on the face of the record which, if ruled on, may result in a reversal of the verdict on appeal.
arson: The malicious, willful, and unlawful burning of a building or other property. Several states divide arson into first degree, second degree, and third degree depending on the time of the burning and the na-

ture and occupancy of the structure. At common law, structure had to be the dwelling place of another.

article: A separate and distinct part of a document, such as a distinct paragraph in a constitution or statute.

articles of incorporation: The document filed with the state upon the formation of a corporation. It lists, among other things, the purpose of the corporation, its place of business, and the names of its directors. Also called "certificate of incorporation."

artifice: A trick; a contrivance; a fraudulent device used to accomplish some evil.

artificial person: An entity created by law which has some of the rights and duties of a natural person, *e.g.,* a corporation.

as is: A phrase denoting a thing is being sold just as the buyer sees it, with no promise from the seller that it is in perfect condition. The buyer takes all risk as to the quality of the item.

asportation: The unlawful carrying away of something. It is an essential element to constitute a crime of larceny.

assault: The attempt or threat, accompanied by the apparent present ability, to inflict bodily harm on another; the display of force as to cause fear of bodily harm. Actual touching is not a requisite of assault as it is of battery.

assay: The testing of ores and metals, especially gold and silver; examination to determine characteristics of weight, measure, or quality.

assessment: The process of determining the value of property for taxation, *e.g.,* a property tax assessment. A special assessment is a burden put upon a piece of land with reference to the benefit the property owner gains, *e.g.,* a special assessment for street repairs. The determination of the amount a person will pay into a common fund, *e.g.,* an assessment of condominium owners for the construction of a swimming pool for the building. In relation to corporations, a call made to stockholders to pay the amount of money mentioned in their subscriptions.

assets: Property of any kind which can be used for the payment of debts. Assets include money, land, personal property, and intangibles such as patents and copyrights.

assign: To appoint to or designate for a particular purpose or duty. To formally transfer one's legal rights or interest in property, as when a deed is assigned to another. To point out or specify, as in to assign mistakes in an assignment of error (*see* assignment of error).

assignment for benefit of creditors: A debtor's transfer of a substantial portion of property to another person in trust for payment of debtor's debts, with the return of any surplus to the debtor.

assignment of error: The complaint made by an appellant in which he specifies the alleged errors made by a lower court and on which he relies for reversal of the decision.

association: A body of persons united for a common purpose. Term sometimes refers to an organization that acts and is treated as a corporation for federal tax purposes although legally it is not one; an unincorporated society. Professionals and nonprofit organizations, for instance, form associations; also certain business trusts are called associations.

assumpsit: Lat. He promised. In contracts, it is a promise, either oral or written but not under seal, by which a person agreed to do or pay for something. Term is used in connection with the recovery of damages for breach of contract.

assumption: Act of taking over; assuming responsibility. *E.g.,* the assumption of a mortgage on a house to make oneself personally liable for the mortgage debt.

assumption of risk: An affirmative defense used by a defendant in a negligence suit in which he asserts plaintiff knew of a danger and voluntarily exposed himself to it. Assumption of risk by plaintiff would relieve defendant of legal responsibility for any resulting injury.

assurance: The act of assuring; a declaration which inspires confidence; a pledge, guaranty, or surety; insurance. A document showing title to real property; a deed. Also, the act of conveying or transferring title.

assured: The person covered by an insurance policy; the insured.

asylum: A sanctuary; a place of safety and shelter from arrest or prosecution. Certain states and countries are places of asylum. Term denotes both the place and the protection it affords. Neutral waters where ships take refuge during warfare. Archaic: An institution for the protective housing of the insane, blind, lame, or destitute.

at bar: Before the court. A "case at bar" refers to the specific case presently before the court.

at large: Free, not restrained or controlled; *e.g.,* an escaped prisoner is said to be at large until apprehended. Unlimited; open to debate. At large elections are those in which all voters cast ballots for a candidate; *e.g.,* U.S. Presidential or Senatorial elections are at large as opposed to state legislative elections which are limited to in-district voters.

attachment: The remedy which involves the taking of property to be held as security by the court for the purpose of satisfying an anticipated judgment. A writ issued by the court to the sheriff ordering him to bring before the court a person guilty of contempt. A document affixed to another.

attainder: A form of punishment involving the elimination of the civil rights of a person guilty of a crime punishable by death. The doctrine of attainder was once used as a punishment for treason, but is no longer constitutional.

attempt: Effort to commit a crime; effort goes far enough toward the actual start of the crime yet falls short of its accomplishment; contemplation and preparation are not enough. Thus the elements of criminal attempt are intent, an overt act coupled with the real possibility to commit a crime, and the failure to accomplish it.

attestation: Act of witnessing the signing of a document, such as a will, and then signing your name as such a witness.

attesting witness: The person who witnesses the signing of a document. *See* attestation.

attorney: A lawyer; an officer of the court who has a duty toward a client and the court for the administration of law. An agent; a person appointed to act formally for another.

attorney-client privilege: A client's privilege to refuse to disclose and to prevent others from disclosing anything said in confidence to his attorney.

attorney general: The chief nonjudicial legal officer in the country or a state who advises the chief executive and other heads of the executive department on legal matters. On the federal level, he is a Cabinet member appointed by the President and confirmed by the Senate, and is the head of the Department of Justice. On the state level, he is sometimes appointed by the Governor, but more often is elected at large.

attorney in fact: An agent with authority to do some particular act, not of legal character, for another. The agent is granted such authority by a written document called "power of attorney."

attornment: The recognition of a third party as an acceptable successor to a contract, especially the agreement in which a tenant agrees to pay rent to a new owner of property.

attractive nuisance: Dangerous piece of property that may be attractive to children; the doctrine which states that a person who has such a possibly dangerous property or condition on his premises has the duty to take reasonable precautions to guard against injury to children attracted to it. The fact that a child is a trespasser does not relieve owner of responsibility for injuries; *e.g.*, a swimming pool is an attractive yet potentially dangerous condition, and its owner has a responsibility to put a fence around it.

auction: The public sale of personal or real property to the highest bidder. The person who conducts an auction is a licensed individual called an auctioneer, and he operates on behalf of the seller.

audit: (Noun) An examination of something, especially financial records, accounts, or tax returns, to determine their truth and correctness. (Verb) To conduct an audit; to examine; to adjust; to ascertain; to verify.

auditor: Person qualified to conduct an examination of financial records; may be a public official or private accountant working for a business. In court, an auditor, also known as a master, examines an account in controversy and reports to the court, which then uses the report's information in rendering its judgment.

authentication: To officially recognize a thing as genuine; in evidence, the act of legally recognizing a document, such as a will, a deed, or a law, to be what it is claimed to be.

authority: The right, permission, or power to act, as in the permission a principal gives to his agent to act in his behalf, or the power a police officer has in the lawful exercise of his duties. Authority can be "express" (*i.e.*, that which is explicitly given as in a document of Power of Attorney); it can be "implied," as in that which can be inferred from a person's conduct or from circumstances; and it can be "apparent," as when a principal permits an agent to act. Judicial precedent, *i.e.*, higher court decisions have authority over those of lower courts. A body with power to act.

authorize: To give the right to act; to empower with authority. Sometimes term connotes "permitted" or "directed" to act.

autopsy: An examination of a corpse usually to determine the cause of death; a post mortem examination.

avails: Profits or proceeds, such as the avails from the sale of land.

aver: (Verb) To state clearly; allege; assert. (*See* averment.) Old Eng. (Noun) Property; especially livestock.

averment: In pleading, a positive statement alleging facts; an allegation.

avoidance: In pleading, the statement in which a person admits facts in an allegation against him, yet also shows why those facts should not have their normal legal effect, *i.e.*, to avoid them. (*See* affirmative defense.) An annulling or voiding of something. Evasion.

avowal: A declaration or offer of proof made outside of the jury's hearing, by a witness not permitted to testify before the jury, in order to have the statement recorded should the case be appealed.

avulsion: The removal of soil by the action of water, and its placement on the land of another. It differs from accretion (*see* accretion) in that avulsion is a sudden, perceptible change, and in that the ownership of the land does not change. Avulsion also denotes the sudden change in the course of a river or stream, and this does not change the boundary line marked by the previous course of the water.

award: (Verb) To give or grant, as when a jury awards damages, or when a contract is awarded to a firm. To adjudge, as when a court rules on a matter in controversy. (Noun) The decision rendered by a tribunal.

B

bad debt: An uncollectible debt, worthless to the creditor, *e.g.,* a loan made with the intention it would be repaid but which appears unlikely to ever be repaid. A bad debt is deductible for tax purposes.
bad faith: Dishonesty in dealing with another person. Term implies a willfulness on the part of one person to trick or mislead another, and is not the same as negligence or mistake. It may or may not constitute fraud.
badges of fraud: A general term used to indicate suspicious circumstances surrounding a transaction, especially suspicion of defraud of creditors. A particular "badge" does not prove fraud but only implies it. *E.g.,* if a transaction takes place to avoid a creditor and in anticipation of a suit, the conveyance is called a badge of fraud.
bad title: A defective title, insufficient to legally convey property, not marketable.
bail: (Verb) To give a security (often money) to procure the release of a person being held for an offense, and to insure that person's future appearance in court. (Noun) The person in the position of a surety (*see* surety) who gives such a security.
bail bond: A written instrument of debt made by a person in custody and by others for him (*see* surety) which procures his release. Surety promises to pay amount mentioned on bail bond should defendant fail to appear in court at a designated time.
bailee: Person to whom property of a bailment (*see* bailment) is delivered. Person who temporarily possesses personal property in trust for another.
bailiff: A sheriff's deputy or court officer who keeps order in a courtroom. Person given authority for the care of another; a guardian. A keeper of the property of another who is responsible to manage it for the best benefit of the owner.
bailment: The delivery of personal property to another under express or implied contract, for some specified purpose, to be returned or accounted for after purpose is fulfilled. "Bailment for hire" is the relationship created upon delivery of goods to someone (bailee) for some purpose in exchange for compensation, *e.g.,* when a broken television set is delivered to a TV repair shop. The lawful possession of property belonging to another, with the duty to account for it, *e.g.,* a finder of mislaid camera.
bailor: Person who gives personal property to another to be held in bailment. *See* bailment.
bait and switch: A deceptive advertising practice in which a retailer entices customers into the store with attractive advertising, and then fails to stock sufficient quantities of the advertised product or disparages the product. Both tactics are done with the intention of selling a higher priced product.
balance sheet: A summary of financial data showing assets, liabilities, and owner equity of all the accounts of a company at a certain time.
bank: A commercial institution which receives deposits of money, cashes checks, makes loans, and handles other money-related matters. Banks are chartered under federal and/or state laws, and are usually incorporated. The raised ground at the edge of a watercourse.
bankrupt: The state of being unable to pay one's debts when due and payment is demanded. A person, partnership, or corporation so unable to pay its creditors. *See* bankruptcy, insolvency.
bankruptcy: A legal procedure, by which a debtor is relieved of his debts. Under the Federal Bankruptcy Act, a debtor's assets may be liquidated to pay his creditors, or, under a provision of the Act, debtor's assets are not liquidated, and debtor is allowed to reorganize, continue business, and pay creditor from future earnings.
bar: A prohibition or barrier to the relitigation of a case which has already been adjudicated; *i.e.,* a court decision sometimes "bars" further action on the same case. A position in a courtroom; a defendant "at bar" stands before the judge. "The bar" is the entire body of lawyers. A case "at bar" is the particular case before the court.
bar association: A voluntary organization of lawyers whose primary purpose is the betterment of the

legal profession. Bar associations are formed on national, state, county, and municipal levels.
bargain: (Noun) A mutual agreement between parties; a contract. (Verb) To negotiate the terms of an agreement.
barratry, barretry: Offense of provoking or exciting quarrels and suits, sometimes done by lawyers for the profit that can be gained from an ensuing lawsuit. In maritime law, act by a master or mariner of a ship, done for a fraudulent or unlawful purpose which results in injury to the ship's owner.
barrister: In England, a legal counselor; a person who argues a case at bar; similar to a trial lawyer in America, except a barrister does not prepare a case from the beginning but gets the case material from another type of legal person—a solicitor.
barter: The exchange of one good or service for another which does not involve money.
basis: The foundation of something; the value of a property on a certain date. The basis of a property is used as a baseline in determining appreciation (gain) or depreciation (loss) of value over time, and is used for taxing purposes.
bastard: An illegitimate child; a child not born during a lawful marriage.
bastardy proceedings (action): Legal action in which the father of an illegitimate child is determined and support obligations are enforced. Same as "paternity suit."
battery: The unlawful, undesired, and unprovoked use of force on another person with the intention to harm or create fear of harm in that person; harmful touching. In tort law, all parts of a person's body and anything closely attached to it (such as clothes or a car being driven) are protected. Assault is the threat to use force; its actual use in an offensive way, even though slight, is battery.
bawd: An operator of a house of prostitution; a madam.
bearer: Person who possesses a negotiable instrument, title, or security marked "payable to bearer," "cash," or is indorsed in blank, *i.e.*, the payee is unnamed. The instrument itself is called a bearer bond or bearer paper.
bench: A court while sitting in its official capacity. All judges together. The place in a courtroom where the judge sits.
bench warrant: A judge's written order to authorities to arrest a person, often issued to bring a person before the court to answer a contempt charge or to appear as a witness.
beneficial interest: An interest, or right to profits, in a property; that interest which one holds entirely for his own benefit; the remainder of an estate after obligations have been met.
beneficiary: Person or organization entitled to benefits in a will, insurance policy, or trust.
benefit of clergy: In Old England, the exemption the clergy possessed from the jurisdiction of the secular courts. It then came to mean the exemption of any church officers from capital punishment, though it did not apply to certain crimes such as high treason. Abuse led to its abolition in 1827.
bequeath: To give a gift of personal property in a will, distinguished from "devise," which is to give a gift of real property, although terms are often used synonymously.
bequest: A gift of personal property given in a will; a legacy; distinguished from a "devise" which is a gift of real property.
best evidence: The best proof or evidence available under the circumstances; primary evidence; the original, *e.g.*, the actual written document, not a copy.
bestiality: Sexual intercourse between a human and an animal; constitutes a crime against nature. *See* sodomy.
beyond a reasonable doubt: Phrase used to refer to the level of certainty required in the mind of an honest, conscientious juror before convicting a person of a crime; it is not absolute certainty, containing not the least bit of doubt (for this is impossible), but that degree of certainty a moral person seeking the truth is required to have; it is the highest degree of proof required in a trial.
bias: Preconceived opinion; a leaning toward one party or side of an issue; a predisposition; a judge's state of mind toward a litigant which tends to sway her judgment may be cause for disqualification.
bicameral system: A legislature divided into two houses, as is the Senate and House of Representatives.
bid: An offer to buy or sell a product or service at a stated price. *E.g.*, building contractors submit bids for work on construction projects, and public agencies accept bids before awarding contracts.
bigamy: Criminal offense committed by marrying a person when one knows his or her previous marriage is still in existence.
bilateral contract: An exchange of mutual promises in which each party is both a promisor and promisee; *i.e.*, each is bound to perform some duty for the other. *E.g.*, the contract for the sale of a car is bilateral because one party promises to pay for the car while the other promises to give it; differs from a unilateral contract in which there is a promise on one side only, usually a promise to pay for a service rendered.
bill: In legislation, a draft of a proposed law which is introduced to the legislature for enactment. A written account of indebtedness stating items sold, services

rendered, or work performed. The first pleading by a plaintiff in equity action; a complaint.
bill of attainder: Any form of legislative action which singles out an individual or group of persons for punishment without trial. Such an act is unconstitutional.
bill of exceptions: A formal written statement of the objections a party has with the rulings, decisions, or instructions given by a trial judge which is submitted for the information of an appellate court.
bill of exchange: A written order made on a second party to pay a third party a certain sum of money; a check, a draft.
bill of indictment: The document containing the accusation(s) against a person before it is given to a grand jury. *See* indictment.
bill of lading: A receipt for the goods issued by a person contracted to transport and deliver them to a specified person or place. It names the person from whom goods are received, states the place of delivery, describes the goods, and states the terms of the contract to transport them.
bill of particulars: An amplification of a pleading or a more detailed statement of the offense charged against a defendant to inform him of the specific nature and extent of a plaintiff's claim. It allows defendant to properly prepare his defense, but does not mention the specific evidence plaintiff will use against him.
bill of review: Proceeding in equity which seeks the reversal or revision of a decree already rendered. It is usually applicable only to correct errors of law on the face of the record, when new evidence is discovered, when new matter arises, or where there is evidence of fraud impeaching the original transaction.
bill of rights: The first ten amendments to the U.S. Constitution which guarantee fundamental rights and liberties of the individual, many of which limit the power of legislature.
bill of sale: A written agreement which transfers title of personal property to another; not the same as a receipt for payment.
bind: To legally obligate, especially by a contract, bond, or decree; to hold responsible for duties or obligations.
binder: A temporary insurance policy issued before determination of risk and the issuing of a final policy. A receipt for a deposit on the purchase of a home which binds buyer and seller to agreed-upon terms.
bindover: The act by which a court requires a person post bond and appear in court, or enter into a recognizance. To transfer a case to a higher court or grand jury after finding probable cause of guilt.
blacklist: A list of persons to be avoided, *e.g.*, employees who have been fired for unacceptable performance or behavior, or troublesome union members. (Verb) To put someone on such a list.
blackmail: Extortion of money by threat to do bodily harm, expose a wrongdoing, or disgrace the character of another.
blank indorsement: The signing of a promissory note or bill of exchange without naming person to whom payment is to be made. It is payable to the person who possesses it (*see* bearer) and is negotiable upon delivery.
blasphemy: Act of maliciously reviling or reproaching God or religion; speaking of God so as to harm or destroy reverence toward Him. At common law, a misdemeanor that is seldom enforced.
blue sky laws: Laws that regulate sale of stock and other securities to protect investors from fraudulent offerings.
board: An organized body of persons which acts in the interest of others by performing managerial, representative, and administrative duties for a corporation or government, *e.g.*, board of directors, board of health, board of aldermen. Regular meals, though term sometimes includes lodgings.
Board for International Broadcasting: Created in 1973, this agency oversees broadcasting by stations serving the U.S.S.R. and free Europe.
bona fide: Lat. In good faith; honest; without deceit. A bona fide purchaser is one who acts in good faith, without notice of adverse claims to title, and who pays seller a valuable consideration. A bona fide possessor is one who holds property with the honest belief that he is the proper proprietor.
bond: An instrument of indebtedness issued by companies and government bodies which pays holder an interest for a specified amount of time. Some bonds have detachable coupons redeemable by the bearer for the interest payments. A contract between a surety and the government which states surety will have defendant appear in court at a specified time, or forfeit bond money; bail bond. A binding agreement, backed by securities, to do or not do something; *e.g.*, a "performance bond" guards against loss due to failure on a construction project. A deed which obligates a person or his heirs to pay a sum of money by a specified date.
bonded warehouse: A government-designated building where imported goods are kept. Owner or lessee of building posts bond to protect government from loss connected with stored goods.
bondsman: A surety; one who posts bond for the release of a person in custody is called a bail bondsman.
bonus: Extra pay given gratuitously to an employee often in appreciation or as an incentive; any extra payment above regular remuneration. Bonuses are given, for instance, for extraordinary performance on

a job, for prepayment of mortgage debt, and to professional athletes.

bookmaking: The taking and recording of wagers, most often on sporting events such as horse races, boxing matches, and football games. It is a form of gambling and is illegal except where permitted by law for specified events.

book value: The net worth of something, such as a company, as recorded in its account books; value of something after deducting liabilities from assets.

bootlegging: The illegal possession, use, transportation, or sale of intoxicating liquor, often done to avoid taxes.

booty: Personal property taken by a land army.

bottomry: A contract in which a shipowner borrows money to repair or equip his vessel, while offering the ship and its cargo as security for the loan. They are usually made by the master of the ship in times of emergency while in a foreign port. A characteristic of a bottomry is that the lender risks losing his money should the ship fail to reach its destination.

boycott: A refusal to do business with a party, usually to express displeasure or to effect a change in that party's practices. A consumer boycott is one in which customers refuse to buy a certain product or deal with a certain company. A group boycott is a conspiratorial refusal to deal with some business with the intent of forcing them out of competition; it is illegal under the Sherman Antitrust Act.

breach: Violation of a law, right, duty or obligation by omission or commission, *e.g.*, failure to perform according to a contract.

breach of contract: Failure to perform, hinderance of another's performance, or repudiation of any of the promises made in a contract, without legal excuse.

breach of peace: General term for an offense which disturbs the public order. It can be by violent acts or words that provoke others to disruptive conduct; disorderly conduct.

breach of promise: Failure to keep a promise, especially a promise to marry; short for "breach of promise of marriage."

breaking: The application of force to a solid object so as to separate it, usually to gain unlawful entry; *e.g.*, picking a lock, opening a window, or even opening a door with criminal intent constitutes a breaking.

bribery: The crime of voluntarily offering or receiving a thing of value with corrupt intent to influence a public official or anyone connected with discharge of public duties, *i.e.*, jurors, witnesses, and candidates for public office, as well as police officers and elected officials.

brief: A concise statement of the facts of a case, relevant laws, and an argument which cites the reasons and authorities counsel will use to support his case. A summary of a large document. A summary of the published opinion of a case.

broker: Agent who acts as a "middle man" between a buyer and seller of realty or personalty such as land, stocks, or bonds.

brothel: A house of prostitution or part of house used as a location for the illicit business of exchanging sex for money; a bawdy house.

brother: A male having the same parents as another person. Half-brothers/sisters have one common parent.

buggery: Sexual intercourse with an animal; sexual intercourse between men; other acts constituting crimes against nature. Generally, same as "bestiality," "sodomy."

building line: A line set a certain distance from the border of a property beyond which a building may not extend.

burden of proof: Obligation to provide evidence necessary to establish a disputed fact or a degree of belief in the mind of the court. Two concepts are involved under burden of proof: burden of persuasion and burden of going forward with the evidence. Burden of persuasion is the ultimate burden of convincing the court of an issue, and it does not shift during the trial. This burden is on the state in criminal proceedings, and the state must establish the elements of its case beyond a reasonable doubt. The burden of going forward with the evidence is on the plaintiff at the start of the trial, and he must present a preponderance of evidence in his favor, *i.e.*, enough to justify trying the case. This burden may shift during the trial; when a plaintiff presents sufficient evidence, the burden then shifts to the defendant to produce counter-evidence.

bureaucracy: An organization with a hierarchy of authority, specialized functions, and fixed positions, rules and procedures; a governmental body of non-elected officials which makes and/or administers policy.

burglary: Entering a building or room with intent to commit a felony, usually theft. Common law required a burglary to be a breaking and entering of a house at night, but modern statutes have broadened the definition.

business judgment rule: States that business managers are immune from liability when making careful, honest decisions under corporate authority.

business record exemption: Exemption to the hearsay exclusion rule which permits routine records, such as police reports to be admitted in court as evidence.

business trust: An unincorporated form of business organization in which property is conveyed to a trustee, *e.g.*, a bank, according to specified terms, to be held and managed for the benefit of a beneficiary.

buyer: A purchaser, especially of movable property (chattels).

bylaws: Rules and regulations of corporations, associations, and other organizations. Sometimes term is used synonymously with "ordinance" to mean the laws or statutes of a locality.

C

C.A.B.: *See* Civil Aeronautics Board.
cabinet: Body of officials which advises a chief executive, *e.g.,* the heads of the major executive departments of the U.S. government, such as the Secretary of State and the Secretary of Defense.
cadaver: A dead human body; a corpse.
calendar: A list of cases to be tried; a docket.
call: Corporate law: A demand made on subscribers for payment of an unpaid portion of shares. Securities: Option to buy an amount of shares of stock at or within a specified time and for a specified price. Conveyance: An object or landmark that serves as a boundary marker.
callable bonds: Instruments of indebtedness redeemable before maturity (*i.e.,* the issuer has the option to pay off debt early); redeemable bonds.
calumny: False accusation of a crime; defamation; libel; slander.
camera: A judge's chambers. A case heard "in camera" is heard in private, with no spectators.
cancel: To make void; to invalidate; to revoke. An instrument is cancelled by destroying it or writing on it so as to show it has been terminated. Regarding wills, the maker's intent to revoke is a necessary ingredient for its termination.
canon: Law or rule, especially of church discipline and doctrine, but also used with reference to inheritance, ethics, and taxation rules and those that guide the construction of written documents.
canon of ethics: Standard of conduct expected of lawyers that includes both a minimum level of conduct lawyers must maintain and ideal principles to which they should aspire.
capacity: The mental ability to comprehend the nature and effect of one's acts, especially in the making of a will or contract or in the commission of a crime. Regarding wills, capacity includes one's ability to understand the nature and extent of one's property and the claims made upon it. Regarding contracts, capacity requires one to be of legal age, of sound mind and sobriety to make a contract. Regarding criminal acts, capacity means one is able to understand the criminality of an act and be able to conform to the law.
capias: Lat. That you take. General term for various writs issued by a judge to the police to take someone into custody, *e.g.,* a "capias pro fine" is a writ authorizing the taking into custody and detention of someone until a fine is paid.
capital: (Noun) All property or monies of a business (*see* assets) such as the machinery a company owns to make its product, or the money stockholders have invested in the business. (Adj.) Major; chief; principal.
capital assets: Income tax law: All property owned by a taxpayer except for certain business property such as inventory or real estate.
capital crime: Crime which may be punishable by death.
capital expenditure: Money spent to improve a property, *e.g.,* the construction of a building on a company's property. The expenditure adds to the value of the property, but it is not deductible as an ordinary business expense.
capital gain: Profit made when a capital asset, such as a house or stock, is sold. Capital gains are classified as long term (property held more than 12 months) and short term (property held less than 12 months).
capital investment: Money spent to increase the value of an asset. Money spent to purchase new equipment for a business.
capitalization: All the liabilities of a business such as the stocks, bonds, and debentures it has issued; the total value of those liabilities. The structure of a company in reference to the stocks and bonds issued by it. (Verb) To record an expenditure as a future asset rather than a present expense. A computational method of giving value to a property according to the income it produces.
capital punishment: Punishment by death.
capital stock: All the shares of stock a company has issued or may issue; the amount of money or property investors have contributed to a company. Capital stock represents a company's liability to its investors.

capitulation: Act of surrendering under certain terms. Certain immunities from the law granted to aliens living in a foreign country.

caption: The introduction to a pleading which includes the names of the parties in the case, the title of the court it is held in, the presiding judge, the docket number, and other facts. Sometimes term refers to just the heading on the legal paper, *e.g.,* Smith v. Jones, 34 Cal. App. 3d 234 (1974). The seizing part of common law larceny, the other part being the carrying away.

cargo: The freight carried on a ship, train, airplane, or truck, as distinct from the transport vehicle itself.

carnal knowledge: Sexual intercourse; full penetration of female sex organ by male is not necessary.

carrier: Someone who transports persons or goods for hire. A "common carrier" is one whose regular business is to transport the general public; *i.e.,* one who transports all persons or goods indifferently, *e.g.,* a railroad or bus company. A "private carrier" transports persons or goods in specific instances under contract.

cartel: A grouping of individual companies that conduct similar business in order to gain advantage from the union, such as for the fixing of prices or the creation of a monopoly. Cartels are restricted in the United States under antitrust laws. An agreement between hostile nations made during wartime.

case: A lawsuit; an action; a cause in controversy before the court. The evidence and arguments used to support one side of a lawsuit. In general, the word means a situation, an event, or a happening, as in "in this case."

case law: Law based on judicial precedent rather than legislative enactment; *i.e.*, the body of law founded in adjudicated cases as distinguished from statutes; common law.

case system: The method of studying law by the examination and discussion of past cases.

cash surrender value: The cash amount a life insurance policy is worth when terminated.

cash value: The price a property would bring if sold in an unrestrained, open market by an uncompelled seller to an uncompelled buyer; market value; fair market value; actual cash value.

causa: Lat. Cause, motive; lawsuit, case.

causa mortis: Lat. In anticipation of death, such as a gift causa mortis.

causa proxima: Lat. Proximate cause. The immediate or most closely related cause for a happening. The real cause of an accident (*see* proximate cause). It carries the liability.

causa sine qua non: Lat. Cause without which a thing would not have occurred, used especially in relation to the cause of an injury in a negligence case.

causation: A necessary link between a wrongful act and resulting damage which grounds liability. In tort law, an act must be the "proximate cause" and the "cause in fact" of the plaintiff's injury.

cause: That which produces a result; the reason for something. A legal action, suit, or case.

cause of action: Facts which give a plaintiff the right to bring a legal action against another. *See* claim.

caveat: Lat. Let him beware. A warning or caution, especially given to a judge or ministerial officer to prevent him from performing certain acts. Statement which opposes the probate of a will. Notice filed with the U.S. patent office by an inventor to prevent a patent from being issued to another.

caveat emptor: Lat. Let the buyer beware. A maxim which means the buyer purchases something at his own risk and should examine the item before taking possession of it. It applies to purchases where item is not under strict warranty. This maxim has been weakened by recent laws.

cease and desist order: An order from an administrative agency or court demanding that certain activities be stopped, *e.g.*, an order from the National Labor Relations Board to an employer to stop an illegal labor practice.

cede: To give up; to assign; to transfer. Usually used to mean the transfer of territory from one country to another.

censorship: Restriction of the public dissemination of printed material, movies, plays, or spoken words. Such restriction is sometimes done on the grounds of morality or in order to keep peace and order. Censorship has been challenged as a denial of first amendment rights of freedom of speech and of the press.

census: A counting of people who live in a city, state, county or nation, usually for the information of a government. A census also compiles social and economic information on those counted.

Central Intelligence Agency (C.I.A.): Established by National Security Act of 1947. Agency makes recommendations to U.N. Security Council and gathers foreign intelligence and counterintelligence information.

certainty: Without doubt; clearly known; definiteness.

certificate: A written statement by someone with official status assuring that something has or has not been done, that certain facts are true, or that a legal requirement has been met.

certificate of deposit: A document issued by a bank acknowledging a deposit of money to be paid back with interest.

certificate of stock: A document issued by a corporation acknowledging the interest the stockholder has in the corporation.
certification proceeding: An action by the National Labor Relations Board to determine whether a company's employees want to be represented by a particular union.
certified check: A check drawn on deposits in a bank where the bank guarantees or "certifies" there is enough money on deposit to cover the check. The bank becomes liable for payment of the amount of the check.
certiorari: Lat. To make sure. A writ issued by a superior court to an inferior court ordering the inferior court to produce records so that they may be examined for any irregularities, jurisdictional problems, or errors apparent on the face of the record. Most commonly used to refer to United States Supreme Court. The writ acts as a discretionary device for the Court to choose the cases it wishes to hear.
cession: Act of giving something up, especially property or rights. *See* cede.
C.F.T.C.: *See* Commodity Futures Trading Commission.
chain of title: The history of a title to a piece of property which traces the successive conveyances starting with the earliest known owner and ending with the present owner.
challenge: To object, to call into question, or to take exception to something, especially a person serving as a juror, but also to the personal qualifications of a judge to hear a case. There are two types of challenges to a juror: peremptory and for cause. Peremptory challenges do not need to state causes for the objections, whereas a challenge for cause does require causes to be stated.
chambers: A judge's private office; also rooms in a courthouse where court officers can conduct business which need not be done in court.
champerty: A bargain made with a party to a lawsuit in which a third person, called a champertor, offers to pay for the litigation in return for part of any award given. It is a form of maintenance and is illegal.
chancellor: In some states, a judge in the court of chancery. The highest executive officer of a university. An ecclesiastical officer who assists a bishop in matters of church law.
chancery: Equity; jurisprudence exercised in a court of equity—*i.e.*, matters decided according to reason, good conscience, and fairness as distinct from strictly according to law.
change of venue: The removal of a suit begun in one location to another location often done because of prejudice in one venue which may hinder a fair trial.
Chapter Eleven: Term used for a bankrupt company. Under bankruptcy laws, company is allowed to continue in existence while it pays current debts.
charge: An accusation. A lien, claim, or encumbrance on land which gives the chargee a right to payment of debts owed him. The liability on an estate imposed in a will for the payment of testator's debts on legacies. A judge's summation of a case and instructions to a jury on matters of law, given before the verdict is rendered.
charge d'affaires: Fr. A diplomatic representative to a foreign government; a substitute for an ambassador.
charge-off: An accounting term for the elimination of an item from assets, such as an uncollectable debt; a write-off.
charitable: For the public good, for the promotion of the general welfare, not for private profit. For something to be called "charitable," such as a trust or a bequest, it must be for the benefit of general public, not for a specified person or persons. Charities are for the benefit of the poor, the advancement of education, for the advancement of religion, and other causes beneficial to society.
charter: A document that establishes a corporation setting forth the laws that will govern it; the corporation's constitution; also an act by a legislature which creates a corporation. A document issued by a sovereign power which grants a group of people certain rights, liberties, and powers such as the "Magna Charta." The organic law of a city or town. To hire a vehicle, airplane, or ship for transportation purposes.
charter-party: A written contract between a merchant and a shipowner for the transportation of goods.
chattel: An item of personal property as opposed to real property. If the item is moveable and is not attached to or has no connection with land, it is called a personal chattel, *e.g.*, car, stereo (*see* personalty). An interest concerning property is called a real chattel, *e.g.*, leasehold estate.
chattel mortgage: A mortgage on personal property rather than on real property, *i.e.*, the putting up of personal property as security for payment of money or performance of some other act; a bill of sale with a defeasance clause, *i.e.*, a clause that cancels the lien on the property when all payments have been made. Used before existence of U.C.C.
check: A written order made on a bank for payment of money from funds the writer of the check has in his account with the bank to be paid on demand to the party named on the check. The check must be signed by the maker of the demand, and contain an unconditional promise to pay a certain sum in money to the order of the payee. A check is evidence of the draw-

er's promise to pay, and if it is a bad check (*i.e.*, there are insufficient funds on deposit to cover the amount drawn) the holder may sue for the amount owed him. *See* certified check, draft, promissory note.

Chief Justice: The senior or principal judge of a court which has three or more judges sitting together. *E.g.*, there is a Chief Justice of the Supreme Court as well as of the court of appeals.

chose: A personal chattel; personal property. *See* chattel, chose in action, chose in possession.

chose in action: A claim or right to possess something not presently in one's possession, such as money owed one in a debt. It includes the right to recover the item by lawsuit. Also, the thing itself that is recoverable by suit.

chose in possession: A personal property in one's possession including the right to possess and enjoy it.

C.I.A.: *See* Central Intelligence Agency.

circuit court: A court with jurisdiction in several districts or counties; some are immediate appellate courts and some are trial courts. *Compare* district court.

circumstantial evidence: Secondary facts from which a primary fact may logically be inferred; evidence gained not from direct observation of facts or personal knowledge, but from deductions made from related facts and circumstances; indirect evidence. Such evidence is capable of supporting a decision in a case if it consistently and reasonably points to one conclusion.

citation: A writ issued from a court of jurisdiction compelling a person to appear in court at a specified time; a summons. An order from a police officer for a person to appear in court, *e.g.*, traffic citation. The reference to the legal authority for a point of law which includes the case name, the volume of the report or reporter, the page number on which it appears, and court—if more than one is in reporter, *e.g.*, *Skalnik v. Town of Sperry*, 527 P.2d 860 (Okla. 1974).

cite: To summon a person to appear in court. To refer to a passage in a book, especially to the legal authority which supports one's argument; to quote.

citizen: Person who is a member of a political community, who enjoys its rights and privileges, and who owes allegiance to its government. United States citizens are persons born in the United States or its territories, persons born to U.S. citizens while they are abroad, persons naturalized according to law, as well as municipalities, local governments, and national banks.

civil: Branch of law pertaining to rights and remedies as opposed to criminal law, *e.g.*, torts, contracts, real property.

civil action: A suit brought to protect a private right or to redress a wrong, as distinguished from a criminal proceeding; equitable action; legal action.

Civil Aeronautics Board (C.A.B.): Created in 1938 to regulate airlines and interstate air commerce, including rates and fares. Abolished as of January 1985.

civilian: A private citizen; a person not in the armed services. A person well versed in the civil law.

civil law: Body of law that a nation or state has established for itself as distinguished from natural law (*see* natural law) and international law; municipal law. Law determining private rights and liabilities as distinguished from criminal law. Roman law as set forth in the Justinian Code and distinguished from England's common law and the Church's canon law.

civil rights: Rights granted by positive law (*i.e.*, law established by legislative enactment or tacit acquiescence), as distinguished from civil liberties which grant rights by negative law (*i.e.*, law that restricts governmental power); specifically, rights guaranteed by the Constitution or by statutes such as those against discrimination on the grounds of race, religion, or national origin.

civil service: Governmental employment excluding that in the armed forces.

claim: The assertion of a right to property, money, or remedy (term is used as noun and verb); the facts giving rise to the assertion; cause of action.

claimant: Person who makes a claim or asserts a right. *See* claim.

clandestine: Secret, hidden, usually for an illegal purpose. *E.g.*, a clandestine mortgage is a second mortgage given on a property while concealing the first, and clandestine introduction is the secret introduction of an item into a country in order to avoid customs.

class action: A lawsuit brought on behalf of a plaintiff and an ascertainable group of persons the plaintiff represents. For a class action to exist the group of persons must: share a common interest with the plaintiff, be too large to feasibly appear in court, and benefit in some way from a successful outcome of the plaintiff's suit.

classified information: Information designated by its source (usually the government) to be for limited distribution.

clause: A single part of a legal document be it a paragraph, subdivision, sentence, or part of a sentence.

Clayton Act: An amendment to the Sherman Antitrust Act, enacted in 1914, which extended the prohibition against monopolies, price discrimination, certain mergers, and exclusive dealing contracts between companies.

clean hands: A maxim in equity law that holds that a person seeking equitable relief must not have acted unfairly in relation to the transaction at issue. If the action appears to arise out of an illegal or immoral matter, the person bringing it is said to have "unclean hands," and the court will not grant relief to such a person.
clearance: In maritime law, the right of a ship to leave port. In contracts involving the showing of motion pictures, the amount of time between the close of the showing of a film in one theater and its start in another. An amount of space needed around a moving vehicle, such as a train or bus.
clear and convincing proof: The degree of proof required to produce a firm belief concerning the truth of facts in the mind of the person(s) trying matters in issue; the degree of proof is greater than the "preponderance" (*see* preponderance) required in most civil cases, and less than "beyond a reasonable doubt" (*see* beyond a reasonable doubt) required in criminal cases.
clear and present danger: Constitutional doctrine concerning speech which is not protected by the first amendment guarantee of freedom of speech. Restrictions may be imposed if the speech provokes an illegal action or presents a danger to society. *E.g.*, yelling fire in a crowded theater and using "fighting words" are not protected.
clearinghouse: An association through which banks exchange checks and make adjustments on accounts. Also, an association within a stock or commodity exchange which handles daily records of the transactions between its members.
clear title: Title free from any obstruction, incumbrance, burden, or limitation; good title; marketable title.
clemency: The reduction of the punishment given a criminal by an executive commuting the sentence or by pardon; mercy; leniency.
clerical error: A "mechanical" error, or error of technique, as opposed to a judicial error, *e.g.*, a typing or copying mistake, a failure to properly record elements of a case, or an inadvertent omission of a clause from a document.
client: One who retains a lawyer for legal advice, representation in court, or for other legal matters.
close: (Noun) A piece of land enclosed by a boundary, whether clearly visible such as a fence, or invisible and found only in the title. (Verb) To end a case.
close corporation: Corporation owned and run entirely by one person or by a small group of persons; family corporation. Such a corporation need not meet some of the usual requirements of a corporation such as annual meetings and stockholders' election of officers.
closed season: A time of year during which the hunting or fishing of a particular type of animal is prohibited.
closed shop: A company which requires its employees to be members of a particular union. They were declared illegal by the Taft-Hartley Act.
cloud on title: An outstanding claim or encumbrance on the title to a property which casts doubt on the validity of that title. Such a claim itself may be valid or invalid.
co: Prefix meaning with, jointly, together, or in conjunction with. An abbreviation for company or county.
code: A systematic collection of laws, statutes, or rules that have been enacted by the legislature, *e.g.*, commercial code, penal code, motor vehicle code.
Code of Professional Responsibility: Rules of conduct for the legal profession written by the American Bar Association and adopted by most states. The Code presents general ethical standards as well as strict rules of conduct. Violations may be punished by suspension or revocation of one's license to practice law. *See* canon of ethics.
codicil: A supplement to a will which adds to, subtracts from, restricts, qualifies, or modifies the will. A codicil must be written in clear, distinct language and executed according to testamentary rules.
codification: The process of systematically collecting and arranging by subject the laws of a particular locality.
coercion: Threat, intimidation, or force used to pressure a person to act against her will, *e.g.*, coercing another to commit a criminal act by threatening her with bodily harm or death. Testamentary law: Coercion is pressure which causes testator to act against her free will, *e.g.*, pressuring her to include an undesired beneficiary.
cognizance: The exercise of jurisdiction, *e.g.*, the power to try and rule on a matter. Judicial notice or knowledge; *i.e.*, the recognition of the truth of facts without evidence, such as a law of nature, is recognized to be true without having to prove it.
cognovit note: A promissory note signed by a debtor that gives an attorney the right to enter a judgment against him should he fail to pay his creditor on time.
cohabitation: To live together as husband and wife. It may or may not include sexual relations. To illegally have sexual intercourse.
co-heir: One who inherits property jointly with another; one of several persons to whom an inheritance descends; joint tenants; tenants in common.
coinsurance: A clause in an insurance policy which makes the insured person responsible for a percentage of the property not specifically covered in the policy. This scheme divides the risk between the in-

surer and the insured (thus the term coinsurance), and it encourages the policyholder to carry greater coverage.

collateral: Secondary; auxiliary. Parallel; on the side. Property offered as security for the performance of an obligation, such as a bank account offered to back a loan.

collateral attack: A challenge to the integrity of a judgment, decree, or order brought in an action separate from the one which rendered the original judgment, decree, or order. It is not an appeal or review, and although it seeks to avoid or defeat the judgment, it must have a stated purpose other than that of impeaching the judgment; *e.g.*, a challenge to proper jurisdiction often constitutes the basis for a collateral attack.

collateral estoppel: Doctrine stating that issues litigated and determined in a proceeding are binding for the parties involved should those issues arise in any subsequent proceeding. A defendant may plead collateral estoppel to an issue to prevent double jeopardy. *See* double jeopardy, res judicata.

collateral security: Additional security attached to an obligation to insure its performance, *e.g.*, valuable jewelry offered in addition to a bank account as collateral for a loan. It is subsidiary to the principal obligation and runs parallel to it; *i.e.*, if it is sold, its proceeds go to pay off the original debt.

collation: The comparison of a copy to the original; also the report by the person who made the comparison. "Collation of advancements" is the grouping of the assets of an intestate to determine the value of what he has already given to some heirs during his lifetime (advancements) so that the estate may be fairly distributed among all the heirs.

collective bargaining: A procedure by which employers and representatives of their employees negotiate a bargain regarding conditions of their employment such as wages, working hours, benefits and working conditions. The procedure is used to settle labor disputes, and must be conducted in "good faith," *i.e.*, with an open and honest desire to solve the differences between them.

collision: The striking together of two objects

colloquium: That part of a libel or slander complaint which connects the offensive words of the defendant to the plaintiff.

collusion: A secret agreement between two or more persons to commit a fraudulent act; term especially applies to manufacturing evidence to obtain a divorce.

color: Appearance or semblance, something that seems true, but is not actually so; a prima facie right. In pleading, the hiding of facts behind insufficient legal theory, *i.e.*, grounds that are apparently valid but are actually insufficient.

colorable: That which appears to be true or real but is not actually so; counterfeit; feigned.

color of office: Appearance of having official authority to act while not actually possessing it; an act so performed.

color of title: Mere appearance or semblance of good title; any fact or instrument which gives the appearance of passing good title but which, due to some defect, actually does not pass good title, *e.g.*, a counterfeit deed has only color of title; apparent title.

combination: The union of two or more persons for a common purpose; a union of persons to achieve an unlawful end; conspiracy. Patent law: An invention produced by uniting other inventions, some or all of which may have already been patented. The combination may be patented if it produces a new and useful result, and not a mere aggregate of the results of its parts.

comment: A statement of opinion by a judge or counsel based on alleged facts. If a judge comments on the credibility of a witness or weight of the evidence, he or she must make it known it is his opinion.

Commerce Clause: Article I, section 8, clause 3, of the U.S. Constitution which states, "Congress shall have the power to regulate commerce with foreign nations, and among the several states and with the Indian tribes."

commercial code: A compilation of laws dealing with most aspects of commercial transactions such as sales, bank deposits and collections, letters of credit, and investment securities. It was compiled in 1954 by the National Conference of Commissioners on Uniform State Laws and the American Law Institute and has been adopted by all states except Louisiana; Uniform Commercial Code (U.C.C.).

commercial law: Law relating to the rights of those engaged in commerce and trade.

commercial paper: Negotiable instruments; written documents that serve as money; bills of exchange, *e.g.*, checks, bearer bonds, certificates of deposit, and promissory notes.

commission: Authority from the government empowering someone to perform certain acts, such as the authority an officer in the navy or a police officer has to perform his duties; the authority to take a deposition. A public board or administrative body. An amount of money paid to an agent for his services, such as that paid to a stockbroker. The performance of a criminal act.

commitment: The order or process by which a person is sent to jail or to a mental institution. A promise to do something.

committee: A body of persons entrusted with authority to consider, determine, or manage some matter or to perform a duty. The guardian of an insane person.
commodity: A thing produced, bought, or sold; an article of commerce; movable item; personal property. Farm or mining products, such as wheat or iron ore, that are traded on a Commodity Exchange.
Commodity Futures Trading Commission (C.F.T.C.): Created in 1974; regulates trading on the 11 U.S. futures exchanges and actions of commodity exchange members.
common law: Law based on judicial principles found in court decisions rather than law based on legislative enactment. It originates and derives its authority from usage and custom rather than statute. In England, that law distinguished from Roman Law, Civil Law, and Ecclesiastical Law. In the U.S., common law is that background law of England and the American colonies before the American Revolution. Generally, common law is the system of legal concepts upon which laws are based. It is adaptable by judges to the changing needs of society.
common-law marriage: One created without ceremony by mutual agreement to form a marriage relationship, cohabitation as husband and wife, and an assumption of marital obligations. Such a marriage is invalid in many states.
community property: Property owned jointly by a husband and wife, each having a one-half interest; it includes property acquired by either spouse during the marriage (except by gift, devise, legacy, or descent). In states with community property systems, income earned by either spouse is owned jointly and equally by each. In common law systems, it is owned by the person who earns it.
commutation: Act of changing, altering, or substituting one thing for another. In criminal law, it is the act of lessening the punishment given to a convicted criminal. In commercial and civil law, it is the act of substituting one form of payment for another such as accepting an amount of money for performance of a job.
compact: An agreement or contract, especially of a serious nature. Compacts are made between nations to settle disputes, as well as between persons to create enforceable rights and obligations.
company: An association of persons united to perform a business or commercial activity and made a legal entity by a charter or incorporating document. It may divide its interest into transferable shares sold to the public in order to raise capital. Some companies are incorporated for religious or charitable purposes and do *not* sell *shares*. *See* corporation, partnership, firm.
comparative negligence: A doctrine that compares the relative degree of fault attributed to a defendant and a plaintiff in a negligence suit; it states that a plaintiff may recover damages from a defendant in a negligence suit even though the plaintiff may be guilty of some negligence himself, provided that the negligence of the defendant was greater. The damages awarded the plaintiff will be diminished in proportion to the degree of negligence attributed to him.
comparative rectitude: A principle applied in divorce cases that compares the relative degree of responsibility attributed to each spouse for the marriage termination. Relief is awarded to the person least at fault.
compensation: Payment for injury or loss sustained; giving something of equal value for something lost; making of amends; recompense. Payment for work performed.
compensatory damages: Those recoverable for the precise injury sustained; damages that make an injured party whole as opposed to punitive, nominal, or exemplary damages. Compensatory damages include medical expenses, pain, mental suffering, and injury to one's reputation.
competent: Having the proper legal qualifications, ability, or authority; having the capacity to understand and act reasonably.
competent evidence: Evidence which is legally admissible; it is relevant and is of the proper form required to assist a jury in determining a point in question.
complainant: Person who makes a complaint; one who initiates a lawsuit; plaintiff; petitioner.
complaint: Criminal law: A formal charge made under oath before a magistrate stating that a person has committed a crime or offense. (*See* affidavit.) Civil law: A statement of the plaintiff's claim for relief and the grounds on which it is based; the original pleading in a civil action.
compliance: Act of complying, obeying, or submitting to someone or something, as in "compliance with the law."
composition: An agreement between a debtor and his creditors whereby the creditors accept a lesser amount than is owed them in exchange for some consideration, such as immediate payment. There are two types of composition agreements: a "composition with creditors" in which creditors voluntarily release the debtor from some part of his obligation, and a "composition in bankruptcy" in which creditors must, by law, release the debtor. *See* accord.
compos mentis: Lat. Of sound mind; sane.
compounding a felony: Refusal by a party injured in a felony to prosecute or inform against the offender in

exchange for some considerations, such as a cash bribe.

compound interest: Interest on interest, *i.e.,* interest added to principal creates an aggregate sum upon which interest begins to accrue.

compromise: An agreement to settle differences by making mutual concessions; it can be made in or out of court. (Used as noun and verb)

comptroller: An official who examines and audits accounts, keeps records, supervises the collection of money, and reports on the financial status of a public body or private company.

compulsion: The exertion of physical or mental force to compel a person to act against his will. *See* coercion, duress.

compulsory process: Process which compels a person to appear in court; the constitutional right a defendant has to call a witness into court. Subpoenas, summons, and warrants of arrest are writs utilized in this process.

compurgator: In old Anglo-Saxon law, one of several neighbors of an accused person who swore he believed in the defendant's innocence. A compurgator is the forerunner of a juror in English law.

concealment: The withholding of information which one in honesty and good faith is bound to reveal, *e.g.,* the concealment of a hidden medical problem from an insurer.

concerted action: Action involving joint plans, arrangements, and agreements between persons pursuing some goal; conspiracy. In labor relations law, it is a joint action by employees to further a common goal, such as a work stoppage to present a wage grievance; concerted activity.

concession theory: In corporations law, a theory which views a corporation as "indivisible, immortal, and [which] rests only in intendment and consideration of the law." *10 Coke 1, 32 (1613).*

conclusion of law: Conclusion reached by a judge after applying the law to the facts in a case, as distinguished from conclusion of fact, which is a conclusion drawn by a jury from evidentiary facts: final judgment or decree. A judge's statement as to what law applies to the facts found in a case. In pleading, it is a statement which does not plead the facts, for instance, a defendant's reaction to the facts.

concubine: A woman who lives with a man as his wife yet who is not married to him.

concur: To agree with; *e.g.,* a concurring opinion of an appellate judge is one that agrees with the majority opinion though it may be for different reasons. To happen simultaneously, as in "the two events concurred." To act jointly with other claimants in making demands against an insolvent debtor.

concurrent: Running together, as concurrent prison sentences are served at the same time, which differs from consecutive sentences which are served one after the other. Agreeing with, as a concurrent opinion held by a judge agrees with a majority opinion, but is based on different reasons. Acting in conjunction, as in, concurrent causes act together at the same time to produce a result. Having the same authority. *See* concurrent jurisdiction.

concurrent jurisdiction: Authority possessed by two or more different courts to hear and decide on the same matter within the same territory. The choice of which court will be used is left up to the plaintiff.

condemn: To sentence a person to death upon conviction of a capital crime. To declare unfit for use. To take private property for public use. *See* condemnation.

condemnation: The process of taking private property for public use under the power of eminent domain. The owner's consent is not necessary, but just compensation must be paid. *See* expropriation; *contrast with* confiscate.

condition: A possible future event, the occurrence of which creates a right or attaches a liability. Contract law: A provision in a contract that limits or modifies the duties under the contract. A clause in a will which suspends, revokes, or modifies the bequest. Real estate law: A qualification, restriction, or limitation annexed to a conveyance of land which states that the estate will commence, be enlarged, or be defeated upon the occurrence or nonoccurrence of an event, or the performance or nonperformance of an act. A condition can be express, *i.e.,* made known by clear, direct words; or implied, *i.e.,* known indirectly or inferred from surrounding circumstances; or constructive, *i.e.,* judicially imposed. *See* condition precedent, condition subsequent.

conditional: Depending on the occurrence or nonoccurrence of a possible future event; contingent.

conditional bequest (legacy): A gift of personal property by will that either takes effect or is defeated depending on the occurrence or nonoccurrence of an uncertain future event.

conditional fee: An estate in land conditioned to terminate on the occurrence of some particular event which may or may not occur; also known as "fee conditional," "fee simple conditional," and "base fee."

conditional sale: A sale of goods whereby the buyer takes possession of the goods but does not have ownership until they are paid for in full.

condition precedent: A condition that must exist before a right or obligation is created. The term is used in real estate law to refer to a condition that must exist before an estate can take effect. It is used in contract law to refer to an event that must occur or an act that must be done before a contract becomes effective. In insurance law, the term refers to a condition that must exist before a policy is effective. *See* condition.

condition subsequent: A condition which, after occurring, cancels a right or obligation. In estate law, a condition subsequent is one attached to an estate already vested, and which will make the estate conveyed liable for defeat if a breach of the condition occurs. In contract law, it will void a contract if the specified event or action occurs. In a lease, a condition subsequent will give a landlord the right to revoke the lease. *See* condition.

condominium: A jointly owned, multiple-unit building whose residents have exclusive ownership of a single unit (apartment) and ownership as a tenant in common of all the common areas, facilities, and grounds. A system of owning a building.

condonation: Voluntary forgiveness of a spouse's actions that may constitute grounds for divorce, with the implied condition of future good behavior. It is a valid defense in a divorce action.

confederacy: An association of nations united for their mutual benefit; confederation. An association of persons united for an illegal purpose; conspiracy.

confession: An admission of guilt. A confession is admissible as evidence against a defendant only if it is given voluntarily. A confession may be indirect or implied, *i.e.,* inferred from the defendant's conduct or pleading.

confession and avoidance: Pleading in which a person confesses (admits) the truth of an allegation against him but seeks to avoid the effect of the admission by presenting new matter; affirmative defense.

confession of judgment: Entry of a judgment against a debtor who has agreed such a judgment will be entered should he fail to pay his debt on time. The procedure saves the time and expense of a normal legal proceeding, but has been prohibited in many states due to abuse and due process considerations; cognovit note.

confidence game: A swindle whereby the swindler falsely represents himself or some fact, gains the victim's confidence, and abuses that confidence, usually to enrich himself.

confidential communication (information): Privileged communication intended only for the knowledge of a particular person, *e.g.,* communication between client and attorney or between husband and wife.

confidential relation: Relationship in which one person puts trust and confidence in another to act in good faith for his best interest. It arises where one person has an influential or superior position over another because of the confidence placed in him by the person in a dependent position. *E.g.,* confidential relations exist between client and attorney, employee and employer, principal and surety, child and parent, and many other relationships. *See* fiduciary.

confirmation: (Noun) An affirmation; a contract or document affirming something. (Verb) To give approval; to make firm or binding. A confirmation of estate is a conveyance of an estate or right in land in which a voidable estate is made unavoidable or made larger. A confirmation of sale is the probate court's approval of an executor's sale of estate property.

confiscate: To take private property for public use without compensation. *Contrast* expropriation.

conflict of interest: A term describing a situation in which a public official's private interests clash with his duty to serve the public interest. A conflict of interest may disqualify the official from acting on a particular matter, such as a judge from hearing a case in which he has a monetary interest.

conflict of laws: Differences and inconsistencies in the laws of different localities; the system of jurisprudence which determines which law applies or reconciles inconsistencies of conflicting laws when the jurisdiction of different states or countries is involved. Such matters are often decided by determining which jurisdiction had the most significant interest in the matter in controversy.

confusion of goods: A mixing of the personal property of different persons so as to make the individual property of each indistinguishable. The mixing may be accidental, but if it is willful and tortious, the person who did the mixing suffers the loss of his property.

conglomerate: A corporation that controls a number of companies not in competition with one another.

conjugal rights: Marital rights which include the right to companionship, love, sex, and joint property.

connivance: Secret consent to the commission of an illegal act. In divorce actions, it is plaintiff's corrupt consent to offense charged against defendant.

consanguinity: Blood relationship; kinship; having common ancestors. Consanguinity is either lineal (*i.e.,* being directly descended from another), such as a son is from his father; or collateral (*i.e.,* being related but not directly descended from the other), such as cousins are related.

consent: Free, voluntary agreement by one who has proper physical and mental capacity; it is an act of reason and deliberation; acquiescence; a unity of opinion.

consent decree: A decree in equity court sanctioning an agreement between parties; an agreed judgment. An agreement by a defendant to stop certain activities.

consequential damages: Indirect damages or losses not flowing immediately from an act, but rather from the consequences of the act, *e.g.,* loss of business as a result of a fire. Damages resulting from special conditions which are not ordinarily predictable. Some contracts have provisions against consequential damages which limit liability for injuries caused by unusual, unpredictable circumstances. Same as special damages.

conservator: A guardian appointed by the court to take charge of the property or manage the affairs of an incompetent person.

consideration: The thing of value each party to a contract agrees to give in exchange for what he receives; the reason a contract is made. Consideration is necessary to make a contract binding. The term includes both the benefit gained by one party and the corresponding responsibility undertaken by the other. *E.g.,* if a builder makes a contract with a homeowner to build an addition to the homeowner's house, he undertakes the responsibility to do the job in exchange for the promise he will be paid an agreed-to amount. The homeowner's promise to pay for the addition is consideration for the builder's promise to do the work, and vice versa.

consignment: The handing over of goods by their owner (consignor) to a carrier for delivery to a third party (consignee); bailment for hire. Also, the goods so sent. Commercial law: Sending goods to an agent to sell.

consolidation: A joining together of separate parts into one, such as a consolidation of companies to form a new corporation (also called a merger), or the joining of suits to be tried as one.

consortium: Marital rights, the company, companionship, affection, and aid one spouse gives to another. "Loss of consortium" may be grounds for a lawsuit, for example, by the spouse of a person negligently injured in an accident, or if disaffection occurs as a result of an intentional interference with a marriage. Civil law: The joining of several persons as parties to one action.

conspiracy: An agreement of two or more persons made for the purpose of committing an illegal act, or for the purpose of doing a lawful act by unlawful means. Each person must know the purpose of the conspiracy and agree to join in the plans to further that purpose. Many jurisdictions require that some overt act accompany the planning for conspiracy to exist.

conspirator: One of the persons involved in a conspiracy. A conspirator may simply agree with another person's criminal aims, or he may actually aid in the planning, commission, or attempted commission of a crime.

constable: A municipal or county officer who keeps the peace, serves writs, and executes court process (*see* process). Constables have been replaced by sheriffs.

constitution: A system of basic laws and principles by which a nation, state, corporation, or other organization is governed. It may be unwritten, but the term generally refers to a written document containing those laws and principles.

constitutional law: The branch of law that involves the interpretation and application of the fundamental laws and principles stated in the U.S. Constitution. Those laws and principles apply to the organization, function, and power of the government, and to the rights of the governed.

constitutional right: Right guaranteed by the U.S. Constitution or by a state constitution which is not to be violated by any legislative acts.

construction: Act of determining the meaning of something that is unclear, such as a statute, law, or written document. There is strict (or literal) construction which determines exact, technical meaning, and liberal (or equitable) construction which expands on and interprets the meaning of a statute or law.

constructive: That which is not so in its essential nature, but which is regarded as such in the mind of the law; not actual, but legal. Constructive is used as an adjective with many terms to mean that which, through inference, presumption, or interpretation, the law holds as existing. *E.g.,* "constructive eviction" is a situation where a landlord causes a tenant to leave his premises without actually asking him to do so, *e.g.,* by turning off the heat in winter. "Constructive fraud" lacks the element of intentional dishonesty of purpose actual fraud requires, but the law regards it as fraud because its consequences in equity are similar to fraud. A "constructive trust" is one raised by a court of equity against a person who obtains or holds legal title to property through fraud, abuse of confidence, or some other unconscionable conduct, that is, title which in good conscience he should not hold.

consul: An officer assigned to a foreign country to promote and protect a government's economic interests and the interests of its citizens in that country.

consumer: One who purchases, rents, or uses a product or service primarily for personal rather than business purposes.

consumer credit: Credit offered to individuals for personal, family, or household purposes as opposed to business purposes.

Consumer Product Safety Commission (C.P.S.C.): Created in 1972—responsible for reducing unreasonable risks of injury associated with consumer products.

consummation: The completion of something, such as an agreement by the mutual signing of a contract. The act of making a marriage "complete" by having sexual intercourse.
contemplation: Expectation; anticipation; consideration of an action with the thought that it will occur. *E.g.,* "contemplation of bankruptcy" refers to the expectation a business will fail. A transfer or assignment of an asset made in contemplation of bankruptcy is made with the intention of protecting the asset from the distribution that results from the bankruptcy proceedings. Acts done in "contemplation of death" are those done in anticipation of death, such as the transfer of property to avoid inheritance taxes. In such transfers of property, death need not be imminent, but thoughts of death must be the primary motive for the transfer for it to be said that it was made in "contemplation of death."
contempt: Intentional disobedience of or disdain for a known order from a court or legislative body.
contempt of court: Conduct which tends to interrupt the dignity and order of a court or the administration of justice; intentional disobedience of a court order. There is direct contempt which openly disregards the authority of the court in its presence, and indirect (or constructive) contempt which disrupts the administration of justice outside the courtroom.
contentious: That which involves an argument, contest, or dispute between adversaries. A trial is a contentious proceeding. "Contentious jurisdiction" is jurisdiction concerned with hearing and ruling on disputed matters.
contest: To challenge, to dispute, to call into question, such as to contest a will. To oppose, to defend, to resist, such as to contest a lawsuit in court.
contingent: Liable or possible, though not certain, to occur due to dependence on some possible future event; provisional. *E.g.*, with a "contingent claim" liability does not exist until the occurrence happens. A "contingent estate" is a right to property that vests only after the occurrence of a specified event. A "contingent fee" is one paid to a lawyer depending on the amount awarded in a civil suit, which may be nothing if the suit is lost. *See* conditional.
continuance: The adjournment or postponement of a court action to a future time or date. A continuance may be granted at the request of one or both of the parties to the action, or it may be ordered by the court for its own reasons.
contra: Lat. Against; in opposition to; contrary to; disagreeing with.
contraband: Goods that are illegal to produce, possess, export, or import; goods which a neutral country is not permitted to carry into a country at war.
contra bonos mores: Lat. Against good morals.
contract: An agreement between two or more parties which creates legally binding obligations. A valid contract must involve competent parties, proper subject matter, consideration (*see* consideration), and mutuality of agreement and of obligation. The Uniform Commercial Code defines contract as "the total legal obligation which results from the parties' agreement." Contracts are classified in many ways, some of which follow:

Express or implied. An express contract is openly expressed in writing or orally. An implied contract is one inferred by law to exist because the parties' conduct or surrounding circumstances indicate a contractual relationship exists.

Bilateral or unilateral. A bilateral contract is one involving mutual promises between parties. A unilateral contract is a one-sided promise where one party undertakes an obligation without a reciprocal promise or obligation being made or undertaken.

Executed and executory. An executed contract is one which has been carried out, *i.e.*, where both parties have met their obligations. An executory contract is one where an obligation is to be carried out in the future.
contra pacem: Lat. Against the peace.
contravention: Act of going against or breaking a law or agreement.
contribution: That which one person does or gives to meet his share of a jointly-held responsibility. The right to demand a person bear his portion of a shared burden, such as a jointly held debt or a concurrently caused injury. (*Contrast* indemnity.) Civil law: A division of the proceeds of the property of an insolvent debtor among his creditors.
contributory: (Adj.) Additional; supplementary; auxiliary. (Noun) A person who is a member of a joint stock company and who is liable to contribute to the assets of the company when it is being wound up.
contributory negligence: Lack of ordinary care for one's safety on the part of an injured plaintiff which, when added to the negligence of another, contributes to the cause of an injury. It is an affirmative defense to a negligence charge, but it has often been replaced by the doctrine of comparative negligence.
controversy: A definite, concrete issue concerning legal relations among parties whose interests conflict. The term is used in article III of the U.S. Constitution to limit the exercise of judicial power to concrete cases involving the legal rights of adversary parties, that are based on alleged facts, and that would result in a decision granting specific relief. A civil proceeding as distinguished from a criminal proceeding (called a case).
contumacy: Intentional disobedience or defiance of a judicial order, whether in or out of court, *e.g.*, refus-

al to appear in court when summoned to do so.
conventional: That made by agreement between parties rather than by law, *e.g.*, a conventional lien or a conventional estate.
conversion: Tortious act of depriving an owner of his property without his permission and without just cause. An illegal taking, detention, use, assumption of ownership, or destruction of the property of another all constitute conversion. A change of real property into personal property, or vice versa; equitable conversion. Act of exchanging one type of security for another.
conveyance: A transfer of title to real property. (Verb is convey) The deed or written instrument which transfers title to real property; deed of conveyance.
convict: (Verb) To adjudge a person guilty of a crime. (Noun) Person in prison after being found guilty of a crime by a court.
conviction: A final judgment of guilt reached after a criminal trial which is based on a guilty verdict, a guilty plea, or a plea of "nolo contendere." Term often includes the subsequent act of imposing punishment on the guilty person.
cooling time: Criminal law: That time between provocation and reaction which allows a person to become calm and composed, and thus become able to comprehend the results of his actions. Labor relations: Time provided for settling disputes between labor and management. Divorce law: An automatic period between the initiation of a divorce action and the divorce hearing. A time during which a buyer may cancel a purchase.
coparceners: Persons who jointly acquire an estate by descent. They are co-heirs who jointly and severally hold an interest in an entire estate. "Coparcenary" is an estate so jointly inherited and held. Coparcenary differs from joint tenancy in that it can only come about by descent, whereas joint tenancy can be created by a written instrument.
copyright: Statutory protection of an artist's or writer's work giving the creator (or the holder of the copyright) the right to regulate the publication, multiplication, or use of the copyrighted material for a certain period of time. It is an incorporeal right; *i.e.*, a right to something intangible as opposed to tangible, such as a right to land. "Common law copyright" is one that exists for unpublished material.
coram nobis: Lat. In our presence; before us. A writ of appeal which brings before the court then hearing a case errors of fact, and seeks relief from the consequences of those errors. It differs from a writ of "coram vobis" (before you) in that the latter is directed by a court of review to the trial court. These writs have been abolished by *Federal Rule of Civil Procedure 60(b)*.
co-respondent: A codefendant in an equity suit. Person charged in a divorce action with having committed adultery with the plaintiff's spouse.
corner: Controlling a large quantity of a commodity for the purpose of manipulating its price. This is done by buying, for future delivery, a greater quantity of the commodity than is at the time available in the market. The buyers withhold the commodity from sale until increased demand for it artificially pushes its price up.
coroner: A public official who conducts inquiries into violent deaths or deaths that occur under suspicious circumstances. A "coroner's inquest" is the name of the investigation conducted by such an official.
corporal punishment: Physical punishment; punishment inflicted on the body, such as beating or slapping. The term may also include imprisonment.
corporation: An artificial person (*see* artificial person) created by and operating under law, thus possessing only the properties its charter gives it; a legal entity having an existence and personality distinct from that of the individual members that form it, but having the capacity of acting as a single person in matters related to its purpose. There are "public" and "private" corporations. Public corporations are created by the state for political purposes, *e.g.*, a town government or a school district. Public corporations also refer to those that sell shares to the general public. Private corporations are created by private persons for nongovernmental purposes. Their shares are not sold to the public at large. *See* close corporation.
corpus delicti: Lat. Body of the crime. The substantial fact a crime has been committed; the thing upon which a crime has been committed coupled with proof a crime has indeed been committed, *e.g.*, in a murder case, the body of the victim and proof that the victim died by a criminal agency.
corpus juris: Lat. Body of law. The substance of the law. A book or books containing a compilation of the law. "Corpus Juris Secundum" is an encyclopedic work on American law.
corroborate: To strengthen, confirm, or support; *e.g.*, corroborating evidence is that which supports evidence already presented.
corruption of blood: A doctrine of feudal English origin which prevented a person from inheriting or passing property to his heirs because of attainder (*see* attainder). It has been abolished.
costs: Money paid by the loser to the winner of a court action to cover the expenses incurred by the litigation. Generally, costs do not include attorney's fees. Charges and fees that statutes require be paid

for the services of court officers, witnesses, jurors, and others.
co-tenancy: Ownership of property by two or more persons who have unity of possession, *i.e.,* a right to possess the entire property. Term includes joint tenancy, tenancy in common, and tenancy by the entirety (*see* joint tenancy, tenancy in common, and tenancy by the entirety).
counsel: An attorney; counselor. Advice given regarding legal matters.
count: In indictments, an allegation of a distinct offense; a charge. In civil procedure, the statement of the specific cause of the action.
counterclaim: A counter demand made by a defendant against a plaintiff (*i.e.*, between opposing parties in the original action) in a civil suit. It is not a defense, answer or denial, but an independent cause of action made to diminish or defeat the plaintiff's claim. A counterclaim may be compulsory, arising out of the subject matter of the claim against the defendant, or permissive, not arising out of that subject matter. *See* set-off; *compare* cross-claim.
counterfeit: To forge, fabricate, or unlawfully copy something with the intention of deceiving another by passing the copy as the original. Used also as a noun and an adjective in reference to the thing so fabricated.
countermand: To revoke or cancel an order previously given. An order which is inconsistent with a previous order countermands the first order by implication. Used also as a noun.
counteroffer: An offer made in response to an offer which changes the terms of the original offer, *e.g.*, by making acceptance dependent on the performance of a condition.
countersign: To sign a document in addition to a principal signature so as to attest to the document's validity. The signature itself is called a countersignature.
county: A geographical subdivision of a state made for political, judicial, or administrative purposes. In some jurisdictions, counties have incorporated in order to facilitate the administration of local government.
course of dealing: The history of business conduct between parties which establishes a basis of understanding their behavior.
court: A governmental institution charged with the administration of justice according to laws or principles of equity. The place justice is administered. A judge or all judges.

Courts are classified as "superior" and "inferior." Superior courts have general original jurisdiction in the first instance (*i.e.*, unlimited jurisdiction in their jurisdictional area) and have a degree of control over lower courts. Inferior courts have limited jurisdiction (can only hear certain types of cases) and are subject to review by higher courts. Courts are also classified as civil and criminal. Civil courts adjudicate controversies between individuals involving private rights. Criminal courts adjudicate cases involving criminal laws. A court of equity administers justice according to principles of equity.
court-martial: A military court established to adjudicate cases of members of the armed forces. (Verb) To prosecute before such a court.
court of appeals: A court which hears cases on appeal from the lower courts. *See* appellate court.
Court of Claims: A federal court that hears and determines claims against the United States Government. These claims may be founded upon acts of Congress, regulations of executive departments, contracts with the government, and upon matters founded upon the Constitution.
covenant: A written agreement; a promise or obligation contained in an instrument under seal, such as a deed. The term is often used in relation to land, such as a "covenant for quiet enjoyment," which is a promise by the conveyor of land that he will protect the buyer against lawful claims made on the land. A "covenant of seisin" is a promise made by a grantor of property that he lawfully possesses the property and has the right to convey it. Covenants are classified in many ways. "Covenants in gross" are those that do not run with the land, *i.e.*, they do not pass to succeeding owners. "Covenants running with the land" do pass to succeeding owners. "Covenants against encumbrances" are promises made by the grantor stating that an estate has no burdens on it, such as claims or liens.
coverture: At common law, the status of a married woman which combines her civil existence with her husband's. Coverture gives the husband equal control over his wife's property (as is the case in community property jurisdictions). Modern statutes have changed this and have given the woman complete control over her own property in many jurisdictions.
C.P.S.C.: *See* Consumer Product Safety Commission.
credit: (Noun) The trust or confidence a buyer gains from a seller based on the buyer's ability and reputation for payment. It allows a person to pay for a purchase over time or to borrow money. The time allowed a buyer to pay for a purchase. The amount of money at one's disposal, *e.g.*, in a bank account or other security. In accounting, money one is owed; opposite of debit. (Verb) To acknowledge payment of a debt.
credit bureau: A firm that collects information on the character, reputation, and credit rating of persons

or corporations for distribution to subscribers, such as banks; commercial agency; credit agency; mercantile agency.

creditor: Person to whom a debt is owed; one who extends credit to another; anyone to whom an obligation is owed; opposite of debtor.

creditor's bill (or suit): An equity proceeding whereby a party who has been found by the court to be owed a debt (judgment creditor) seeks to collect on that debt from the assets of the debtor (judgment debtor) which cannot be reached by execution, *i.e.*, the seizure and sale of the assets. *See* execution.

crime: A violation of penal law. Crimes are classified in many ways, most generally as misdemeanors and felonies. They are classified as "mala in se" (immoral or wrong in themselves) and "mala prohibita" (prohibited by law but not necessarily immoral). Crimes are also petty and major, infamous and not infamous, and those which involve moral turpitude and those that do not.

crimen falsi: Lat. A crime involving some element of deceit, fraud, or untruthfulness, *e.g.*, embezzlement, perjury, forgery. At common law, such a crime disqualified its perpetrator from appearing as a witness.

criminal: (Noun) One who has been found guilty of committing a crime. (Adj.) Pertaining to or having the character of a crime. As opposed to civil which pertains to private rights and remedies, criminal generally pertains to law that protects society at large from harm.

criminal conversation: Adultery; sexual intercourse with a person not one's spouse. It is a tortious activity which entitles the injured spouse to damages. *See* alienation of affection.

criminal law: The branch of law which defines what public wrongs are considered crimes and assigns punishment for those wrongs.

criminal negligence: Omission or commission of an act which a reasonable, prudent person would do or not do under similar circumstances. Such negligence endangers another's life or safety and is punishable as a crime. *E.g.*, reckless driving with complete disregard for the safety of others is criminal negligence that may be punishable as manslaughter if the death of another occurs.

cross-action: An independent action by a defendant against a plaintiff or codefendant which grows out of the subject matter of the plaintiff's suit. Same as "cross-complaint." Term is often used interchangeably with cross-claim, but accurately, a cross-claim is between parties on the same side of the action.

cross-claim: A claim made by a person against a party on the same side of an action. Cross-claims arise out of transactions or occurrences that are the subject of the original suit, a counterclaim to the original suit, or the property involved in the original suit. *Compare* counterclaim, cross-action.

cross-examination: The questioning of the opposition's witness in order to test the truth and accuracy of that witness's testimony given on direct examination.

cruel and unusual punishment: Excessive punishment which inflicts unnecessary pain, such as beating, torture, or starvation; punishment not in proportion to the crime. The death penalty is not cruel and unusual punishment per se, although some states have held it to be so. The eighth amendment prohibits cruel and unusual punishment.

cruelty: Willful and malicious infliction of physical or mental pain. Term is used in divorce actions to mean that conduct that inflicts physical suffering, mental distress, or fear of bodily harm on one's spouse so as to seriously harm the marital relationship. Cruelty to animals inflicts unnecessary suffering on animals and is a misdemeanor.

culpable: Worthy of blame; morally at fault. "Culpable negligence" is sometimes defined as more than ordinary negligence in that it is a conscious and wanton disregard of one's legal duty or of the rights and safety of others.

cumulative: Additional; added together; consecutive. "Cumulative sentences" are served one after the other, as distinguished from "concurrent sentences" which are served at the same time. "Cumulative evidence" is additional evidence which serves to prove a fact already proven by other evidence: corroborating evidence. A "cumulative remedy" is a remedy (*see* remedy) added to one already in force.

curia: Lat. A court or judicial tribunal.

curtesy: At common law, a husband's right to his deceased wife's estate, dependent upon the birth of a child capable of inheriting the estate. A "curtesy initiate" exists when such a capable child is born, but before the wife dies. After her death, the right is called a "curtesy consummate." *Compare* dower.

curtilage: Space around a house often, though not necessarily, enclosed by a fence or shrubbery; also "curtillium."

custody: Care or control of a person or piece of property, *e.g.*, the custody a guardian has over the child under his or her care or the custody a person has of a car loaned to him. Custody is not possession (which entails the exercise of dominion and control) but is a mere keeping and caring. Also, a person whose liberty is restricted, in prison or out, is said to be "in custody."

custom: A practice which, through long, repetitious use and common acceptance, has gained the status of unwritten law in a particular area. "General custom" prevails throughout the country and is called common law. "Particular custom" or local custom applies to a smaller locality, such as a town.

customs: Duties on imported or exported goods. Governmental branch that oversees the importation of goods into a country.

cy-pres: Fr. As near as possible. A doctrine which allows the court to carry out a will or trust which, for some reason, is impossible to carry out as directed. In such a case, the court will follow the general intention of the testator as nearly as possible. This doctrine is commonly applied in regard to gifts to charity.

D

damage: The loss or harm caused by the negligence, design, or accident of one person to another person or his property. Damage is distinguished from injury in that injury is the wrong committed whereas damage is the harm suffered. *See* injury, damages.

damage feasant: Doing damage. The term originally meant the harm caused by trespassing animals.

damages: The monetary compensation awarded to one who suffers a loss or detriment which is the fault of another. Damages are classified in several ways. "Actual damages" are awarded for the real loss suffered, and the term is synonymous with "compensatory damages" and "general damages."

"Exemplary" or "punitive damages" are awarded in excess of actual damages to punish the defendant.

"Nominal damages" are awarded as a token for an infringement of a right, *i.e.*, a small amount awarded where no substantial loss has been suffered or where the plaintiff cannot show the amount of his injury, but where the law recognizes that some slight injury has occurred.

"Incidental" or "consequential damages" are awarded to compensate for costs incurred by a buyer which are incident to a breach of contract by a seller, or vice versa.

damnum: Lat. Damage.

damnum absque injuria: Lat. Damages without injury. A loss suffered where there is no cause for legal action.

day in court: The right to appear in court to answer a complaint or to defend a right; due process. The opportunity to appear in court to present claims or defend rights; the day one is to appear in court.

deadly weapon: Any instrument which can cause death or serious bodily harm whether it is designed to do so (*e.g.*, gun, knife) or merely capable of doing so (*e.g.*, hammer, ax).

death: The ending of life; the cessation of all vital life signs such as brain function, movement, respiration, heart beat, reflexes, and responsiveness to external stimuli. The precise definition of death varies, yet most states' definitions involve the cessation of brain function.

"Civil death" means a person loses all civil rights, such as when he is sentenced to life imprisonment. "Natural death" is that which results from natural causes as distinguished from violent death. "Presumptive death" is presumed death due to long, unexplained absence.

debauchery: A broad term for excessive indulgence in sensual pleasures, such as unlawful sexual behavior or habitual drunkenness; sexual immorality.

de bene esse: Lat. Conditionally; provisionally; for the present. Phrase applies to a thing done in the present in anticipation of future use. *E.g.*, de bene esse evidence is taken out of court and before a trial to prevent it from being lost, due to the death of a witness, for instance.

debenture: A certificate, promissory note, or bond acknowledging or creating a corporate obligation, usually unsecured. A "mortgage debenture" is one where specific property or funds are used as security.

debit: Bookkeeping term for sum charged as due or owing. As a verb, word means to enter an amount on the left-hand side of a ledger as being owed the account.

de bonis non administratis: Lat. Of the goods not administered. When an executor dies without completely administering an estate, the administrator appointed to succeed him is granted administration de bonis non.

de bonis propriis: Lat. Of his own goods. Term used for a judgment against an executor or administrator which is settled out of that person's property and not out of the estate of the deceased. It is rendered, for instance, when the executor or administrator has wasted the deceased person's property.

debt: That which is owed to another, whether money, services, or goods; an obligation one person owes to another.

debtor: One who owes a debt; one who is under obligation to pay money to another.

decedent: A deceased person, especially one who has recently died.
deceit: A fraudulent representation whereby one person, while having knowledge of the falsity of a material fact, intends to deceive another, thereby causing the latter to suffer damage due to his acting on the misrepresentation.
declaration: Act of declaring, asserting, or formally stating. *See* declaration of intent. An unsworn statement made out of court, such as a "dying declaration" where the victim of a homicide speaks about the circumstances surrounding his fatal injury. The formal complaint by a plaintiff where the cause of action is stated.
declaration of intent (or intention): A formal statement made before a court by an alien intending to become a U.S. citizen. *8 U.S.C.A. §731.*
declaratory judgment: A statement of the court declaring the rights and duties of the parties in a case or stating an opinion on a question of law without awarding relief. This judgment is binding whereas an advisory opinion is not.
decree: A decision in a court of equity, admiralty, or probate which includes the remedy ordered to correct the injustice. A distinction once was made between decrees and judgments, the former referring to decisions in a court of equity and the latter to decisions in a court of law, but today judgment commonly applies to both.
decree nisi: A provisional decree that takes absolute effect unless a reason can be shown why it should not.
de die in diem: Lat. From day to day.
deed: A written instrument which transfers real property or the right to real property. A "bargain and sale deed" is a conveyance with a consideration regarding its use attached. A "quitclaim deed" releases and conveys only the interest the grantor has in the property involved. A "warranty deed" insures the validity of the title. The covenants of title are warranty of seisin, quiet enjoyment, and right to convey, freedom from encumbrances, and defense of title as to all claims.
deed of trust: A conveyance of title by written instrument creating a trust in real property which is used as security for performance of an obligation, such as payment of a debt on land. It is similar to a mortgage, though it differs in form. The deed of trust is executed in favor of a disinterested, third-party trustee, whereas a mortgage is executed to the creditor directly. *See* mortgage.
deed poll: A deed made by and obligating only one party as opposed to an indenture which obligates two or more persons.
deem: To hold; construe; adjudge; treat as if. *E.g.*, a fact deemed to be true is treated as if true.
de facto: Lat. In fact; in actuality; *e.g.*, a de facto corporation exists in actuality though it may not meet all the legal requirements of a corporation. De facto is used in contrast with de jure, which means lawful.
defalcation: Failure to account for or pay money entrusted to one when due. Term is broader than misappropriation and embezzlement in that it does not necessarily imply criminal fraud. The making of a claim against a claim. *See* recoupment, counterclaim.
defamation: The publication of material injurious to a person's good name and reputation. Includes both libel and slander.
default: Failure to perform a legal duty; neglect; omission. *E.g.*, a default on a mortgage is the failure to pay on the loan when due, and a default in legal proceedings is the failure to perform a procedural step, such as to appear or plead in an action when required to do so.
default judgment: A judgment entered against a defendant who fails to appear in court or to enter a plea when required to do so.
defeasance: An instrument attached to some other deed or estate which cancels or defeats the latter; a collateral deed containing conditions which, when met, cancel the original deed. A "defeasance clause" is a clause in a mortgage which states that the mortgage is ended when all payments on it have been made.
defeasible: Subject to being canceled, annulled, revoked, or avoided upon the occurrence or nonoccurrence of a future event or action. *E.g.*, a mortgage is a defeasible instrument because it is subject to cancellation upon its being paid in full.
defect: A deficiency; a lack of completeness or perfection; the absence of a requirement needed to make something legally sufficient. A defect can be in a product, in performance, or in a title.
defendant: The person accused in a criminal case or sued in a civil action.
defendant in error: The party who, after prevailing in a lower court, becomes a defendant in an appellate court due to alleged errors of law in the lower court.
defense: All the evidence and argument offered on behalf of a defendant to refute a plaintiff's charges or to diminish or defeat his recovery.
deficiency: An insufficiency, a lack of something. The difference between the amount a taxpayer shows he owes on a tax return and the amount the taxing body says is owed.
deficiency judgment: A judgment in favor of a creditor which imposes personal liability on a mortgagor for the amount of debt remaining after the sale of his property to satisfy the debt.
definitive: Final; conclusive; that which ends something, such as a lawsuit.

deforcement: The holding of land which rightfully belongs to another. Term includes abatement, discontinuance, disseisin, and intrusion, but is broader, and it especially applies to cases where the rightful owner has never had possession.
defraud: To cheat; to trick; to misrepresent material facts with the intent to deprive another of property, right, or interest. *See* fraud, deceit. Omissions or concealments which breach a duty, trust, or confidence, and which injure or take advantage of another.
degree: A level, step, or grade, such as in first and second degree murder or first and second degree relatives.
de homine replegiando: Lat. For replevying a man. A writ to release a person from prison or from the custody of a private person where that person (*see* surety) becomes responsible for the released person's appearance in court. Analogous to writ of habeas corpus.
de jure: Lat. Lawful; by right; legitimate; *e.g.*, de jure segregation is that intended by law. De jure is used in contrast to de facto, which means in fact.
del credere: Italian. Of belief or trust. An agent who sells goods for another on credit and guarantees that the purchaser will pay for the goods.
delegate: (Noun) A representative; an agent; a person authorized to act for another, such as a delegate at a political convention. (Verb) To authorize; to relegate, as in "to delegate power."
delegation: A body of representatives or delegates. The act of authorizing a person to act for others. Civil law: A species of novation whereby another person takes on the obligation of the original debtor. The consent of the three parties to the substitution is required in a delegation, whereas in other species of novation, consent is required of only the two parties to the new arrangement. *See* novation.
delegatus non potest delegare: Lat. A delegate cannot himself delegate; *i.e.,* an agent or representative cannot delegate the authority granted to him without the express consent of the person whom he represents.
deliberate: (Verb) To plan, consider, or think over beforehand. (Adj.) Carefully considered; well thought out; planned, as opposed to spontaneous. A crime is deliberate when its perpetrator carefully considers the motives, nature, and consequences of the crime before deciding to commit it.
delictum: Lat. A tort; wrongful act; an injury. A "delict" is a crime or misdemeanor.
delinquency, delinquent: The condition of failing or omitting to perform a legal duty, such as to pay a debt. "Delinquent" as a noun is the person who so fails; as an adjective, it refers to the object of the delinquency, *e.g.*, a delinquent tax. A "delinquent child" is an underage person who commits a crime.
delivery: The act of transferring possession of goods or title to property. Delivery of goods may be actual or constructive; *i.e.*, implied by law, such as where goods are stored in a warehouse and access to the warehouse is given to the purchaser of the goods. In a transfer of title, delivery takes place when the grantor intends to convey title and puts the deed into the control of the grantee. *Compare* conveyance.
delusion: An unfounded, irrational, or absurd belief held against evidence of its falsity. An "insane delusion" is the product of a diseased or deranged mind.
demand: (Noun) An assertion of a legal right; a claim; a forceful request to perform an obligation owed to one, such as to pay money. (Verb) To assert a legal right; to claim as being owed to one; to seek relief.
demand note: A promissory note which does not state a specific time for payment but rather is payable on demand, *i.e.,* when it is presented.
demesne: His own. Domain; held in one's right, and not of a superior. Term comes from the land the lord of a manor kept for his own use. It is used today in the phrase "seised in his demesne as of fee" meaning a person has a corporeal inheritance (having physical substance). This is distinguished from an incorporeal hereditament (having no physical substance) which is said to be "seised as of fee."
de minimus: Lat. Of small, unimportant matters.
de minimus non curat lex: Lat. The law is not concerned with trivial matters.
demise: (Noun) A conveyance or transfer of an estate in fee for life, or at will. Synonymous with "lease" or "let." (Verb) To transfer an estate by inheritance or succession. Death.
demonstrative evidence: Evidence that is shown directly to the court or jury with no intervening testimony; real, tangible evidence that appeals to the senses, *e.g.*, a gun.
demur: To object in a pleading to the sufficiency at law of the opposing party's pleading. *See* demurrer.
demurrage: A payment due the owner of a ship when it is delayed in port beyond the time allowed in the contract for its hire. Term also applies to railroad cars, and exists to expedite the loading and unloading of freight.
demurrer: A defendant's allegation in a pleading that the legal consequences of the opposition's plea are insufficient to compel him to answer, even though the defendant admits the matters of fact alleged against him are true.

A "special demurrer" specifies the defects in *form* of the plaintiff's pleading. A "general demurrer" does not specify defects but rather is worded in general terms, and is an objection to the *substance* of the pleading.

In modern procedure, the demurrer has been abolished and replaced by a motion to dismiss. *Federal Rule of Civil Procedure 7(c).*

denial: In pleading, a refuting of the charges made against one; a contradiction; a traverse. Denials can be general and refute all allegations made in a complaint, or specific and address a particular allegation.

denizen: A person whose status is between that of a natural born citizen and an alien. He lives in a foreign country and has many but not all of the rights of a citizen.

de novo: Lat. Anew; afresh; a second time. *E.g.*, a trial de novo is a new trial which tries a matter as though it had not been heard before.

departure: A deviation from a previous pleading, whether in the substance of the pleading, its legal basis, or by way of a reply, rejoinder, or subsequent pleading. A disagreement between a pleading and the evidence offered to support it. *See* variance.

deponent: Person who gives a deposition; one who gives a sworn testimony; a witness; an affiant.

deportation: The expulsion of an alien from one country usually to the country from which he came; banishment; exile.

depose: To make a deposition; to give sworn testimony. To forcibly remove from office, particularly a sovereign.

deposit: An amount of money given as security for the performance of an obligation, often the purchase of something. A deposit is given as an indication of the buyer's earnest intention to purchase the property, and may be applied to the purchase price and is forfeited if the depositor withdraws from the obligation. A bailment of goods kept by a bailee and returned at the bailor's request. The placing of money in a bank; the money so deposited.

deposition: The pretrial, sworn testimony of a witness taken out of court in response to oral examination or written interrogatories and recorded in writing for use in court. The adversary is given an opportunity to cross-examine the deponent during the questioning. *Federal Rules of Civil Procedure 26 et seq; Federal Rule of Criminal Procedure 15. See* interrogatories; *compare* affidavit.

depreciation: Reduction in the value of a property due to deterioration caused by use, weather, or the passage of time. An amount taken as a deduction on tax returns for reduction in the value of property.

deputy: A person authorized to act in place of another; a delegate; an agent; a substitute for a public officer who may perform all the duties of that person.

derelict: Abandoned, deserted. Maritime law: A vessel abandoned without hope or intention of recovery. Land left permanently uncovered by receding waters. Intentionally abandoned personal property. A person without substance or apparent purpose in life; a bum; a vagrant. *See* dereliction.

dereliction: The process by which land is gained when waters that covered it recede; the land so uncovered. Voluntary abandonment of property. Neglect of duty.

derivative action: A suit by a stockholder on behalf of a corporation to enforce a corporate right or remedy a wrong. The corporation is a necessary party to the action and recovery is made to the corporation.

derogate: To lessen or detract from so as to impair.

derogation: A partial repeal or abolition of a law by the passage of a subsequent law.

descendant: A person who proceeds directly from the body of another, *i.e.*, one's child, grandchild, great-grandchild, etc. A person to whom an estate descends.

descent: The transfer of real estate by inheritance and the operation of law, not by will.

desertion: Abandonment of one's duty, such as that which one owes to one's spouse or child, or to one's military post, with no intention of returning.

de son tort: Lat. By his own wrong. *E.g.*, an executor de son tort is a person who, without authority, acts as an executor of an estate.

detainer: Lawful detention of a prisoner to insure the prisoner's availability for turning him over to other authorities at the end of his term. Act of keeping property from a person who is legally entitled to it. An "unlawful detainer" is the illegal keeping of goods or real property which may have been originally acquired lawfully, such as when a tenant refuses to leave an apartment after his lease has expired and he has been asked to leave.

detention: Act of holding a person or thing, such as a suspected criminal or a stolen automobile.

determinable: Liable to be determined, settled, or ended after an amount of time or when a certain contingency occurs. A "determinable fee" is an interest in land which may last forever or until an event stated in the grant of devise which creates it occurs, *e.g.*, an estate granted to a widow until she remarries.

determination: A final decision, as in the court's determination of a lawsuit. Contract law: The extinguishment or ending of an agreement by judicial order after a contract has been affirmed. An ending in general. An estimate. Tax law: An allowance or disallowance in correcting an error in taxation.

detinue: At common law, an action to recover personal property, in specie, unlawfully held by another, plus damages caused by its detention.

detriment: In general, term means loss or harm; in contracts it is that which a person gives up in exchange for a promise by the other party. *See* consideration.

devastavit: Lat. He has wasted. Mismanagement of a decedent's estate by its executor or administrator which results in a loss to the estate. Such a violation of duty makes said person personally liable for the loss.
devest: To deprive. *See* divest.
deviation, deviant: A departure from the normal course of travel, operation, or procedure. In employment, it is an employee's departure from his normal duties or scope of employment. In insurance, it is a departure from the risks a policy covers without just cause. The adjective is "deviant."
devise: A gift by will; specifically a gift of real property although term sometimes is used to refer to personal property. (Verb) To dispose of real property by will. *Compare* bequest, bequeath.

A devise may be contingent (does not vest until a future event occurs) or vested at the death of the testator.

Devises are classified as specific (mentions a particular piece of land), general (does not mention a specific piece of land but refers to land without additional words attached to qualify it, *e.g.*, "all my lands"), and residuary (all the land left after the debts on the estate have been settled). *See* residue.
devisee: Person to whom real property is given by will.
devolution: Transfer of property from one person to another by operation of law. The transfer of a right, liability, title, estate, or office.
devolve: To pass or be transferred from one person to another, *e.g.*, the transfer of an estate from a decedent.
dictum: Abbreviation for "obiter dictum," "a remark by the way." An opinion, observation, or remark by a judge which is not necessary for the decision of the case. Plural is "dicta."
digest: A collection or compilation of books, articles and cases arranged for reference purposes. The American Digest System is the master index system used in the U.S.
dilatory: Tending or intended to cause delay.
dilatory pleas: At common law, a class of defenses based on a matter not connected with the merits of the case but which serve to delay action on it while not impeaching the right of action itself. Pleas challenging jurisdiction, and those regarding matters of procedure or the capacity of the defendant or plaintiff are dilatory as long as they do not defeat the plaintiff's cause of action or result in any relief against the plaintiff. Dilatory pleas have practically disappeared in modern practice. *See* demurrer.
diligence, diligent: Attentiveness; care; prudence. The law distinguishes three degrees of diligence to describe the degree of care various persons exercise in their own affairs: ordinary (prudent person), slight (less than prudent), and extraordinary (exceptionally prudent person). The adjective is "diligent."
diminution: A reduction; an act of taking away or making less. Term is used in phrases such as "diminution of salary" and "diminution in value."
direct: (Adj.) Immediate; proximate; without any intervention or influence; *e.g.*, the direct cause of an accident is the primary reason the accident occurred. In the usual course or order; opposite of cross, collateral, or remote. (Verb) To command, order, instruct, or advise.
direct attack: A challenge to have a judgment reversed, corrected, vacated, annulled, voided, or enjoined, made in a proceeding for that express purpose. It differs from a collateral attack which challenges a judgment in a proceeding instituted for another purpose.
direct contempt: Acts done or words spoken in the presence of the court which tend to interrupt the administration of justice or embarrass the court.
directed verdict: A jury verdict ordered by the court. In civil cases, a party may receive a directed verdict if the opposite side does not present a prima facie case or a necessary defense. *Federal Rule of Civil Procedure 50(a)*. In criminal cases, a directed verdict may only be for acquittal. *Federal Rule of Criminal Procedure 29*.
direct evidence: Evidence from a person who actually witnessed the matter in question with his own senses. It is distinguished from indirect or circumstantial evidence.
direct examination: The examination in chief of a witness by the party who called him to the stand.
director: Person elected or appointed to manage the affairs of a corporation. Directors act as a unit called the board of directors.
directory: Instructive; directive; that which is for advisory purposes alone, and carries no obligatory force. A directory provision in a statute should be complied with as nearly as possible, though in fact it is optional. A mandatory provision must be complied with and it carries consequences for failure to do so.
disability: Lack of legal capacity to perform an act, such as a minor's incapacity to sue, an insane person's inability to make a contract, or a married person's incapacity to remarry without first dissolving the previous marriage. A physical or mental incapacity to perform one's work; loss of earning power due to such an incapacity. Under Social Security Act: Inability to perform substantial gainful activity due to mental or physical impairment.
disaffirm, disaffirmance: To repudiate; to refuse to accept; to revoke a consent previously given, as in to revoke a voidable contract. Noun is "disaffirmance."

disbar, disbarment: To deprive an attorney of the right to practice law by suspending his license. Disbarment is an act of the court taken because of illegal or unethical conduct by an attorney.

discharge: (Verb) To release, dismiss, free, or relieve. *E.g.*, to discharge a bankrupt is to release him from liability on his debts; to discharge a worker is to dismiss him from employment; to discharge a person held on accusation of a crime is to set him free; to discharge a jury is to relieve it from further consideration of a case. To perform a duty. (Noun) A document by which a contract, such as a mortgage, is ended. A proceeding which releases a bankrupt from his debts.

disclaimer: A renunciation or rejection of a claim, right, or office, *e.g.*, a refusal to accept a right or an interest in an estate offered to one, or a defendant's renunciation of any claim to the thing demanded by the plaintiff.

disclosure: A revelation; an act of making known. A thing revealed. As used in the Truth in Lending Act, term refers to the manner in which certain necessary information is to be conveyed to a person seeking credit.

discontinuance: A voluntary termination of a suit by written notice from the plaintiff or by a court order by a judge; a voluntary dismissal; a nonsuit. The abandonment of work on a project. A "discontinuance of an estate" is a termination or suspension of an estate tail due to a grant by a tenant in tail which was larger than such tenant was entitled to convey. *See* tail.

discrimination: The unequal treatment of persons where no reasonable distinction exists among them. Federal statutes prohibit discrimination in employment based on sex, race, age, religion, and national origin.

disfranchise: To deprive a free citizen of a right or privilege especially the right to vote. *See* franchise.

dishonor: To refuse to accept or pay a check or other negotiable instrument. *E.g.*, a bank may dishonor a check if there is not enough money in the drawer's account to cover it.

disinherit, disinheritance: To deprive an heir of his inheritance. This can be done by writing a clause to that effect in one's will. Noun is "disinheritance."

disinterested witness: An impartial, unbiased witness; one who has no interest in the outcome of the case.

dismiss, dismissal: To discharge or discontinue a suit or action. A "dismissal" is the order or judgment which discharges or disposes of a suit, action, or motion, and may be with prejudice (*i.e.*, based on the merits of the case and barring further action on same), or it may be without prejudice (*i.e.*, not based on the merits and not barring subsequent action).

disorderly conduct: A general term for behavior that tends to disturb the peace or shock public sense of morality.

disorderly house: A term of broad definition meaning a place where illegal or publicly offensive practices are frequently carried out, *e.g.*, a house of prostitution or a gambling house.

disparagement: A discrediting, belittling, or degrading of someone or something. Disparagement may be of goods for sale (*see* bait and switch) or of title, which casts aspersions on a title to property. In old English law, term meant the discredit one sustained by marriage to someone below one's rank or character.

dispensation: Permission to do something usually forbidden; exemption from a law; an allowance to omit something commanded.

disposition: The giving up of something; a relinquishment; a disposal, settlement, or final determination of some matter, such as the disposition of an estate, a debt, or a case. The sentencing phase of a criminal proceeding. Frame of mind; temperament.

dispute: A controversy; a demand made or right asserted which is refuted by another party. The subject of a controversy.

disqualify: To render unfit or ineligible, as in to disqualify a juror due to his prejudices.

disseisin: The wrongful dispossession or taking and putting out of an owner from his real property which he presently possesses and enjoys. A disseisin may be a deprivation of the owner of the rents and profits of his property. *See* seisin.

dissent, dissenting opinion: To disagree; a judge's disagreement with the majority opinion rendered.

dissolution: Act or process of ending, dissolving, or breaking up, as in the dissolution of a contract when the contracting parties themselves cancel it, the dissolution of a corporation when the corporate entity is dissolved, or the dissolution of a marriage by divorce.

distrain: To take and keep the personal property of another to be returned upon the performance of an obligation, *e.g.*, a landlord's taking of a tenant's personal property for nonpayment of rent; any detention of personal property. *See* distress.

distress: The act of taking personal property without legal process from a wrongdoer by the party injured, done to secure performance of an obligation the wrongdoer has undertaken. The act is regulated by statute regarding a landlord's taking of a tenant's property. The taking of personal property to enforce tax payment. Property distrained.

distribution: The giving out of something in portions, such as the remainder of an estate after taxes and debts have been paid to the heirs of a person who dies leaving no will. The division and giving out of the capital assets of a corporation to stockholders.

district: A subdivision of a geographical area for administrative, judicial, political, or electoral purposes, *e.g.*, a congressional district.

district attorney: The prosecuting attorney who represents the United States government in a federal judicial district (U.S. District Attorney) or the state in a state judicial district (State's Attorney).

district court: A federal trial court of record having general jurisdiction over a particular geographical area; U.S. District Court. An inferior state court having general jurisdiction, although in some states jurisdiction is limited.

disturbance (disturbing the peace): General term for any act which annoys or agitates another person or interrupts the quiet and orderliness of a neighborhood or a gathering. At common law, a wrong done to an incorporeal hereditament by obstructing the owner from enjoying it, *e.g.*, to put a fence across a piece of land a person has the right to use.

diversity of citizenship: A ground used to invoke the jurisdiction of the federal courts when parties on different sides of a controversy involving more than $10,000 live in different states, or when one party is an alien. *See* the judicial powers granted the United States under article III, sec. 2 of the U.S. Constitution.

divest: To take away, deprive, or get rid of something as in to divest one's property by selling it; to cause a loss of a right or interest in an estate which has already vested in a person.

dividend: A sum from the surplus earnings of a joint stock company divided and paid periodically to stockholders. A payment to creditors in a bankruptcy proceeding.

divisible contract: A contract susceptible to division into two or more independent parts; severable contract. The separate parts may be considered as independent agreements contained in one instrument, the breach of one not affecting the whole contract.

divorce: A legal separation of husband and wife. A divorce may be absolute (a complete termination of the marriage allowing each person to remarry), or limited (separation of spouses not allowing either to remarry). The latter is also called a legal separation. *See* annulment.

dock: (Noun) The place in some courtrooms where a prisoner stays during trial. (Verb) To diminish; to deduct from, especially wages due to an employee, *e.g.*, for tardiness.

docket: A brief record of the proceedings of a case. A book containing brief entries of court proceedings. Also used as a verb meaning to enter court activity in a docket. A list of cases for trial or appeal.

doctrine: A rule or principle of law developed through court decisions.

document: Anything with a message on it that can be read, *e.g.*, a deed, contract, receipt, map. (Verb) To support with documentary evidence.

document of title: A paper recognized by businesses as granting its holder the right to receive, hold, or dispose of goods mentioned on the document, *e.g.*, a bill of lading, a warehouse receipt, a dock warrant.

doing business: The carrying on of business for which a corporation was organized. To determine whether a foreign corporation is doing business within a state, it must be determined that the corporation has certain minimum contacts with the state that made it amenable to the courts and/or susceptible to the taxes of that state.

doli capax: Lat. Capable of distinguishing between right and wrong. This capacity makes one amenable to the criminal laws.

doli incapax: Lat. Incapable of distinguishing between right and wrong. The law recognizes persons under age seven as doli incapax, and thus they cannot be convicted of a crime.

domain: Absolute ownership and control of land; the land so owned. The state's power to control private land for public use is called the "right of eminent domain." Public parks are said to be in the "public domain."

Domesday Book: An ancient record published in the time of William the Conquerer (1081-1086), consisting of surveys of the lands in England.

domestic: (Adj.) Pertaining to home, whether one's house, home state, or country. (Noun) A household servant.

domicile: One's permanent home; legal residence. A person has only one domicile though he may have several temporary residences. For a place to be called one's domicile, one must have an intention of making it one's permanent home. The determination of one's domicile is important because it determines one's voting district and the taxing body under which one falls. *See* residence.

dominant tenement (estate): A tenement or estate whose owner benefits from an easement on another estate (servient estate). *E.g.*, *A*, the owner of a piece of land, sells half of it to *B*, his neighbor, yet retains the right to build a driveway across the land to get to the street. *A* holds the dominant estate, *B* the servient estate.

dominion: Ownership and control of something, which includes the right to claim it and the power to dispose of it. Sovereignty. Civil law: Dominion may be "proximate," meaning the owner has possession of

the property, or "remote," meaning a person owns something but is not yet in possession of it.
domus sua cuique est tutissimum refugium: Lat. A man's house is his safest refuge.
donatio: Lat. A gift, donation. A voluntary transfer of title and possession of property without consideration.
donee: One to whom a donation or gift is given; a grantee.
donor: One who makes a donation or gift.
dormant: Inactive, silent, in abeyance, such as a "dormant claim" where title vests in no one, or a "dormant judgment" which remains unexecuted for such a long time that it must be revived before it can be executed.
double damages: Twice the damages normally awarded for certain kinds of injuries. Such damages are awarded according to statute and often for punitive reasons.
double entry: A bookkeeping method which shows every transaction both as a credit and a debit.
double jeopardy: A provision in the fifth amendment of the U.S. Constitution which prohibits the prosecution of a person a second time for the same offense.
doubtful title: Title whose validity is in doubt; title which exposes its holder to litigation.
dower: A widow's portion or interest in her husband's real estate; a woman's right to one-third of her deceased husband's lands or tenements of which he was seised in fee simple or fee tail at any time during their marriage. Abolished in a majority of states. *See* curtesy.
draft: A negotiable instrument which instructs a second party (drawee) to pay a third party (payee) a sum of money, *e.g.*, a check or bill of exchange.
drawee: The party on whom a draft is drawn, *e.g.*, a bank.
drawer: The party who draws a draft, *i.e.*, one who makes a bill of exchange or signs a check.
droit: Fr. Law, right, justice.
drug addiction: Condition of habitual, uncontrolled use of narcotics.
duces tecum: Lat. Bring with you. A "subpoena duces tecum" is a writ requiring a witness to bring to court any documents, records, or other evidence relevant to a controversy.
due: Owing; payable, as when a debt is due it is time for it to be paid. Just; proper; lawful; sufficient; as in "due care" or "due process of law."
due care: The standard of care one legally owes to another under a certain set of circumstances; that degree of care a reasonable and prudent person would exercise under the circumstances. Failure to exercise due care is negligence.
due date: The day on which an obligation must be met, such as the payment of a tax or debt.
due process of law: A flexible term for the fair and orderly administration of justice in the courts. Essential to the concept is the right a person has to be notified of legal proceedings against him, the opportunity to be heard and to defend himself in an orderly proceeding, and the right to have counsel represent him. Basically, due process is the fundamental fairness principle at the core of the Anglo-American system of jurisprudence. Due process also refers to the actual legal proceedings which serve to protect and enforce individual rights and liberties.

The phrase is expressed in the fifth amendment to the U.S. Constitution: ". . . nor [shall any person] be deprived of life, liberty, or property, without due process of law," and also in the fourteenth amendment which applied the principle to the states.
duplicity: The technical fault of combining multiple causes of action or defenses in one plea, multiple offenses in one count of an indictment, or multiple incongruous subjects in one legislative act. Deception, double-dealing.
duress: Unlawful threats of harm or other pressure used to force someone to act against his will; illegal imprisonment or legal imprisonment for illegal purposes. An act performed under duress relieves a person from the legal effect his actions would normally have. *E.g.*, a contract signed under duress is not binding. *See* coercion.
duty: Obligation, as in the duty one has to perform under a contract; obligatory conduct, as in the duty of care one owes to others to avoid negligent injury to them. A tax on imports and exports.
dwelling: The house or building in which a person or persons live, *e.g.*, apartment building, trailer house. Buildings attached to a house are also part of the dwelling.
Dyer Act: National Motor Vehicle Theft Act. The act makes it a crime to knowingly transport, receive, conceal, barter, or sell a stolen motor vehicle in interstate or foreign commerce.
dying declaration: Statements concerning the cause and circumstances of a homicide made by the victim who was aware his death was imminent. These statements, introduced into evidence by a witness who heard them, are a common exception to the hearsay rule, and are admissible on the grounds of trustworthiness and necessity. The witness's credibility, though, is subject to demeanor examination and cross-examination.

E

earned income: Money gained from work as opposed to that gained from invested capital, such as stock dividends.
earnest: That which is given to secure a contract. "Earnest money" is a sum a buyer pays to a seller to demonstrate buyer's intention and ability to fulfill a purchase contract, *e.g.*, a small downpayment on a house. This money is often forfeited if buyer defaults.
earnings: Income; money earned from work performed or services rendered, without the aid of capital. The term, though, has come to include profits gained from the employment of capital in a corporation.
easement: The right to use part of the land owned by another for a special purpose. Its use must be consistent with the general use of the property by the owner. The tenement with this right is called the "dominant tenement" and the one which bears the burden is the "servient tenement."
eavesdropping: Secretly listening to another's conversations without consent, whether by electronic devices or by standing outside someone's window and listening under the "eaves." This is a common law offense.
ecclesiastical courts: Religious courts established in England which mainly deal with spiritual matters of the established church.
e converso: Lat. Conversely; on the other hand. Equivalent to "e contra."
ecumenical: Universal, worldwide, especially applied to the entire Christian church.
edict: A command or proclamation by a sovereign that carries the effect of law.
E.E.O.C.: *See* Equal Employment Opportunity Commission.
effect: (Noun) A result; consequence; the product of a cause. (Verb) To accomplish; to execute; to make, as in "to effect a sale."
effects: Personal property; any chattel or movable personal property, although term may also include real property.
egress: A means of getting out; an exit.
ejectment: An action to recover possession of land claimed by another. To recover, plaintiff must show defendant is in wrongful possession of the property and that plaintiff has a present legal right to possession of same. Also called an "action to recover possession of land," "summary process," "eviction," and "forcible entry and detainer."
ejusdem generis: Lat. Of the same kind or class. The "ejusdem generis rule" of construction states that when general words follow an enumeration of specific persons or things, the general words are to be interpreted as being in the same category as those specifically enumerated.
election: The act of choosing, as in the election of a candidate to office, a widow's election of whether she will accept what her husband left her in his will or what is provided by statute, or the election of one of several remedies at law.
elector: A qualified voter.
electrocution: Execution by passing an intense electric current through a convict. Verb is "electrocute."
eleemosynary corporation: Charitable; given as alms. An "eleemosynary corporation" is a private corporation created for religious or charitable purposes.
element: A basic or essential part, as "breaking and entry" are elements in the crime of burglary. An ancient belief held that the universe was composed of four basic elements: earth, water, air, and fire. Now the term means the forces of nature, especially those in violent weather.
eligible: Legally qualified to be selected, as in to be eligible to be elected to public office, or to be eligible to become a citizen.
elisor: Person appointed to perform the duties of a sheriff or coroner when that officer is unable or disqualified to act. An elisor is used especially in the execution of writs of venire which summon a jury.
emancipation: Generally, the act of setting free. Specifically, that time when a parent relinquishes control over a minor thus ending the legal duty to support him and granting him full right to his earn-

ings. This usually occurs at the age of majority. Emancipation may be express or implied by conduct.
embargo: A government's order prohibiting the passage of ships or certain goods into and out of its ports, sometimes issued for purposes of war, and sometimes for the control of commerce. A common carrier's refusal to carry certain kinds of freight, or to carry freight between two points.
embezzlement: The fraudulent taking for one's own use the money or property of another by a person who originally acquired it lawfully. For a crime to constitute embezzlement, a fiduciary relationship must exist between the wrongdoer and the victim, the wrongdoer must have come to possess the money or property through that relationship, and he must have acted with fraudulent intent.
emblements: Crops grown annually by labor of a tenant (*e.g.,* corn, wheat, garden vegetables) and not those that grow spontaneously. The doctrine of emblements states that a tenant has the right to take any crops he has been growing, even after his tenancy has ended.
embracery: The offense of attempting to corruptly influence a jury. Person guilty of this crime is an "embraceor."
eminent domain: State's power to take, or authorize others to take, private property for the common good provided that just compensation is paid for it. In theory, the state has superior dominion over all land, and its "owner" holds it mediately or immediately and must surrender it when the state reasserts its dominion over it. The process of so taking land is called "expropriation" or "condemnation."
emolument: The profit, gain, or advantage arising from office or employment. It includes salary, fees, and benefits.
empirical: That which is based on observation, experiment, or experience.
employee: A person who works for another for salary or wages, and whose work is under the employer's control and direction. The specific definition varies according to statute. Synonymous with "servant."
employer: One who hires another person to work for him, and who is in the position to control and direct that work. Formerly called "master."
employer's liability acts: Statutes which define an employer's liability for injuries suffered by employees while on the job. Many of these statutes state that an employer is still liable even though the worker's negligence may have contributed to the injury, *e.g.*, Federal Employers' Liability Act and Workers' Compensation Acts.
emptor: Lat. A buyer. Used in phrase "caveat emptor" meaning "let the buyer beware."
enabling clause: That clause in a statute or constitution that states by what power it is enacted and enforced, *e.g.,* "Congress shall have the power to enact and enforce this article by appropriate legislation." *U.S. Constitution, amendment XV.*
enabling statutes: Any statute which grants new power to do something. An old English statute that gave certain persons the power to make leases for life or for 21 years.
enact: To establish by decree or law; to put into effect.
enacting clause: Preliminary clause in a legislative act which states the authority by which it is made.
en banc, in banc: Fr. In full bench. Term refers to situation where all qualified judges of a court take part in a case. This is usually done for important cases in the appellate court.
enclosure: Land enclosed by some visible obstruction such as a fence or hedge. (*Compare* close) An obstruction that surrounds land. In old English law, the act of freeing land from rights of common and vesting it in one absolute owner. Also "inclosure."
encroach: To intrude unlawfully upon the land, property, or authority of another, usually in a gradual, secretive manner. *E.g.,* to fence in part of another's land is to encroach upon it.
encroachment: Act of unlawfully extending one's property boundaries onto the property of another. A fixture that illegally intrudes upon a street or highway. Easement: Act by the owner of an easement which alters a dominant tenement so as to create an additional burden upon a servient tenement.
encumbrance: A claim or interest in land held by a person other than its owner, *e.g.,* a mortgage, lien, easement. It does not prohibit passing title, but it does lower the land's value. An encumbrance may also be on personal property, *e.g.,* a chattel mortgage. Also "incumbrance."
endorsement: Act of signing the back of a negotiable instrument to transfer it entirely to another person. An "accommodation endorsement" is one where the endorser extends credit to the holder of the instrument without consideration. A "blank endorsement" is one which does not specify to whom the instrument is payable, and thus is negotiable by the bearer. A "restrictive endorsement" is conditional, *i.e.,* there are restrictions placed on it as to how it can be transferred. Also "indorsement."
endowment: Money or property given to a person or institution the income from which is to be used for a specific purpose; the act of setting up such a fund. The assignment of dower.
enfeoffment: Old English term for transferring full ownership in land by a ceremony called "livery of seisin." Today, term means act of investing a person

with a fee (estate in real property); the deed by which a person is so vested with possession. Also "feoffment."

enforce: To put into effect; to carry out; to cause the performance of; to execute, such as to enforce a contract. To compel obedience.

enfranchise: To make free. To give the right to vote.

engrossing: The making of a clear, legible copy of a document. The cornering of the market on a commodity and gaining of a monopoly.

enjoin: To command with authority; to order that something be done or not be done; to require; to issue a writ of injunction. *See* injunction.

enjoy: To have and use with satisfaction; to have the economic benefit of. "Enjoyment" is the exercise of a right, such as the right to peacefully occupy one's property.

enlarge: To increase, expand, make larger. To free someone from custody or prison. "Enlargement" or "enlarger l'estate" is a type of release which enlarges an estate and conveys the interest of a remainderman to a tenant.

enroll: To record; to register; to enter into the records of a court or legislature.

enrolled bill rule: Rule that states that a duly passed and signed bill shall not be questioned as to its enactment.

entail: (Verb) To limit the succession to real property to the issue, or certain classes of issue, of an heir; to create an estate tail. (Noun) A fee limited to the issue of an heir's body; a fee tail. *See* fee tail.

enter: Real property: To go onto land to take possession of it. To become part of something, as in to enter a conspiracy. To formally put into the records, as in to enter a transaction into a ledger, or to enter an appearance in court.

entering judgment: The formal entry of a court's decision into the court records by the court clerk. This record serves as incontestable evidence of the court's judgment.

enticement: Act of wrongfully persuading or inducing a person to do something, *e.g.*, to persuade a child to enter a car for unlawful purposes.

entirety: Whole; not divided; *e.g.*, property "seised of the entirety" by a husband and wife is held wholly by both, and neither can convey it without the consent of the other. "Entirety of contract" means the contract is not divisible or severable.

entitle: To give right or title to. To qualify for. "Entitlement" is the right to claim something, such as social security benefits.

entity: An existence, a being, be it actual or artificial, *e.g.*, a person, corporation, or trust.

entrapment: Act by police or other government officer of inducing a person to commit a crime he had not contemplated nor would have committed if not for the inducement. It is done to obtain evidence needed to initiate prosecution against the person, and constitutes an affirmative defense if proven by the defendant.

entry: Act of writing down an item in a record book, such as a court record or business ledger; the item so entered. The act of going into another's house to commit a crime. The slightest entry of a person, or an instrument used by him for criminal purposes, is sufficient to constitute the "entry" requirement for burglary.

enumerate: To count; to list. "Enumerated" means mentioned specifically or designated.

enumerator: Person who takes a census.

enure: To take effect; to serve to the benefit of a person, as in, "The benefits of the insurance policy enured to *A*." Also "inure."

Environmental Protection Agency (E.P.A.): Federal agency created in 1970 to monitor environmental quality and enforce pollution control laws.

E.P.A.: *See* Environmental Protection Agency.

Equal Employment Opportunity Commission (E.E.O.C.): Created by Civil Rights Act of 1964—established to eliminate employment discrimination.

equal protection of the laws: Constitutional guarantee (fourteenth amendment) that the law shall equally protect all persons under the same circumstances. This does not imply that the law cannot classify persons for specific reasons (*e.g.*, taxation), but only that the classification cannot be arbitrary.

equitable: Fair, just, based on principles of equity.

equitable estate: A right or interest in an estate the title to which is held by another. The distinction between an equitable estate and a legal estate is that the holder of an equitable estate has the right to the beneficial use and enjoyment of it, whereas the holder of a legal estate possesses title but not necessarily the right to use and enjoyment. *E.g.*, the beneficiary of a trust has an equitable estate.

equitable estoppel: Doctrine which prevents a person from asserting a right he otherwise would have had because of the effect his conduct would have on another. That is, if *A* relies on *B*'s acts and conduct and would be injured if *B* repudiates his acts and conduct, fairness (and the law) holds that *B* should be prevented from so repudiating. Same as "estoppel in pais."

equity: Fairness; justice according to principles of fairness and not strictly according to formulated law. "Courts of Equity" are those which administer justice in equity. They originated in England to handle cases where courts of law were inadequate. Today, law and equity have combined, and courts of equity

have generally been abolished. The value of property minus all encumbrances on it.
equity of redemption: Right a mortgagor has to redeem an estate after forfeiture. The mortgagor must pay the mortgage debt costs, and interest.
erasure: Rubbing out or obliteration of words from a written instrument. Also the space where the written words were removed from the document.
ergo: Lat. Therefore, consequently, because.
erroneous: Involving error: deviating from the law. "Erroneous judgment" means a court had the power to act but exercised that power wrongly.
error: A mistake in application of law or in matters of fact. "Error" is also short for "writ of error" which is a writ that authorizes a higher court to review the decision of a lower court for errors that appear on the face of the record.
escalator clause: Clause in certain contracts that provides for an increase in the contract price for specified reasons, *e.g.*, a clause in a labor contract which ties wages to the cost of living; a clause in a construction contract that ties the cost of a building to the price of wood, cement, or labor; a clause in a lease executed subject to price control regulations.
escape: Act of voluntarily and unlawfully fleeing from custody.
escheat: The transfer of property to the state because its owner died leaving no one legally entitled to claim it. The property so transferred.
escrow: A document, stock, money or other property given to a third person (escrow agent) to be held by him until the occurrence of an event or performance of a condition, upon which time the agent delivers it to the grantee or obligee, *e.g.*, a deed to land held until its purchaser pays for it in full.
esquire, esq.: A title given to members of the bar and to others.
essence: That which is necessary or essential; the vital element of something, such as a contract. Where "time is of the essence" in a contract, one party must perform on the contract by a certain date or within a period of time for him to be able to require performance by the other party.
Establishment Clause: The provision in the first amendment of the U.S. Constitution which prohibits the state from enacting laws that establish religion, or those that prohibit the free exercise of religion. The provision prevents the state from favoring one religion over another, from forcing a person to believe or disbelieve any religion, from spending public funds for religious schools, and from allowing prayers to be said aloud in public schools, among other things.
estate: The interest a person has in real property. This interest varies from absolute ownership to naked possession (actual possession without color of title). All the property, whether real or personal, in which one has in interest, *e.g.*, a decedent's estate.
estate at will: A leased estate held at the will of the lessor for an indefinite period of time, *i.e.*, either party is able to end the lease at any time he wishes. An estate at will may be by express contract or by implication of law. Also "tenancy at will."
estate by entirety: Estate held jointly by a husband and wife by virtue of the unity in marriage, and which goes to the surviving spouse upon the death of the other.

The difference between an estate by entirety and a joint tenancy is that the latter may be vested in a number of persons, each of whom have a partial interest in the property, where the former is vested in only two who are regarded as one by law, and each of whom have a right to the entire estate. Also "tenancy by the entirety."
estate for years: An estate in land that will end after a fixed period of time, whether weeks, months, or years, *e.g.*, a leasehold estate. Also "tenancy for years" and "tenancy for a term."
estate tax: A tax on the right to transfer a deceased person's property. It is based on the value of the entire estate. An "inheritance tax" is the opposite, *i.e.*, it is a tax on the right to receive property, and is based on the value of the property each heir receives.
estoppel: A bar which prevents a person from denying or asserting anything that contradicts what he has, in contemplation of law, established to be true. The elements of estoppel are: (a) reliance on the acts or representations of another, (b) a deception of that person, and (c) a change of position to the detriment of the person who so relied on the acts or representations.

The three categories of estoppel are: 1) Estoppel by record, which precludes the denial of truth established in a judicial or legislative record, 2) Estoppel by deed, which prevents a party to a deed from denying its existence or the truth of any facts in it, and 3) Estoppel in pais, or equitable estoppel, which prevents a person from denying something his conduct led another to believe.
et al.: Lat. Abbreviation for "et alii," meaning "and others."
ethics: Body of principles of good conduct, especially pertaining to a group or people or a profession.
et ux.: Lat. Abbreviation of "et uxor," meaning "and wife."
eviction: Dispossession; act of making a tenant surrender possession of property. Eviction may be by an assertion of paramount title, by disturbing tenant's enjoyment of property thus causing him to leave, by reentry (for breach of a covenant in the lease), or by legal proceedings by the landlord.

evidence: All the means legally presented at trial to persuade the court or jury as to the truth of a matter in question. Evidence includes testimony by witnesses, records, photographs, and exhibits. Although "evidence" and "proof" are used interchangeably, there is a distinction between the terms: "Evidence" is the *means* by which the truth or falsity of a matter is established, and "proof" is the *result* of evidence, although not all evidence establishes proof.

ex: Lat. Preposition meaning from, out of, by, on, on account of, or according to. Also a prefix meaning "former" and "without."

examination: The questioning of a person under oath, whether by written or oral interrogation. Also, an investigation or search. Examinations are made of witnesses at trial, of persons charged with crimes, of persons filing for bankruptcy, of inventions submitted for patents, and of abstracts of title.

examiner: Person authorized to conduct an examination.

ex cathedra: Lat. From the chair; with authority.

exception: Act of excluding someone or something that would otherwise be included. The thing so excluded. Formal objection to a trial court's ruling made to enter the disagreement into the record, and subsequently to be used in appealing the case. Under the rules of procedure in federal courts and most state courts, exceptions have been replaced by objections. *See Federal Rule of Civil Procedure 46.*

excessive: That which is greater than what is usual and proper, *e.g.*, excessive bail, excessive force.

exchange: A barter; a trade; a transfer of property for property, not for money, although some money may be paid in addition to the property exchanged. An organization or association that provides a place where securities are bought and sold, *e.g.*, New York Stock Exchange, Chicago Board of Trade. A transfer of funds between persons distant from one another at a price agreed upon or at a price fixed by commercial usage.

excise tax: A tax on the manufacture, sale, or use of commodities, or on licenses to pursue certain occupations or on corporate privileges. Also known as "license tax" and "privilege tax."

exclusionary rule: Rule that prohibits illegally obtained evidence from being admitted at trial, *e.g.*, evidence obtained in an illegal search.

exclusive: Pertaining to one subject only; not shared. A court with "exclusive jurisdiction" has power in certain areas or over certain persons to the exclusion of all other courts. Same as absolute jurisdiction. "Exclusive agency" is the right an agent has to do business in an area to the exclusion of all others. "Exclusive license" is the exclusive right to produce and sell a patented product.

ex contractu: Lat. Arising out of a contract. An action ex contractu arises from a breach of promise in a contract. It is one of the two divisions of obligations and causes of action. *See* ex delicto.

exculpate: To clear or tend to clear of alleged guilt; to provide a justification or excuse. The adjective is "exculpatory."

exculpatory clause: A clause in a trust instrument that relieves a trustee from liability when he has acted in good faith.

excuse: (Noun) A reason for doing or not doing something; a reason for being exempt from a duty or obligation. (Verb) To exempt someone from a duty.

ex delicto: Lat. From a tort or wrongful act. An action ex delicto arises out of fault or malfeasance. Commonly called "ex maleficio." It is one of the two divisions of obligations and causes of action. *See* ex contractu.

ex dolo malo non oritur actio: Lat. From fraud no action arises. A court will not hear an action based on an illegal or immoral act.

execute: To perform; to carry out; to complete; to make, as in to execute a contract or an obligation.

execution: The carrying out of something, such as a court order; the putting of something, such as a contract, into effect. The act by which the state puts a person to death.

executor: Person appointed by a testator to carry out the directives of his will. This may be done expressly or by implication. A woman so appointed is an executrix. When a person is appointed by the court to administer a decedent's estate, he/she is called an administrator/administratrix.

executory: Something not yet executed or performed; that which requires some performance or occurrence for its completion. *E.g.*, an "executory devise" is a gift by will that does not take effect until a future contingency takes place. "Executory interest" vests only after the happening of a specified condition.

executrix: Female executor.

exemplary damages: Damages awarded in excess of actual damages, *i.e.*, more than is required to compensate plaintiff for injuries sustained. Such damages are awarded to punish defendant, to discourage him and others from committing acts similar to the one for which he is being punished, and to provide some solace to plaintiff for mental anguish and shame. Same as "punitive damages" and "vindictive damages."

exemption: Freedom from a responsibility or duty that one would ordinarily have, *e.g.*, jury duty or military service. A privilege granted by the state to a debtor exempting some of his property of liability to his creditors. A deduction allowed from gross income

on income tax returns, *e.g.,* for self, dependents, or blindness.
ex gratia: Lat. Out of grace; as a favor.
exhibit: (Noun) An object displayed in court as evidence, such as a document, photograph, or gun. A paper attached to a document. (Verb) To display or show.
ex moro motu: Lat. Of his own mere motion; of his own accord; voluntarily without request.
ex officio: Lat. From his office; solely by virtue of office. Powers ex officio are powers necessarily implied by one's office.
exonerate: To free from alleged guilt; to find no fault.
exoneration: Act of clearing someone of alleged guilt. A removal of a burden; a release from liability, such as an exoneration of part of an estate where liability for payment of debts is removed from one part of the estate (*e.g.,* real property) and placed on another (*e.g.,* personalty). The right to be reimbursed for debts one pays for another. It is similar to "indemnity" though indemnity is usually based on a contract.
ex parte: Lat. For, by, or in behalf of only one party. *E.g.,* an ex parte injunction can be granted in an urgent situation to one party without notifying the party bound by the injunction.
expatriation: Voluntary act of giving up citizenship of one's country and becoming a citizen of another. Such an act ends all civil and political rights the expatriate had in his original country.
expectancy: Something which one expects or hopes for but which one has no present right to possess. *E.g.,* an heir has an expectancy interest in the property he hopes to inherit, yet no interest vests in him until its owner so states it and dies. "Expectancies" are estates in anticipation, and they are of two sorts with regard to the time of their possession and enjoyment: A "remainder" is an expectancy interest created by the act of the parties to the estate, and a "reversion" is an expectancy interest created by an act of law.
expectant heir: Person who hopes and expects to inherit property, or person who actually has a vested or contingent remainder in property.
expert witness: One whose special knowledge of a subject enables him to express opinions and draw conclusions in his testimony at trial. Persons without such knowledge are not allowed to do so, and are restricted to testifying only to the facts.
ex post facto: Lat. After the fact. Opposite of "ab initio."
express: Clear, definite, or actual; conveyed in explicit terms; *e.g.,* an express contract, an express warranty. Contrasted with "implied."
expressio unius est exclusio alterius: Lat. The expression of one thing is the exclusion of another. This maxim is used in interpreting documents and laws, and means that when certain persons or things are specifically mentioned, it can be inferred that those not specified are excluded.
expropriation: The compulsory purchase of property by the state under its power of eminent domain. Same as "condemnation." Act of surrendering or renouncing a claim to property.
ex rel.: Lat. Abbreviation for "ex relatione," meaning "upon relation"; on the information of. Suits instituted by the state on its behalf, but at the instigation and on the information provided by an individual who has a private interest in the suit are said to be instituted ex relatione. Captioned: "State of Illinois ex rel. Smith v. Jones."
extend: To enlarge; to broaden; to expand; to carry out past a previous limit. To extend credit means to allow a person to defer full payment on a purchase.
extension: A lengthening of time allowed to meet an obligation or of time for which a contract is valid. *E.g.,* the extension given to a debtor allows additional time for payment of debts. The extension of a contract makes an existing contract operative for a greater length of time, and is distinguished from a renewal which requires a new contract be made.
extenuating circumstances: Facts tending to contribute to an illegal act, but which reduce the damages or penalty against the wrongdoer because he had little or no control over those facts.
extinguishment: The ending or cancellation of something, such as a contract, debt, or interest in property.
extortion: Offense committed by someone who employs threats to unlawfully obtain money or other property from another. At common law, extortion applies to public officials who use the color of their office to corruptly take money or property. Extortion differs from robbery in that the threat to the personal safety of the victim is less in extortion than in robbery. Synonymous with "blackmail."
extradition: The surrender by one country or state to another of a person accused or convicted of a crime in that other country or state.
extrajudicial: That which is outside of a regular court proceeding, *e.g.,* extrajudicial oath, extrajudicial confession. That which is outside a court's jurisdiction.
extraordinary remedies: Writs issued to redress or prevent a wrong where ordinary actions in law or equity are insufficient. *E.g.,* a writ of habeas corpus might be issued for a child being kept by someone who does not have custody. A writ of mandamus will order a public official to do something. A writ quo

warranto will inquire into the right of a public official to act. These remedies have generally been abolished and replaced by regular court action.

extraterritoriality: A quality some laws have which make them operative outside the state or country which enacted them. Extraterritoriality gives a country jurisdiction over its citizens in a foreign country.

extremis: Short for Latin "in extremis," in extremity. Term is used to indicate a situation of extreme circumstances, especially that of imminent death.

extrinsic evidence: Facts outside the body of a document, such as oral statements. Extrinsic evidence is normally inadmissible in defining the boundaries of an instrument. *See* parol evidence rule. Such evidence is always admissible for purposes of intrepreting an agreement.

extrinsic fraud: Fraud which is additional or supplementary to the issues tried in a case where judgment is rendered. Such deceit may have prevented one party from presenting his case in court, and would provide grounds for equitable relief against the judgment rendered. Also "collateral fraud."

eyewitness: One who testifies as to what he has seen.

eyre: A journey. In old England, a court of judges who traveled throughout the kingdom.

F

face: Material that appears on a document or statute without any explanation, modification, or addition. Front of check or money order where payor writes the particulars of the instrument. The surface of anything.

face value: The value stated on the face of a security or insurance policy, *e.g.*, the value at maturity or death. The value upon which interest is computed. The value that can be ascertained from a document without aid from extrinsic facts or evidence. Par value.

facias: Lat. That you do; what you have caused.

facio ut des: Lat. I do that you may give; a type of contract in which one agrees to do something for wages or an agreed sum of money.

facio ut facias: Lat. I do so that you may do; a type of contract in which one party agrees to do or refrain from doing something in return for the other party's promise to do or refrain from doing something.

facsimile: An exact copy.

fact: Something that took place; an act; something actual and real; an incident that occurred; an event; a thing done; something that exists and is real as opposed to opinion or supposition; events which are proven in the evidence heard by a court and upon which the law operates.

facta sunt potentiora verbis: Lat. Deeds, facts, or accomplishments are more powerful than words.

factor: An agent who possesses and seeks to sell goods belonging to a client or principal in exchange for a commission. The commission is called a factorage.

factum: Lat. A deed or act; fact; central fact or act upon which a question turns; statement of facts.

factum a judice quod ad ejus officium non spectat non ratum est: Lat. An action of a judge which is unrelated to his office derives no force from his being a judge.

failure of consideration: The neglect, refusal, or inability of a contracting party to perform or furnish the agreed-upon consideration after making and entering into a contract, *e.g.*, the thing of value contemplated as consideration becomes worthless or is destroyed.

failure of issue: Dying without children.

fair comment: A defense to an action for libel based on the common-law right to comment, within limits, upon the conduct of public officials without being liable for defamation. Plea states that even if the statements made were untrue they were not intended to create ill-will or be malicious, but rather were intended to state the facts as the writer honestly believed them to be.

fair hearing: Flexible term used to describe trial-like decision-making process of administrative agencies which contemplates the taking of testimony, with the right of cross-examination assured to the parties, and the rendering of findings of fact supported by evidence. The hearing does not have to use full trial rules or procedures, but it must be conducted in a manner consistent with due process.

fair market value: The amount a willing buyer would pay and a willing seller would accept, neither being under a compulsion to buy or sell and both having reasonable knowledge of the relevant facts. The price goods would bring in the ordinary course of trade.

fair trade acts: Laws permitting manufacturers to establish minimum resale prices for namebrand goods sold by a retail storekeeper.

fair use doctrine: Principle which allows a person other than the owner of a copyright to use the copyrighted material in a reasonable manner without the consent of the copyright owner.

false: Not true; intentionally untrue; wrongful, unjust.

false arrest: Tort consisting of unlawful restraint or deprivation of a person's liberty; arrest without proper legal authority; illegal arrest. False arrest may also be a criminal offense.

false imprisonment: Intentional tort involving the unlawful restraint of the physical liberty of another. If the restraint is imposed by the use of purported le-

gal authority and results in an arrest, then there is a false arrest as well as false imprisonment.
false pretenses: Untrue statements or misrepresentations made in order to obtain valuables by defrauding the owner.
false return: A report made by a sheriff or other court officer in which false statements are made. Income tax return which has false information on it.
falsify: To prove to be false or incorrect. To counterfeit or forge; to alter fraudulently.
falsus in uno, falsus in omnibus: Lat. False in one thing, false in everything. Maxim that if a jury believes that a witness has testified falsely in one matter, it may disregard his entire testimony as being false.
family purpose rule, family car doctrine: Principle of tort law in some states which holds that the owner of a "family car" is liable for injury caused by its negligent use by members of the family.
Farm Credit Administration: Established by Farm Credit Act of 1971 to provide adequate and dependable credit to farmers.
fault: Negligence; an error or defect of judgment or conduct; any deviation from prudence or duty; any shortcoming or neglect of care or performance resulting from incapacity or perversity; a wrongful act; neglect of obligation or duty; mismanagement, bad faith; the responsibility for a misdeed or for negligence. Defect or imperfection. Wrongful act, omission, or breach. *See U.C.C. §1-201(16).*
F.C.C.: *See* Federal Communications Commission.
F.D.I.C.: *See* Federal Deposit Insurance Corporation.
fealty: Obligation of fidelity which feudal tenant owed to his lord.
feasance: Doing an act, performing a duty.
F.E.C.: *See* Federal Election Commission.
federal: Joined in a union having a central and predominate authority. In the United States, the national government as opposed to state government.
federal common law: Laws established by the federal courts, uninfluenced by laws and legal decisions made by state courts. The use of federal common law was restricted by *Erie Railroad v. Tompkins*, 304 U.S. 64, 82 L.Ed. 1188, 58 S.Ct. 817, 114 ALR 1487.
Federal Communications Commission (F.C.C.): Created by the Federal Communications Act of 1934. Regulates radio and television broadcasting within the U.S.
Federal Deposit Insurance Corporation (F.D.I.C.): Established in 1933 to insure deposits in Federal Reserve System member banks.
Federal Election Commission (F.E.C.): Established by the Federal Election Campaign Act of 1971 to monitor campaign practices in federal elections.
Federal Emergency Management Agency (F.E.M.A.): Established in 1978 to make flood insurance and reinsurance available nationwide.
Federal Home Loan Bank Board (F.H.L.B.B.): Established in 1932 to provide a flexible credit reserve for member savings institutions engaged in home mortgage lending.
Federal Labor Relations Authority (F.L.R.A.): Created in 1978 to provide leadership in establishing policies and guidance relating to federal labor-management relations.
federal offenses: Violations of federal statutes. Congress defines the offenses and prescribes the punishment; *e.g.*, treason, income tax evasion, smuggling, and kidnapping across state lines.
federal question: Issues of law which involve the construction of the United States Constitution, federal laws, or treaties. The federal courts have original jurisdiction over such matters.
Federal Reserve System: Created by the Federal Reserve Act of 1913 to establish a general monetary policy and banking system for the United States.
Federal Trade Commission (F.T.C.): Established by the Federal Trade Commission Act of 1914 to regulate business practices and enforce provisions of the various antitrust laws.
fee: A charge for services performed by government employees or by professionals for services performed or to be performed. An estate in property. The term generally denotes complete ownership which entitles the owner to sell the property or to devise it to his heirs.
fee simple: An estate in land without any limitations on it which gives the owner the absolute power of disposition. Today there is a presumption that an estate is given in fee simple unless there is a clear intention to give a more limited estate. Also called "fee" or "fee simple absolute."
fee tail: An estate conveyed by deed or will to an heir and a fixed line of future heirs by the owner of the estate; an estate of inheritance which passes only by lineal descent. Generally indicated by the words "to *A* and the heirs of his body." Almost universally abolished by statute in modern times.
fellow servant rule: Common law rule that an employer is not liable for injuries caused to one employee by the negligence of another employee. Fellow servants were said to assume the risk of each other's negligence. Employer's Liability Acts and Workmen's Compensation statutes have repealed the fellow servant rule in most jurisdictions.
felo de se: Lat. A felon with respect to himself. A suicide victim; a suicide victim in a jurisdiction where killing oneself is a felony.

felon: One who has been convicted of a felony and has not yet finished serving time for it.
felonious homicide: The killing of a human being without justification or excuse. The term includes suicide.
felony: A major or high crime, as distinguished from a misdemeanor. Crimes are declared to be felonies by statute or by common law. As defined by statute, a crime with a sentence of one year or more with imprisonment or punishable by death. Formerly, every offense at common law which caused a forfeiture of land or goods.
F.E.M.A.: *See* Federal Emergency Management Agency.
feme (femme) covert: Fr. A married woman.
feme (femme) sole: Fr. An unmarried woman.
fence: Person who buys stolen property to resell at a profit. A hedge, ditch, wall, or other structure intended to enclose a piece of land, divide a piece of land into distinct portions, or separate two contiguous estates.
feoffment: Common law method of conveying the title to real estate which includes livery of seisin.
feud: A grant of land made by a superior to a tenant in return for services in exchange for the superior protecting the tenant. An inherited right to occupy and use the land of a feudal estate. Long continued hostility between two families or two branches of the same family.
feudal system: System of property law from the Middle Ages in England and Europe by which a superior or lord granted the use of land to a tenant in exchange for his services. In return the lord was bound to protect the tenant.
F.H.L.B.B.: *See* Federal Home Loan Bank Board.
fiat: Lat. Let it be done. A decree; an order by a judge or other competent legal source.
fiction: An assumption of law that something that is or may be false or nonexistent is true or real. Legal fictions are assumed or invented for the purpose of accomplishing justice.
fictitious name: An alias; a name taken which is different than a person's real name for the purpose of deceiving someone.
fidelity bond: Bond which guarantees payment of a loss if a bonded employee embezzles or absconds with money or valuables in his care; insurance on a person against that person's dishonesty.
fiduciary: Person entrusted with the duty to act for the benefit of someone else. Fiduciary must exercise a high degree of care and must subordinate his own personal interests in the event that there is a conflict; *e.g.*, trustee, director of a corporation, executor.
fieri facias: Lat. That you cause to be made. Writ of execution commanding a sheriff to seize goods to pay off a debt. Also referred to as "fi. fa."
fifth amendment: Amendment to the United States Constitution contained in the Bill of Rights. Fifth amendment provides the privilege against self-incrimination.
file: The court record of a case. To present a legal document to a public official, usually a court clerk, for the purpose of having it placed on permanent record and preserved.
filiation proceeding: Judicial proceeding to establish the paternity of a child born out of wedlock and to compel the putative father to contribute to the child's support. Also called "affiliation proceeding," "bastardy proceeding," or "paternity suit."
filum: Lat. A thread; line; boundary; edge.
final: Conclusive; end, ultimate, last; completed; terminating all controversy, doubt, or dispute.
final decision: Judgment of a court which terminates the litigation in the court which renders it. A final decision settles the dispute between parties unless or until it is set aside or reversed by a higher court. Also called "final judgment" or "final decree."
financial statement: Report summarizing a company's or a person's financial condition, including assets and liabilities.
finding: Decision of a court or jury on issues of fact, which discloses the grounds upon which a judgment rests.
finding of fact: Determination of an issue by the court or jury based on evidence submitted by opposing parties in a lawsuit.
fine: Pecuniary penalty imposed as a punishment for the commission of an offense. In a criminal case, a fine may be imposed instead of or in addition to imprisonment.
firm: A partnership or company; an unincorporated business; a business entity, concern, or enterprise. The name or title under which a partnership transacts business.
firm offer: Written offer which will be held open by a merchant for a certain length of time to buy or sell goods. A firm offer requires no consideration in order to be valid and if no length of time is stated then the offer is irrevocable for a reasonable time, not to exceed three months. *U.C.C. §2-205.*
first impression: First discussion, consideration, or examination; new. A case or question is of "first impression" if it presents a new problem to the court and, therefore, cannot be decided by existing precedent.
first instance, court of: Trial court where a lawsuit is first heard as opposed to a court of appeal.

fiscal: Broad term referring to financial matters in general, *e.g.*, fiscal report; belonging to the public treasury. A fiscal year is a period of twelve consecutive months used by a business or state as an accounting period for annual reports.
fixed assets: Property which is essential to operating a business and which will not be consumed or converted into cash during the current accounting period, *e.g.*, land, machinery, and buildings.
fixed charges: Expenses which must be paid whether or not a business is operating, such as rent, taxes, insurance premiums, and depreciation.
fixtures: Items which were once personal property, but which have become so annexed to or physically attached to realty that they are considered to be part of the real property.
flagrante delicto: Lat. In the very act of committing the crime.
floating capital: Funds used to meet current expenses.
flotsam, flotsan: Goods cast overboard in order to save a ship, goods lost from a vessel, or the debris of a shipwreck found floating at sea.
F.L.R.A.: *See* Federal Labor Relations Authority.
f.o.b.: Abbreviation for "free on board." Indicates that the selling price of goods includes transportation costs. Title to goods usually passes from seller to buyer at F.O.B. location. *See U.C.C. §2-319(1).*
forebearance: Refraining from action when entitled to act. Act of creditor of holding off demanding payment on a debt that is due.
force majeure, force majesture: Fr. A higher force; superior, unyielding force; irresistible, natural, or unavoidable force, *e.g.*, floods, earthquakes, lightning, storms, governmental intervention resulting from necessities of war. Also called "vis major."
forced sale: Sale of property by compulsion. Forced sale is usually ordered by a judge to pay off the court's judgment and is done according to rules set by the court.
forcible detainer: The forcible detention of land or buildings by one who is not the owner and is not entitled to possession.
forcible entry: Entering land or buildings with force, threats, or actual violence for the purpose of taking possession thereof.
foreclosure: Cutting off or termination of a right to property. "Foreclosure" describes both the process and the result and is usually done by the person who holds the mortgage. In addition to taking the property away from the mortgagor and ending his rights in it, the property is usually sold publicly to the highest bidder to pay off the mortgage debt.
foreign: Belonging to another nation, country, jurisdiction or subject matter.
foreman: Spokesperson selected by a jury from among its members. Person in charge of other employees.
forensic: Belonging to, pertaining to, or used in courts of justice.
forensic medicine: Medical knowledge or medical practice involved with court testimony or legal matters. Medical jurisprudence.
foreseeable: Capable of being known in advance, *e.g.*, a reasonable anticipation that injury might result from certain acts or failure to perform certain acts. *See Palsgraf v. Long Island Railroad*, 248 N.Y. 339 (1928).
forfeit: To lose the right to some benefit, privilege or property because of a neglect of duty, an offense, or a breach of contract.
forge: To create a false instrument by making it in imitation of another one with intent to defraud and deceive; to counterfeit a document or signature; to counterfeit or falsify by imitation.
forgery: Criminal offense of making a false document or altering a real one with intent to commit fraud, *e.g.*, false signature, alteration of the amount of a check, misuse of a document.
form: The manner or order of a pleading or legal document as opposed to the essential material of the action or content. Opposite of substance. Model used by attorneys for drafting an instrument, pleading, order, judgment, or other legal document.
forms of action: Procedural devices required for technical categories of personal actions at common law, *e.g.*, trespass, trover, replevin, assumpsit. "Civil action" is the only type of action now for civil suits in most jurisdictions.
fornication: Unlawful sexual intercourse between two unmarried people. Term is often defined by state statute and the offense is usually a misdemeanor.
forswear: To swear to that which the swearer knows is untrue.
forthwith: Immediately; as soon as the nature of the case will permit; as soon as possible; without delay.
fortuitous: Unforeseen; happening by chance or accident; unexpected; unavoidable; inevitable.
forum: Lat. Court of justice; place where legal remedy can be sought.
forum non conveniens: Lat. Inconvenient forum. Doctrine which allows a court which has jurisdiction over a case to decline to hear the case out of fairness to the parties if there is another court available which would be more convenient.
four corners: The face of a written instrument. Under the "four corners rule" the intention of the parties is to be gathered from the document as a whole rather than from isolated parts of it and without aid from extrinsic testimony.

franchise: Special privilege conferred on an individual or a corporation by a government. The privileged use of a trade name and the right to market another's product or services. The privilege is usually granted by the owner of the trade name in exchange for consideration, *e.g.*, brand-name gas stations and fast-food restaurants. The right to vote. Also called "elective franchise."
frank: To send material through the mail without paying postage; the mark or signature used to indicate that a letter or package goes through the mail free of charge. Free.
fraud: Deception, deceit; trickery. An act using deceit such as intentional distortion of the truth or misrepresentation or concealment of a material fact to gain an unfair advantage over another in order to secure something of value or deprive another of a right. Fraud is grounds for setting aside a transaction at the option of the party prejudiced by it or for recovery of damages. "Actual fraud" involves a deliberate misrepresentation or concealment. A court may infer "constructive" or "legal fraud" either from the nature of a contract or from the relationship of the parties.
fraudulent: That which is done with intent to defraud; something which results in or from a fraud.
fraudulent conveyance: Conveyance or transfer of property to another with intent to deceive creditors by defeating their claims by putting the debtor's property out of their reach.
free: Unrestricted; not subject to legal constraint of another; at liberty to act as one pleases; without restraint or coercion.
free and clear: Unencumbered. Title to property that is free of liens or other possible hindrances; a good or marketable title.
freedom of speech: Constitutional right to say what one wants without government regulation or restriction. This right is not absolute, but is limited to prevent abuse; *e.g.*, laws against defamation, obscene or blasphemous matter, or incitement to violate criminal law.
freehold: An estate "in fee" or an estate "for life"; an estate of land without a fixed period of duration. An "estate in fee" is owned by the holder and his heirs forever; a "life estate" is owned by the holder for his life or for the life of another. A "determinable freehold" is owned in fee until the occurrence of some condition (which may not occur).
friendly suit: An action which both parties agree to take to court in order to obtain a desired judgment about a doubtful question of law, or to confirm the parties' agreement; *e.g.*, a creditor's suit against the executor of an estate to obtain equal distribution to all the other creditors, a suit by an infant to affirm a settlement since the infant is not competent to agree to a settlement.
friend of the court: A person who is not a party to the lawsuit but gives the court, on the behalf of the public interest, information or arguments to aid the court in its decision. Also known as an "amicus curiae."
frisk: A quick patting-down of a suspect in order to detect concealed weapons.
frivolous: Lacking a valid legal right or disputed fact situation relevant to the pending issue; insufficient for the court to rule upon. A pleading or claim is frivolous if it presents no issue or injury, is meant solely to delay the action or embarrass the other party.
frolic: When an agent or employee performs acts outside the scope of his employment, he is "on a frolic of his own." *E.g.*, a truck driver who drives off the delivery route for personal activities is on a frolic.
frontage: The length of property along the street or sidewalk. Thus, "frontage assessments" for paving, sidewalks, curbs, and sewers are made in proportion to each owner's share of frontage.
fructus industriales: Lat. The fruits of industry. The crops grown through human agriculture, as opposed to those grown in nature.
fructus naturales: Lat. Natural fruits. Goods produced in the course of nature, *e.g.*, metals, wool, pearls, milk, etc.
frustra probatur quod probatum non relevat: Lat. That which is proved in vain, because when proved it does not help.
frustration: In contract law, doctrine that when a condition fails to occur which frustrates the performance of one party and which both parties knew was essential to the performance of the contract, performance is excused and the contract may be terminated, unless a party warranted that the condition would occur. *E.g.*, a contract to televise baseball games will be excused when the game is rained out.
F.T.C.: *See* Federal Trade Commission.
fugitive: In criminal law, one who escapes after arrest, prosecution, or imprisonment. A "fugitive from justice" is one who, after committing a crime, flees the state or conceals himself from criminal justice officials within the state.
full faith and credit: Requirement in the United States Constitution that each state must recognize the legislative acts, records, and judicial proceedings of the other states, giving them "full faith and credit." *Article IV, Section 1.* One state's final judgment in a case is thus conclusive in every other state if it is conclusive in that state.

fund: Generally, some collection of money, bonds, notes, securities, or other assets, set aside for a particular purpose, *e.g.*, to pay debts, to purchase particular goods and services, to earn interest. To establish such a fund; to capitalize in order to earn interest.

fungible goods: Goods which are alike in every particle, *e.g.*, oil, milk, flour, sugar. *See U.C.C. §1-201(17).*

furiosi nulla voluntas est: Lat. A madman has no will.

future estate: An estate in land without present possession of the land, with the possibility of future possession, *e.g.*, a remainder or a reversion.

future interest: An interest in land or money which will begin in use or possession some time in the future, *e.g.*, a trust which holds money for the beneficiary until he attains the age of twenty-one.

futures contract: A contract to sell goods or commodities at a future time at a specific price. The buyer agrees to pay that fixed price and the seller agrees to deliver the goods although the parties do not actually contemplate delivery, but rather that the contract calls for a settlement between the parties according to market prices. If the value of the commodity has risen, the seller pays the buyer the amount of the increase; if the value of the commodity falls, the buyer pays the seller the decrease.

G

gallows: A raised platform from which convicted criminals guilty of serious crimes are hanged. The superstructure consists of two raised supports with a beam laid horizontally across the supports.
G.A.O.: *See* General Accounting Office.
gaol: English common law term for jail.
garnish: To acquire a portion of a person's wages or assets in accordance with a garnishment action. To warn or summon.
garnishee: A person against whom a garnishment action is successfully brought; a debtor whose wages or assets are attached to pay off an obligation.
garnishment: The legal process by which a person's wages or assets, under the control of another person or a corporation, are used to pay an obligation owed to a third party. Frequently, the rights and procedures in a garnishment proceeding are fixed by statute.
General Accounting Office (G.A.O.): Federal agency which reports to Congress and whose primary duties are to audit and oversee government programs and to review and investigate their operation.
general assignment: Transfer of all of a debtor's assets to a trustee who has authority to liquidate the debtor's assets and distribute the proceeds to creditors.
general creditor: A lender whose loan is secured only by a general promise to repay the debt.
general demurrer: Answer of a defendant to an action filed by a plaintiff in a civil proceeding that denies the substance of the plaintiff's suit but does not state any specific objection; response by a defendant to a civil action that alleges that plaintiff's pleadings are insufficient at law to support the cause of action pleaded.
General Services Administration (G.S.A.): Created by the Federal Property and Administration Services Act of 1949 to coordinate the acquisition and disposition of all government property.
general verdict: Decision by a jury that finds in favor of the plaintiff or defendant in a suit but that does not address the specific fact issues in dispute; the ordinary form of a verdict; to be distinguished from a special verdict, where the jury decides facts only.
gerrymander: To arrange or draw the boundaries of a political district with the intent to achieve an unlawful purpose, *e.g.*, to draw the boundaries of a legislative district with the purpose of precluding members of a racial group from exercising their constitutional rights to vote and run for office. To manipulate; to rig.
gestation: The period in which a female bears a fetus from time of conception to time of birth. At common law, 280 days.
gift: Present; gratuity; donation of real or personal property by one party to another.
gift causa mortis: Lat. Gift made by a person in contemplation of his impending death.
gist: The principal basis in law for a cause of action without which the suit could not be brought. The basis of an argument, its substance.
good behavior: Proper conduct; lawful conduct. As used in criminal sentencing the term refers to the procedure whereby a criminal's proper conduct while in prison will be credited against the time remaining in his sentence.
good cause: Legally adequate reason; lawful basis for an action; a satisfactory excuse.
good faith: A desire to act in a conscientious and equitable manner with regard to the rights of others; the lack of a desire to take unfair advantage of another.
goods: Merchandise; commercial wares; personal property.
good will: An intangible asset which represents the favorable attitude of clients or customers of a business toward the operation of the business; the value of a business enterprise above and beyond the value of the business' tangible assets which represents the enterprise's reputation with the public and its managerial ability.
grace period: Contract law: The period stated in an agreement, or set by statute, in which performance on the agreement is permitted beyond the date of obliga-

tion of performance as stated in the agreement; *e.g.*, in insurance contracts, the period in which insurance coverage continues in force even though the most recent premium has not been paid.

graft: Corruption involving public officials; any attempt by a public servant to use his public office for his personal pecuniary gain.

grand jury: A group of citizens empaneled by the state to investigate and hear evidence concerning specific events and individuals and, after hearing the evidence, to determine whether indictments should be brought against persons investigated in the proceedings. A "grand jury" is usually much larger than a trial jury.

grand larceny: The crime of stealing or converting another's personal property with the intent to permanently dispossess that person of the property. To be considered a crime of this nature the value of the property taken must exceed a minimum value set by statute.

grandfather clause: A provision in a statute or an agreement that permits those engaged in certain activities before the adoption of the statute or agreement to carry on with those activities even though the conduct is now prohibited by the statute or the agreement.

grant: To give; to transfer; to permit; to give one's consent to an arrangement, *e.g.*, to transfer real estate by a written contract. A transfer of real property; a conveyance of real property, *e.g.*, a written contract that transfers title to real property.

grantee: A person who receives a grant of real property.

grantor: A person who makes a grant of real property.

gratis: Lat. Free; without reward, *e.g.*, an action performed freely or without compensation.

gratuitous: Dispensed or transferred without compensation or financial remuneration being given.

gratuity: A gift; a donation; a good or service freely given or given without financial remuneration.

gravamen: The essential part or quintessence of a legal argument or cause of action.

gross: Whole; aggregate; overall total exclusive of any deductions. Great; extreme; excessive; extensive.

gross income: Total revenue; the aggregate of earnings exclusive of any deductions.

gross negligence: The purposeful failure to discharge a duty of care owed in reckless disregard of the consequences as they may affect another's life or property.

ground rent: The payment made to a person for use of his real property; the payment made by a lessee to a lessor under the terms of a lease. Under the terms of a sale or transfer of title to real property, a perpetual payment paid to the grantor of the property and his heirs.

G.S.A.: *See* General Services Administration.

guarantee: A person who receives a guaranty. The written instrument or contract of guaranty.

guarantor: A person who gives a guaranty. A person who is secondarily liable for another's obligation or debt as established by contract.

guaranty: A promise or pledge to fulfill another's obligation in case of that person's default upon that obligation; an agreement to be secondarily liable for the debt(s) of another upon that person's default on that debt.

guardian: A person legally responsible for managing the affairs of a person legally incompetent to administer his property or properly assert his rights; such as, a person who handles the affairs of a senile individual.

guest: A paying visitor or patron at a motel, hotel, or restaurant. One who is not a member of an organization or association and attends its functions.

guest statute: A state law which provides that a gratuitous passenger in an automobile involved in an accident may recover for his injuries against the driver of the automobile only upon a showing of gross negligence or other conduct that exceeds ordinary negligence (*e.g.*, willful and wanton).

guilty: Culpable; responsible for perpetuating a crime; at fault for engaging in a crime or some other type of misconduct.

H

habeas corpus: Lat. You have the body. Legal proceeding whereby a writ is brought in order to determine whether a person in the custody of legal authorities is being lawfully detained.

habendum clause: The clause in a deed or a written instrument that transfers title in property and which names the parties to the transaction and defines the nature and quality of ownership in the property that the grantee receives. The clause usually begins with the words, "To have and to hold."

habitability: Status of a dwelling which signifies that it is capable of being safely lived in; the situation where a residence is livable.

habitation: The act of living or residing at a certain location. A residence; a dwelling; place of abode.

half brother, half sister: Persons who share only one common parent, *e.g.*, persons who have the same father but different mothers.

hallucination: A delusion; a false sensory perception not caused by any external stimulus but rather by some internal influence.

hamlet: A burg; a small village or town.

hard cases: Legal proceedings which because of their facts or the equities present are difficult to apply well-accepted rules of law to, and as a result, a court will deviate from those well-accepted precepts to render its decision.

Hatch Act: Federal law which prohibits government employees from engaging in specified political activities.

headnote: Descriptive summary of a legal argument or principle present in a case that comes before the court's printed opinion.

head of the family (head of the household): Person who exercises control over members of a family unit, supervises their conduct and affairs, and provides for their general support.

hearing: Session or proceeding conducted under fixed rules where evidence is taken on a given subject and whose purpose is to arrive at some conclusion on the basis of the evidence heard, but it is not a trial that affixes guilt or liability, *e.g.*, a legislative proceeding to determine what changes should be made in defense policy.

hearsay: An oral or written assertion, or conduct which carries with it an assertion, made or carried out by someone other than a witness testifying at a legal proceeding, and which is offered as evidence in court to establish the truth of the matter asserted.

heir, heiress: A person who will receive the estate and property of another upon that person's death; a person entitled to receive an inheritance at a future date.

heir apparent: A person who has the right of inheritance to an estate or position so long as he outlives his ancestor or the current holder of the position.

hereditament: Something capable of being inherited or transferred by legal succession.

heretofore: Prior to this moment; before this time; previous to this instance.

hermaphrodite: A person having both male and female reproductive organs.

hierarchy: A group of persons in an organization classified according to their rank, position or level of authority; such as, the classification of the officials of a religious sect.

high seas: The open waters of the oceans and seas beyond the territorial control of any country.

hoc: Lat. This.

hold: To have dominion and control over property by legal title or possession. To determine or resolve a legal question; to sustain an assertion or position. To obligate a person; to render a judgment which affects the legal rights of a person. To conduct; to administer, *e.g.*, to hold municipal traffic court.

holder: Person who is in legal possession of an investment security or some other financial instrument which is payable to him or the bearer of the instrument when it is due. *U.C.C. §3-303.*

holder in due course: A person who takes an instrument for value, in good faith, and without any notice that it is overdue or has been dishonored or of any defense against it or claim to it on the part of any person. *U.C.C. §3-302.*

holding: An ownership interest in an asset or a business enterprise. Decision by a court; rule of law relied on by a court in making its decision in a case.
holding company: Corporation formed to hold equity interests in other corporations and that controls the management of those corporations through the exercise of its equity interests in the corporations.
hold-over tenancy: Possession of real property that exists where a lessee remains in possession of property that he has leased after the term of the lease has expired.
holograph: A handwritten legal document, most often a will or deed, affecting the estate of a person, written entirely by that person and not witnessed by other persons.
home rule: Power granted to local and municipal authorities by state governments to manage their own affairs as established by legislative act or constitutional provision.
homestead: The domicile of a family and the surrounding property, *e.g.*, a farmhouse and the adjoining land and buildings.
homicide: The taking of another person's life; the killing of a person. The purposeful or intentional taking of another's life is criminal homicide (*e.g.*, murder, manslaughter, etc.).
honor: To accept a financial instrument or security as payment for an obligation owed. To make payment with a financial instrument or security on an obligation owed.
honorable: Title of respect given to judges or elected or appointed public officials.
honorarium: Fee or recompense given to a person for services performed but for which no fee is legally or traditionally required; such as, a fee given to a person who speaks at the commencement exercises of a university.
hornbook: Text which summarizes the fundamental precepts of law and cases in a particular legal area.
hostile witness: Witness who is adverse or antagonistic to the interests of the party that called him to testify.
hotchpot: The combining of assets and property of different parties in order to partition and split it equally between the parties.
house: Dwelling; residence; abode; home. Term that describes a legislative assembly; name given one of the two elected bodies of a legislature.
housebreaking: The unlawful entry into another's residence; burglary.
household: A family unit that resides together. That which belongs to a family or a residence, such as, the home's furnishings and effects.
hue and cry: The loud uproar and clamor that authorities and others made as they pursued criminals under the old English common law and which put all on notice that heard the clamor that they must join in the pursuit of the criminals.
hung jury: A jury whose members are so divided and split in their beliefs that they cannot reach a decision.
hypothecate: To mortgage resources as collateral for an obligation or debt owed; to pledge assets as security for an indebtedness.
hypothesis: A premise or theory advanced by a party at a criminal trial; a theory, assumption, or supposition.
hypothetical question: A query asked in regard to a specific event or situation that is based on a combination of conjecture, assumed circumstances, and proven facts.

I

ibid.: Lat. The same; in the same place (book, page, case). Short for "ibidem." The term indicates that a phrase or word can be found in a book already quoted or in a case already cited.
I.C.C.: *See* Interstate Commerce Commission.
id.: Lat. The same; the same thing. Abbreviation of idem. This term is used in a citation to avoid repetition of an author's name and title in a second successive reference to that item.
idem est non esse, et non apparere: Lat. Not to appear is the same as not to exist.
identical: The same exactly.
identification: Establishment of identity. The proving that a person or an item before the court is the same as it is charged or alleged to be.
idiot: One who is mentally deficient from birth and whom the law therefore considers to be hopelessly incapacitated mentally.
i.e.: Lat. That is; that is to say.
ignoramus: Lat. We are ignorant. We ignore it. (Noun) An ignorant person. (Verb) To ignore; not to know. The grand jury would write this word on the back of an indictment when they considered the accusation against a prisoner to be groundless or unconvincing.
ignorantia legis neminem excusat: Lat. Ignorance of the law excuses no one. A defendant may be punished for a prohibited act even if he did not know that the act was illegal.
illegal: Forbidden by law; contrary to the law.
illegitimate: Contrary to law; illegal or improper.
illegitimate child(ren): Child(ren) born to unmarried parents. Child(ren) born to a married woman in a situation where the presumption of legitimacy has been rebutted.
illicit: Illegal; unlawful.
illusory: Falsely appearing to conform to a legal act, *i.e.*, an "illusory promise" resembles a legally binding promise but upon examination is illusory because it does not bind the promisor.
immaterial: Not pertinent to the matter in dispute. Evidence is immaterial if it is not relevant to the issue on trial.
immediate cause: The most recent in a series of causes that directly produces the result (it may differ from proximate cause), *i.e.*, a drunken man drowns after falling into water. His intoxication may be the proximate cause of his death if he would not have fallen into the water while sober, but the immediate cause of his death is suffocation by drowning. *See* proximate cause.
immigration: Act of moving into one country from another for the purpose of permanently settling in the second country.
immoral conduct: Indecent behavior; behavior that is inconsistent with accepted moral standards. This behavior can be grounds for suspending or revoking the license to practice certain professions such as law and teaching.
immunity: A privilege granting exemption from a legal duty such as the immunity of charitable organizations from paying taxes. Freedom from prosecution granted to a witness who agrees to testify in a criminal proceeding.
impair: To make worse; to weaken or to affect injuriously.
impanel: To list the names of persons subject to jury duty. To list the names of jurors for a particular case. To assemble and select a jury for a particular trial.
impanelling: The procedure for selecting and swearing in jurors. The listing of persons chosen to serve on a particular jury.
imparlance: Discussion between the parties to a suit in order to settle the controversy amicably. Time granted to the defendant to plead.
impartial: Favoring neither of the parties; equitable. The Bill of Rights requires that the accused be tried by an impartial jury.
impartiality: Lack of bias or prejudice.
impeach: To accuse, *e.g.*, to charge a public official with wrongdoing while in office. To discredit a person

or a thing, *e.g.*, to call into question the testimony of a witness or the truthfulness of a document.
impeachment: The prosecution of a public official by Congress with the House of Representatives making the accusation and the Senate acting as the trier of fact. Impeachment lies for "treason, bribery or other high crimes and misdemeanors" and can result in the removal of an official from office.
impediment: An obstruction. Contract law: The legal inability to contract for a reason such as insanity. Ecclesiastical law: A situation which affects the validity of the marriage of persons already married or about to be married.
imperative: Mandatory; imposing an obligation.
imperitia culpae adnumeratur: Lat. Lack of skill is considered to be negligence.
impertinence: Irrelevance; a statement in the pleading which is immaterial or scandalous.
implead: To bring into the lawsuit as a party someone other than the original plaintiff and defendant. *See Federal Rule of Civil Procedure 14.* To sue.
impleader: The procedure for joining a person as a party to an action. Under *Federal Rule of Civil Procedure 14*, a mechanism for the defendant to include a third party which may be liable to him for part or all of the defendant's liability toward the plaintiff and thereby determine all liabilities in a single action.
implication: Something implied as opposed to something expressly communicated in words. In wills: A "necessary implication" is sufficient to convey an estate. Here the implication is so strongly probable that any alternative intention of the testator is dismissed. Involvement, as in a crime.
implied: Understood through circumstances or conduct though not communicated in words. *Contrast* with "express."
implied authority: The actual authority of an agent implied from circumstances though not expressly granted by the principal.
implied contract: A nonverbal contract implied by the behavior of the parties. "Implied-in-fact" denotes a contract formed by relying on the conduct of the parties rather than on their words. *E.g.*, an implied-in-fact contract to pay for services exists when one goes to a doctor for treatment even though neither party discusses compensation for the treatment. "Implied-in-law" denotes a contract imposed by law, regardless of the intention of the parties, in order to prevent unjust enrichment. *E.g.*, an implied-in-law contract for payment exists when a doctor gives emergency treatment to an unconscious accident victim although the injured party did nothing to solicit the doctor's help.
implied malice: Malice which the law infers from the conduct of a party. The implication from a deliberate act done for a wrongful purpose. In homicide: Where a killing is committed without any factor such as justification or provocation to excuse the murder or to reduce it to manslaughter.
implied warranty: A legal inference that a merchant guarantees that what he sells is fit for normal use. If the merchant knows that the buyer has a specific purpose for the item, there is an inference that the seller guarantees that the item is fit for that purpose. *E.g.*, if one buys paper bags expressly indicating that they must be able to hold 20 lbs. of weight, there is an implied warranty that the bags sold by the merchant will meet this standard.
impossibility: Something that cannot be done. In contracts: Impossibility of performance due, for example, to the destruction of the subject matter of the contract or to the death of one of the parties; may be a defense to nonperformance. In criminal law: Legal impossibility is a defense to criminal charges when the actions of the accused would not constitute a crime even if fully carried out according to his wishes.
impotence: The physical inability to engage in sexual intercourse. The inability to consummate a marriage is a ground for annulment if the suing party was unaware of the spouse's impotence. In medical jurisprudence: The inability of either party to copulate.
impound: To lock up stray animals in a pound. To place documents or goods in the custody of the court pending a determination of their ownership or authenticity.
imprisonment: The confinement of an individual in a place of detention, usually in a jail or a prison. Any physical restraint or threat of force encumbering the free movement of an individual.
improvement: Any increase in the value of property through the use of labor or the expenditure of money which adds to the property's value by doing more than repairing or restoring the property to its original condition.
impunity: Protection or exemption from penalty or punishment.
imputed knowledge: Knowledge that the law attributes to an individual because the circumstances made the facts easily available and the person charged had a duty to know of them.
imputed negligence: The negligence of one person is assigned to a second party because the second party is somehow responsible for the actions of the first. *E.g.*, the negligence of an employee may be imputed to the employer if the former is acting within the scope of employment. *See* respondeat superior; vicarious liability.
inadmissible: Not acceptable as proof under the law of evidence.

inalienable: Not capable of being transferred or taken away. The Declaration of Independence describes the rights to life, liberty and the pursuit of happiness as inalienable. The U.S. Constitution protects certain fundamental rights such as freedom of religion and freedom of speech.

in bank, in banc: Fr. On the bench. All the judges of the court hearing a case together as a full court. In appellate cases, a litigant can request or the court can move for a consideration of the case by all the judges of a court rather than by a fraction of them. In bank decisions are usually noted at the beginning of the opinion and are often more influential than decisions rendered by a smaller number of judges. Same as "en banc."

in camera: Lat. In chambers; in private. A matter is heard "in camera" in a judge's private chambers or in a courtroom from which all spectators have been excluded.

incapacity, incapacitated: The inability to enter into a legally binding transaction. In contracts: An infant has no capacity to enter into a contract. In Workers' Compensation: Inability to work due either to physical inability to perform or inability to find employment.

incarceration: Confinement in a prison or a jail.

incendiary: (Noun) An arsonist; one who willfully sets another's property on fire. An object capable of starting a fire, *e.g.*, gasoline. (Adj.) Of a fire set by an arsonist.

incest: Sexual intercourse between persons too closely related by blood to be married. Incest is a criminal offense in most jurisdictions, although the degree of prohibited family relationship may vary by statute.

inchoate: Latent; begun but not completed. In crime: A criminal act that was stopped short of completion. The accused may not be prosecuted for the intended crime, but may be charged with the inchoate offense. *E.g.*, attempted murder is an inchoate crime.

incident: A happening or thing of import due to its connection with a main or more important happening or thing.

incite: To instigate; to arouse to action. To induce others to commit a crime.

inclosure: An area of land surrounded by a tangible boundary such as a fence, wall or ditch. Also "enclosure."

income: Money received as profits from business or as salary for employment.

income tax: A tax based on the net or gross incomes of persons or corporations. The sixteenth amendment allows Congress to institute a tax on incomes.

incompatible, incompatibility: Inability to exist together. In many states, incompatibility between husband and wife is grounds for divorce.

incompetency proceeding: A hearing to determine the competency of an individual and whether the state should take charge of him and/or his affairs. If the court deems the individual as incompetent it will appoint a guardian to manage his interests until the incompetent satisfies the court of his competency.

incompetent: A person lacking the legal qualifications to manage his own affairs. Usually an incompetent is of full age and is mentally incapable, *i.e.*, by reason of insanity or chronic illness.

incompetent evidence: Evidence which is inadmissible for some legal reason. A general objection to the admissibility of certain evidence.

incorporate: To combine to form one unit. To create a "corporation," a legal entity recognized by law as an "artificial person."

incorporation by reference: Method of making one document a part of another document by referring to the first in the second, and stating that it should be considered as part of the latter just as if it were actually written out in the first document. The doctrine that a will may incorporate into itself another document which is in existence at the time the will is executed and is sufficiently identified in the will.

incorporeal hereditament: An intangible right which may be inherited that is derived from or involves the ownership of property, *e.g.*, an easement allowing access to another's property or royalties from minerals discovered on one's property.

incorrigible: Incapable of correction or reform. Usually used in reference to a juvenile whose parents cannot manage his behavior or whose conduct cannot be made to conform to the law.

increment: An increase or gain in number or value; that which is gained or added.

in criminalibus probationes debent esse luce clariores: Lat. In criminal cases, the proofs ought to be clearer than light.

incrimination, incriminate: Providing evidence that would implicate someone in the commission of a crime. The fifth amendment protects persons from self-incrimination while testifying.

inculpatory: Probative of guilt. Evidence which tends to establish guilt.

incumbent: Someone who is presently holding an office. Someone who has the legal authority to carry out the duties of an office.

incumbrance: A claim, lien or liability against a property. Any right to, interest in or liability upon real property which diminishes its value but does not prohibit the transfer of title, *e.g.*, an outstanding mortgage, unpaid taxes, or a lien. Also "encumbrance."

incur: To become liable due to an operation of law as opposed to a contract where the party becomes liable by taking an affirmative action. To become liable to or subject to.

indecent exposure: The intentional or negligent exposure of the body's private parts in a public place or within the public view.

indefeasible: That which cannot be defeated, revoked, or made void.

in delicto: Lat. In fault.

indemnify: To insure; to secure against future loss or damage. To reimburse; to compensate for past loss or damage.

indemnity: A contract shifting liability for a loss from one person held legally responsible to another person. An insurance contract to secure a person from anticipated loss or damage.

indenture: A deed, mortgage, or other written instrument, between two or more parties in which the parties assume reciprocal obligations towards each other. The historical practice was to cut the top of the document in a wavy pattern so as to verify its authenticity.

independent contractor: One who undertakes a project for another while retaining control over the means and method by which he accomplishes his goal. The employer has no control over the details of the independent contractor's work.

indeterminate sentence: A prison sentence for the maximum period allowed by law subject to early termination by a parole board after the minimum period has been served. A prison sentence which the court allows the penal authorities to fix within the minimum and maximum time framework established by the court of law.

indicia: Signs; indications that a particular fact or claim is probably true, though not proven certainly; *e.g.*, a document evidencing ownership of property is an "indicia of title." The term is used synonymously with "circumstantial evidence."

indictment: An accusation by a grand jury. A written accusation drafted and submitted to the grand jury by the public prosecuting attorney charging one or more persons with a crime. The grand jury then determines whether the accusation, if proved, would lead to the conviction of the accused. If so, the indictment is adopted by the grand jury and submitted to the court. The indictment also serves to notify the accused of the charges against him with enough precision so that the defendant may prepare an adequate defense.

indigent: One who is needy and poor and has neither property nor persons able to provide support. For social welfare purposes, one is not required to be totally destitute to benefit from public assistance. One must, however, lack the means for a comfortable existence. An indigent defendant who has no funds to hire a lawyer to defend him is entitled to appointed counsel.

indignity: In divorce law, a ground for divorce based on emotional and mental cruelty impacting on the subject's self-respect and personal honor as opposed to physical abuse. Examples of indignities are habitual contumely, studied neglect, intentional incivility, unmerited reproach, malignant ridicule, abusive language, and manifest disdain.

indirect evidence: Circumstantial evidence. Evidence based upon presumptions and inferences from certain facts which leans towards a particular conclusion. *See* direct evidence.

indirect tax: A tax upon some right, privilege, or corporate franchise.

indispensable party: A party whose presence in court is so essential to determining an adequate judgment that any verdict rendered in that party's absence would be incomplete or unjust. A trial cannot proceed unless all indispensable parties are joined, even if the court loses jurisdiction over the case through the joinder.

indorsement: Signature or other marking on the back of a negotiable instrument which transfers the instrument to another. An indorsement transfers the entire instrument, otherwise it is only a partial assignment. A blank indorsement does not specify the party to whom the instrument is payable. Also "endorsement."

inducement: A persuasion or influence using threats or promises. In contracts: The benefit or advantage that the promisor expects to gain from the contract is the inducement for making it. In pleadings: An inducement is an explanatory statement preceding the plea.

in esse: Lat. In being. That which actually exists. In essence.

in extremis: Lat. In extremity. At the end, often meaning near death. Declarations "in extremis" are dying declarations. In extremis may also characterize any situation of extreme circumstances.

infamous, infamy: Shameful or disgraceful. Well known in a derogatory sense. At common law, treason, forgery, and felony were "infamous crimes," indicating particular moral turpitude. One convicted of such a crime was denied the right to testify as a witness. Infamy is the legal status of one convicted of an infamous crime and involves a loss of honor and an inability to testify as a witness.

infant: A person under the age of legal majority—at common law, under 21 years of age, now usually 18 years of age. An infant is subject to various disabilities under the law. *E.g.*, an infant is precluded from suing or being sued unless he/she has a guardian ad litem, and an infant's contracts are generally voidable.

infanticide: The murder of an infant soon after its birth.

inference: A deduction from an admitted fact. In evidence: A fact or claim derived logically from another fact or claim which is accepted as true. Conclusions or deductions are reached through reason, common sense, and human experience rather than merely by guesswork.

inferior court: Any court whose jurisdiction is statutorily limited or special, and whose judgments are valid only if its jurisdiction is established. Any court subject to review by another court in a particular judicial system, *e.g.*, a trial court.

infirmity of mind: A disease or weakness of the mind. Something beyond a temporary disorder.

in flagrante delicto: Lat. In the act of doing the crime; "red-handed."

in forma pauperis: Lat. In the manner of a pauper. In pleadings, the court may allow an indigent party to proceed in forma pauperis and bear no liability for court fees or costs.

information: A written accusation submitted by a public officer specifying charges against an individual. An information differs from an indictment in that the former is presented by a public official on his oath while the latter is presented by the grand jury on their oath. In most states, an information may be used instead of an indictment to bring someone to trial.

informed consent (doctrine): An agreement to allow something to occur based on the knowledge necessary to make an intelligent choice. In tort law: The requirement that a physician avoid possible liability for battery by disclosing to the patient what a reasonably prudent physician exercising reasonable care would disclose to the patient about the nature and risks of a proposed course of treatment, so that the patient may make an intelligent decision about whether to undergo the treatment by balancing the probable risks against the probable benefits.

informer: One who notifies the authorities of a violation of law. In criminal law: An undisclosed person who confidentially communicates material information of a criminal activity which directs government officers in their investigation. The informer is a volunteer and the term does not refer to people who divulge information when questioned by police or when testifying as a witness before the grand jury.

infra: Lat. Under; below; within. In a text, it refers to an upcoming discussion or citation, as opposed to "supra" (above or before) which refers to something already mentioned in a previous part of the book.

infraction: A violation or breach of a law, right, or contract. A particular violation of a statute which the statute specifically identifies as an "infraction" and for which the only punishment is a fine.

infringement: The breach of any law. An interference with the legal rights of another. In copyright law: The unlicensed use of a copyrighted publication by copying it in whole or in part or of a copyrighted article by making, selling, or using it. Also infringement of patent or trademark.

in futuro: Lat. In the future; at a later time. *Contrast* "in praesenti."

ingress: The entering upon some place or something. *See* egress. (Ingress and egress are sometimes used interchangeably.)

ingrossing: The act of creating a perfect copy of a document from a rough draft of it in order to use the copy for its ultimate purpose or to have it in its final form.

inhabitant: One who resides actually and permanently in a particular place and is domiciled there. Corporate law: Corporations are inhabitants of the state in which they are incorporated.

inherit: To receive property from a dead person either by descent (through intestacy laws) or by devise (a will). Technically, to take as an heir solely by descent rather than by devise.

inheritance: All property, real or personal, that is received by heirs from a decedent through the laws of descent and distribution. In popular usage the term refers to property received either through intestacy or by will.

inheritance tax: A tax imposed by the government on all property, both real and personal, transferred from the dead to the living by legacy, will or intestate succession. The tax is on the legal right to acquire property and not on the property itself.

in invitum: Lat. Against the will; without consent.

initiative: The power of the people to propose laws, bills, and constitutional amendments and to enact or reject them by vote, independent of the legislative body. The right of the people to propose laws to be enacted by the legislature. Differs from "referendum," which is the right of the people to approve or reject a law submitted to them for approval.

injunction: An equitable remedy in which the court orders a party to perform or to desist from a particular act. "Mandatory injunction" commands the defendant to take a positive action to accomplish a specific purpose; *e.g.*, the court may order a school to admit a particular student. "Restrictive injunction" forbids the defendant or his agents from attempting or continuing some activity that is injurious to the plaintiff; *e.g.*, the court may prohibit a school from suspending or expelling a student.

"Interlocutory injunction" is any injunction issued prior to trial to prevent irreparable injury to the plaintiff while the court considers whether to grant permanent relief. Granted for a limited time only. Two types: 1. The "preliminary injunction," which is granted after the defendant has received notice and has had an opportunity to participate in a hearing on the issue, and 2. "temporary restraining order," which is granted without notice to the defendant in situations where the plaintiff will suffer irreparably if immediate relief is not granted.

A permanent or perpetual injunction is a final disposition in the suit and is indefinite in length of time.

in jure: Lat. In law; in right. Legally or rightfully.

injuria absque damno: Lat. Wrong or injury without damage. An admitted violation of another's right which has not resulted in any damage to him. This situation will not sustain an action at law if damages must be pleaded as cause of the action. Usually refers to an injury caused through negligence since an intentional injury may entitle one to nominal or punative damages.

injuria non excusat injuriam: Lat. One injury does not excuse another; one wrong does not justify another wrong.

injury: Damage or wrong done to another's person, property, reputation or rights. Not synonymous with "damages," since a right may be infringed without causing any monetary loss. No action at law is maintainable without a legal injury.

in lieu of: In place of; instead of.

in limine: Lat. On the threshold; in the beginning.

in loco parentis: Lat. In place of a parent. In common law, it refers to a person who has replaced a lawful parent by assuming the responsibilities of a parent without adopting the child, *e.g.*, a minor and a residential institution or a court and a ward or orphan.

inmate: A person who resides with others. A prison inmate is a person who is confined therein.

innkeeper: One who keeps a house which provides lodging, food, and entertainment to travelers for compensation.

innocent: Free from guilt or wrongdoing; acting in good faith and without knowledge of defects or incriminatory circumstances.

innuendo: Lat. A hint or insinuation, usually derogatory. In defamation actions, the term refers to the part of the complaint which explains the injurious meaning of words which are not necessarily defamatory on their face.

in odium spoliatoris omnia praesumuntur: Lat. All things are presumed to the prejudice of the despoiler or pirate; every presumption is made against the wrongdoer.

in pais: Fr. In the country. The phrase applies to transactions done outside the court or without a legal proceeding.

in pari delicto: Lat. In equal fault; equally culpable. In contracts: The law of equity will not help either party in an illegal transaction if they are "in pari delicto" but will leave them as it finds them.

in pari materia: Lat. In the same subject matter. In statutory construction: Statutes "in pari materia," relating to the same subject matter, should be construed together in order to derive legislative intent.

in perpetuity: Forever; perpetually.

in personam: Lat. Against the person. In procedure: An action taken against a person which involves his personal rights and is based on jurisdiction over him as opposed to seeking a judgment against property (in rem). Equity courts are said to give "in personam" decisions, meaning that their judgments usually command a person to do or refrain from doing something.

An action for a judgment "in personam" is initiated by giving notice to the affected party either by serving him personally or by substitute service. An example of an action in personam is a lawsuit against an individual who intentionally hit the plaintiff, because the judgment would be against the aggressor himself.

in praesenti: Lat. At the present time; at once; immedately effective.

inquest: At common law, a name for any judicial inquiry. Usually it refers to a body of people appointed by law to investigate matters before them to determine whether a crime was committed. An inquiry made by the jury was also an inquest. The inquiry of a medical examiner or coroner conducted to determine whether a death that has occurred under suspicious circumstances resulted from a criminal act.

inquisition: A judicial inquiry or examination; an inquest. An inquiry by a jury held before an officer of the Crown (inquisitor). An official document recording the decision of the inquiry.

in re: Lat. In the matter of. Used in the title of a judicial proceeding in which there are no opposing parties, but the matter must be decided nonetheless. This may involve the judicial disposition of a thing (*e.g.*, an estate) or of a person (*e.g.*, a neglected child).

in rem: Lat. Actions against a thing (res) and not against a person. A lawsuit in rem involves settlement of a property claim without reference to the individual claimants. This judgment is binding on all claimants to the property, whether they are parties to the action or not.

insanity: Madness; unsoundness of mind. In criminal law, insanity is a defense to criminal charges and relieves one of all responsibility for his actions. However, everyone is presumed sane until the contrary is proved. An affirmative criminal defense.

One test for insanity is the "*M'Naghten* Rule," which defines insanity as a defect of reason, resulting from a disease of the mind, that prevents the individual from knowing the nature or quality of his act or rendering the individual incapable of determining right from wrong.

The American Law Institute has replaced the *M'Naghten* Rule with a test which requires that a person has an inability to appreciate the criminality of his actions or to conform his actions to the requirements of law due to a mental disease or defect. This test has been adopted by most federal courts and by many state courts.

insolvency: The inability to pay one's debts as they become due. The condition of a person or corporation whose liabilities exceed its assets.

insolvent: (Noun) A person who is unable to pay his debts as they become due in the regular course of business. (Adj.) A corporation whose liabilities outweigh its assets is insolvent if it cannot garner sufficient resources to meet its needs either through its own assets or through credit.

in specie: Lat. In kind; in like form, specific, specifically.

inspection: Examination, investigation. "Inspection laws"—The right of public officials to examine regulated articles or conditions in housing or industry to insure compliance with the law. "Inspection of documents"—The right of a party in a legal action to examine and copy documents of the court or of the opposing party, to enter land, or to otherwise gather evidence through the discovery process in preparation for trial. "Inspection rights"—The examination of goods by the buyer, who is entitled to examine purchases to determine whether they conform to an agreement or contract. In inspection law: An examination of an article to determine its suitability for use or commerce, *e.g.*, food inspections.

inspection laws: Regulations authorizing public officials to examine various kinds of merchandise to determine their fitness for use and compliance with prescribed standards in order to protect the public's health, safety, and welfare. For example, inspectors may investigate food for cleanliness or packages for weight and accuracy in labelling in order to admit only marketable goods and to exclude unmarketable goods from sale.

installment: One of the parts into which a debt is divided when payment is to be made at intervals. A regular part payment of a debt.

instant, instanter: Lat. At once; immediately; without delay. When a party is ordered to plead instanter, he must plead on that same day. Usually instanter means within 24 hours.

in statu quo: Lat. In the condition which was. To place a party in the situation that he was in before the controversy or wrongdoing. In contracts: The party in an executory contract who seeks to rescind must first place the other contracting party "in statu quo" (*i.e.*, in the position that he was in at the time of the contract's inception) before rescission can take place.

instigate, instigation: To incite; to stir to some action, especially to commit a crime or to initiate a suit.

institute: (Verb) To start or commence, as in to institute a suit. (Noun) An educational institution providing training for particular work. A treatise on law; *e.g.*, the Institute of Justinian was a treatise on Roman law written by the emperor Justinian. The Institutes of Coke was a four-part treatise on common law written by Sir Edward Coke.

instruct, instruction: To advise; to direct; to order. To give instructions to a jury. A judge will inform a jury of the law applicable to the facts of a pending case as well as point out which party has the burden of proof and any problems of proof to guide the jury in its deliberation. This statement is called a "charge" to the jury. The jury is bound to accept and apply the judge's exposition. To convey information by the client to his attorney.

instrument: A formal document made for a legal purpose, *e.g.*, a will, a contract. An instrument may be used to create or record a legal right, to transfer money or property, or to serve as written evidence of a transaction. A "negotiable instrument" is a document evidencing a right to a payment of money, *e.g.*, a check. In evidence, the term has a broader meaning of anything, including witnesses and animate objects, presented as evidence to the court.

insurable interest: A relationship with a person or an object upon which one can base an insurance policy. Any interest that will directly cause financial loss in the event of loss or damage to the person or object, or financial benefit by its continued existence, is an insurable interest. For example, if one owned a diamond ring and would suffer financially in the event of theft or loss, one has an insurable interest in the ring. However, ownership of the property is not necessary if there is a reasonable expectation of monetary advantage. Also, in the context of life insurance, if one has a reasonable expectation of financial benefit from the life of a person (*e.g.*, a spouse or a business partner), one has an insurable interest on which to base a life insurance policy. An insurance contract must involve an insurable interest; otherwise it is a form of gambling and unenforceable.

insurance: Act of providing against a possible loss from a specified peril by entering into a contract with a party (usually a licensed corporation) that is willing to bind itself to compensate for such loss, should it occur, in exchange for payment. The contract is called a policy. The consideration paid to the insurer or underwriter is called a premium. Types of harm protected against are called risks or perils. The thing or person being protected is the insurable interest. Fire and marine insurance is usually indemnity which means that only such sum is paid by the insurer as is actually lost and the insurer is entitled to stand in place of the insured. In life or accident insurance the insurer undertakes to pay a certain sum to the insured or his legal representative in the event of death or injury.

insured: Any person whose health, life or property is covered by insurance. The owner of an insurance policy.

insurer: An insurance company or underwriter who makes an insurance contract with the insured by assuming the risk or underwriting a policy.

intangibles: Property that has no intrinsic market value but which is evidence of or representative of value or worth. Examples include bonds, stock certificates, and promissory notes. Rights not related to physical articles, but based on relationships between persons that the law recognizes through sanctions.

integration: The act of making whole. In contract law: The adoption of a writing or writings as the full and final expression of the agreement between parties. The writing or writings adopted by the contracting parties. Joining disparate groups (such as races) as equals, as in the desegregation of white and black school districts.

intemperance: Lack of restraint in conduct or habits. Excessive or habitual use of alcoholic beverages. "Habitual intemperance" is the regular consumption of liquor which results in great diminution of the attention that a person can give to his business affairs or which would inflict great mental anguish on an innocent party.

intent, intention, intentional: The purpose, design, or resolve with which a person acts. Since intent is a state of mind, it can rarely be proved directly, but must be inferred from facts or circumstances. In criminal law, the "mens rea" or criminal intent requirement is that a person knows what he is doing and desires or anticipates the results of his act at the time that he commits the offense. Intent, the perpetrator's state of mind at the time of acting, differs from motive, which is what causes a person to act or refrain from acting.

There are two types of intent in criminal law: "General intent" is the intent to commit a crime. Proof of general intent is required in all criminal prosecutions, but does not involve demonstrating that the defendant intended the precise harm which he caused. *E.g.*, shooting into a crowd is proof of general intent to commit murder, even though the accused did not intend to injure any person in particular. "Specific intent" is the intent to accomplish the precise act which the law prohibits. Proof of specific intent is essential for certain crimes, such as "assault with intent to rape."

In torts: An intentional tort requires that the actor desired to cause the consequences of his act or recognizes that these consequences are substantially certain to result from his act.

In documents (*e.g.*, wills), intention is the meaning gathered from the words therein.

inter alia: Lat. Among other things. Used in referring to relevant parts of a statute without citing the whole text, *e.g.*, "the statute provides inter alia."

interest: In property: A legal concern in some property based on a right, title, claim, or legal share. The term usually denotes a right less than full title or absolute ownership in real property. In commercial law: Consideration or compensation paid for the use or retention by one party of another's money. Interest is based on the amount (percentage) charged, the amount loaned, and the length of time of the loan. Interest may be simple or compounded. Simple interest is computed based on the principal only, but compounded interest uses the principal and any accrued interest as its basis for calculation. An interest in legal actions is a legal or monetary concern in the determination of a suit. This interest must be of a present, direct, and immediate character.

interfere, interference: To check; hinder; disturb; trespass; intervene; encroach. To enter into the concerns of others against their wishes. To enter into or take part in the concerns of others. In Patent Law: An interference is a proceeding initiated by the Patent Office to determine the priority of invention among all parties claiming the same subject matter. This takes place when a conflict in patent claims arises, such as when one person claims a patent on the whole or any part of an area already covered by an existing patent or by a pending application.

interim, interim order: Lat. In the meantime; temporary; between. An interim order is a temporary order given until a final order is entered or until some specific event happens, *e.g.*, a temporary injunction.

interlineation: The act of writing between the lines (of an instrument). The writing itself that is found between the lines. An interlineation in a will raises a rebuttable presumption that the writing was made after the will was executed.

interlocutory: Provisional; temporary; not final. A judgment is interlocutory if it does not determine all the issues relating to all the parties, but rather leaves something further to be adjudicated at a later proceeding. An interlocutory appeal is an appeal which does not resolve the controversy, but which is necessary for a later adjudication of the case on its merits.

interlocutory decree: A preliminary or provisional order. A decree made upon some point arising during a suit which is not determinative of the case on the merits, but directs further proceedings in preparation for a final decree. It is a decree made to ascertain a matter of law or fact in preparation for a final decree.

International Court of Justice: The judicial body established by the United Nations. Its jurisdiction includes giving advisory opinions on matters of law and treaty construction when requested to do so by the General Assembly or the Security Council. It may also settle legal disputes between nations who voluntarily submit a controversy for adjudication. Its judgment may be enforced by the Security Council. Its judges are elected by the General Assembly and the Security Council.

international law: The law or customs which regulate the conduct of nations towards each other and towards each other's citizens. The United Nations may establish tribunals to try enemies accused of offenses against international law. There are two kinds of international law: 1. Private international law which determines before which nation's courts a matter should be presented and by which nation's laws a matter should be tried. 2. Public international law is the rules of conduct which independent, civilized states have adopted in their relations with one another.

inter partes: Lat. Between parties. Papers inter partes are documents in which two persons make conveyance to or engagement with the other. Judgment inter partes is a judgment against a particular person and not against a thing or right.

interpleader: A legal proceeding that enables a person holding money or property to compel the claimants to litigate the matter among themselves. When a person who possesses property in which he has no interest but to which two or more parties lay claim and he does not know which party has a right to the property, but is himself sued or expecting to be sued by one or all of the parties, he obtains relief through a court order to interplead; *i.e.*, to have the plaintiffs try their claims among themselves to determine who is entitled to the property. This is called a "stakeholder interpleader." An interpleader is an equitable remedy provided for in *Federal Rule of Civil Procedure 22*.

An example of interpleader is an insurance company having the court order two claimants to the proceeds of a policy to interplead their causes so that the company may turn the proceeds over to the victorious litigant without fear of a lawsuit from the other claimant.

interpolate: To insert words into a completed document which alter its meaning.

interpretation: The discovery of the intention of a writer or of the meaning of a document by studying the words, by conjecture, or by a combination of the two.

A "literal interpretation" ascertains the writer's intention or the document's meaning exclusively from the words used. A "rational interpretation" is a conjecture relying on probability and rationality of what the author intended when the author's language fails to express his intention precisely. A "mixed interpretation" employs both words and educated guesses to fathom the author's intention or the document's meaning when the words of the document are of doubtful meaning or do not express the author's intention when rightly understood.

interrogatories: A group of questions submitted to a party, witness or other person having an interest in the case. In civil actions: A pretrial discovery device in which written questions are submitted by one party to the other party who must reply to the questions in writing and under oath. Unlike depositions, interrogatories can be served only on opposing parties in an action and must be answered in writing. The questions on one or more specific issues of fact necessary to reach a verdict which the court may submit to a jury along with general verdict forms.

inter se: Lat. Among or between themselves. Used to distinguish rights and liabilities between two or more parties to one another from their rights or duties to others.

intersection: A place where two things cross. When applied to streets or highways, it refers to the area common to two streets at the point at which they cross each other as determined by a continuation of the curb. "Intersection" may also apply when one street or highway merges with another without crossing it, forming a "T" intersection. The act of dividing two things by passing a line between them.

Interstate Commerce Act: The Congressional act of February 4, 1887, which regulates commerce between the states, including the transportation of people and property from within one state to another state. The Act attempts to insure that the rates of carriers are reasonable and just by prohibiting unjust discrimination, rebates, pooling of freights, or other monopolistic practices, and that the carriers publish schedules of rates. The Act created a commission (the Interstate Commerce Commission) to carry out these proposals.

Interstate Commerce Commission (I.C.C.): Created by the Interstate Commerce Act of 1887 to regulate interstate transportation.
intervention: The procedure by which a third party not originally a litigant in an action, enters the suit as a matter of right or at the discretion of the court to protect an interest that he has in the subject matter of the dispute. The procedural grounds are delineated in *Federal Rule of Civil Procedure 24*.
inter vivos: Lat. Between the living. Transactions made inter vivos are made while the parties are living and are to take effect while both parties are alive. An inter vivos gift is made while the donor is living and takes effect during the donor's life, as opposed to a gift made "causa mortis" or in contemplation of death.
intestate, intestacy: Without making a will. Strictly defined, a person dies intestate if he dies without making a valid will or without otherwise indicating directions for the disposal of his property. If a person has made a will which has not completely disposed of his property, that individual is said to have died intestate as to that portion of his property not disposed of in his will. A person dies intestate if none of his heirs are available to claim his estate. An "intestate" is one who has died without leaving a valid will.
intestate succession: The disposition of property according to the laws of descent and distribution upon the death of a person who has not left a valid will or who has not accounted for a portion of his estate in his will.
in toto: Lat. In the whole; wholly; completely. If an award is void in toto, then no award is allowed.
intoxication, intoxicated: Drunkenness; the condition of impaired mental capacity due to the excessive consumption of alcohol. In criminal law, voluntary intoxication is not a defense to general intent crimes but may refute the mens rea necessary for specific intent crimes. Involuntary intoxication which renders a person incapable of comprehending the wrongfulness of his conduct would make the actor's behavior involuntary and allow him to avoid criminal liability. (*See* insanity) The state of being poisoned. In driving while intoxicated cases, most states consider intoxication to be either the excessive use of alcohol or of drugs.
intrinsic evidence: Evidence or information learned from a document without any testimony to explain the document or the purposes for which it was written or used.
intrinsic fraud: Fraud occurring during a trial and affecting the adjudication of the issues. Intrinsic fraud may be the result of perjury, false or forged documents, the concealment or misrepresentation of evidence, or bribery of a witness. Usually intrinsic fraud is not sufficient for setting aside a judgment resulting from it since it does not prevent the adversarial process. Fraud used to obtain a transaction which makes the transaction void, *e.g.*, someone signs an instrument without having a reasonable opportunity to discover its essential terms. *U.C.C. §3-305(2)(c)*. Fraud in the inducement.
inure: To take effect; to result. To be of use or benefit to someone, especially used when the benefit is unintended. Property law: To fix one's interest in a property; to vest.
invalid: Void; of no legal effect; inadequate to its purpose; lacking in authority or obligation.
invention: Patent law: The creation of something new by an exercise of mind exhibiting novelty and utility different in kind and in measure from anything done previously. Invention differs from discovery in that it is not the revelation of something which existed and was not known, but rather is the creation of something which never before existed. To meet the requirement of novelty, an invention must be something not obvious to people trained in the field. The article or machine so created.
inventory: A detailed list of goods. A list of goods designating and describing each item and indicating the quantity of each item. The goods themselves, which are on the list. A list of articles constituting an estate or collection drawn up by an executor or an administrator which includes the approximate value of the items.

Under the Uniform Commercial Code, an inventory refers to goods held for sale or lease. The test to decide whether goods are inventory is whether the articles are offered for immediate or for ultimate sale.
invest: To expend capital to acquire property or assets in the hope of securing income or profit for the investor. The word can mean purchasing goods or property for the income that it provides, or purchasing goods or property for their resale value.
investment contract: A transaction or venture where one invests money in a common enterprise where the investor expects, or is led to expect, profits exclusively from the efforts of the promoter or a third party. The contract is based on the investor's reliance on others. A "common enterprise" is the dependent relationship of one party, the investor, on another party's performance of his part of the bargain for the investor's profits.

To be included under the federal securities acts an investment contract requires: 1) an investment of money, 2) a common enterprise, and 3) an expectation of profits solely through the efforts of others.
invitation: The act of a property owner or occupier who solicits or incites another to enter upon, remain in, or make use of his property. An invitation may be

express, as when the owner or occupier uses words to invite another to enter the land or use the property thereon. It is implied when the owner's or occupier's conduct leads another to reasonably believe that the owner expects and intends others to use or traverse the land or the property thereon as they are doing. An example of an implied invitation is the "invitation" of a shop owner to the public to enter his shop to make purchases. Today, most jurisdictions require a standard of reasonable care to all invitees.

invitee: One who is invited onto the property of another, either expressly or impliedly, to conduct business for their mutual benefit or for the benefit of the occupier, or to engage in an activity which the occupier permits to be conducted on his property. *E.g.*, a customer who enters a store is an invitee regardless of whether he makes a purchase. In tort law, a property owner has an affirmative duty to protect the invitee not only against known dangers but also against those dangers which he may discover by exercising reasonable care.

invoice: An itemized, written record of merchandise shipped or sent to a purchaser, including the quantity and value of the merchandise as well as any additional costs. A writing made for an importer specifying the goods imported and their true value.

involuntary manslaughter: The unlawful killing of a human being while committing an unlawful act not amounting to a felony or while committing a lawful act without adequate circumspection and caution. Involuntary manslaughter is killing without malice or premeditation and without intention to kill or inflict serious bodily injury. *E.g.*, a person who hunts game without a license and shoots another hunter by mistake is guilty of involuntary manslaughter since the first hunter did not intend to kill the second hunter but did so while committing a misdemeanor by hunting without a license.

ipse dixit: Lat. He himself said it. An assertion whose authority is based solely upon the individual who made it and not upon any precedent.

ipso facto: Lat. By the fact itself; by the mere fact. As a consequence of an act or fact.

ipso jure: Lat. By the law itself; merely by the operation of law.

irregular, irregularity: Against the rules; improper or insufficient due to a departure from or a neglect of a prescribed rule. An irregularity is a violation or neglect of a prescribed rule or practice. An irregularity may mean a failure to do something necessary for the orderly progress of a suit or the doing of something at an improper time or in an improper manner. An irregularity is also a technical term for a defect in the mechanics of proceedings or in the way an action or defense is conducted.

irrelevant: Not material; unrelated or inapplicable to the issue. Evidence is irrelevant when it has no tendency to prove or disprove any issue involved. Irrelevant evidence is usually objected to and inadmissible at trial.

irreparable injury (damage, harm): The type of injury which cannot be fully remedied by the law and, therefore, requires the equitable remedy of an injunction against the individual about to commit the injury. Demonstrating irreparable injury is usually a requirement for injunctive relief. An injury which is beyond monetary compensation or damages since the damages cannot be measured by any pecuniary standard.

irresistible impulse: A term used in criminal law to mean an uncontrollable desire or urge to commit an unlawful act which cannot be controlled or resisted because a mental disease or insanity has destroyed the actor's self control or freedom of will. As a test for insanity, the irresistible impulse test allows a person to avoid criminal responsibility even though he can distinguish right from wrong and is aware of the nature and quality of his acts if he can demonstrate an inability to refrain from acting due to mental disease.

irrevocable: That which cannot be recalled or withdrawn.

issue: (Verb) To send forth; to put into circulation; to promulgate. To send out officially, as in writs or services of process. (Noun) A legal point of dispute between two or more parties to the litigation which, if it is a matter of law, should be resolved by the court or, if it is a matter of fact, should be resolved by the jury. All who are descended from a common ancestor. In wills, this meaning is usually narrowed to include children alone, depending on the intention of the testator. Most states allow an illegitimate child to inherit from his mother but not from his father. Many states consider an adopted child to be the "issue" of his/her adoptive parents. In securities: The offering for sale of a corporation's stock. The securities, themselves, which are being offered for sale. A series or group of bonds or stock which is put into circulation at the same time.

itemize: To write down in particulars. To declare each item separately. Often used in the context of tax accounting.

itinerant: Wandering; traveling from place to place. Formerly applied to judges who made circuits. Also used in statutes to classify merchants, traders, and salesmen. A person who travels from place to place.

J

jacitation: A false boast; a truthless claim; an assertion that cannot be substantiated. A claim that is disputed by another.

jail: (Noun) A prison; a place of incarceration; the place of confinement where prisoners are held while awaiting trial or as punishment for misdemeanors. (Verb) To imprison; to detain in custody; to place in confinement.

jeopardy: The risk or danger of conviction which a defendant faces from a criminal prosecution.

jetsam: Cargo thrown overboard to lighten a ship in distress, *e.g.*, goods deliberately thrown overboard from a ship, in a storm, to lessen the danger of the ship sinking.

jettison: To cast off or throw overboard from a ship; the act of deliberately removing cargo from a ship in distress, so as to prevent the ship from sinking.

jobber: One who buys merchandise in bulk from manufacturers or wholesalers and then sells it to retailers in smaller lots. One who trades shares on a stock exchange; a dealer in stocks or other securities. A middleman.

John Doe: A name used in a legal proceeding or investigation to designate a fictitious or unidentified person.

joinder: The uniting or joining together of distinct causes of action or persons in a legal proceeding.

joinder of causes of action: The uniting or joining of distinct causes of action in a legal proceeding; under modern rules of civil procedure a party asserting a claim to relief may join as many claims as he has against an opposing party whether they are legal or equitable. *See Federal Rule of Civil Procedure 18(a).*

joint: Undivided; shared; united in interest or liability; such as, a common property interest shared by two or more persons.

joint adventure: Business enterprise formed by a group of persons to carry out a single commercial transaction for profit whereby they pool their property, effects, money, skill, and knowledge.

joint and several: Status where rights and liabilities are shared collectively and also individually among a group of persons.

joint enterprise: Association of persons founded on an express or implied agreement to achieve a common purpose and where there is a community of interest and an equal right of control.

joint liability: Right of any party who is sued to insist that others be sued jointly with him because of their shared liability; contribution.

joint stock company: An unincorporated business enterprise with proprietary interests represented by shares of stock. Also called a "joint stock association."

joint tenancy: Ownership of real property, created under a single deed or instrument, whereby two or more persons have an undivided interest in the whole of the property, an equal right to share in the use and benefits of the property, and attached to which is the right of survivorship.

joint tortfeasors: Two or more persons whose negligent conduct, in concert or individually, united to injure a third person and who are therefore jointly and severally liable for the injury.

jointure: Property or estate granted to a wife upon the death of her husband, as set forth in a prenuptial agreement.

joint venture: Association of persons formed to engage in a particular commercial transaction for profit where there is a community of interest and where the right to share both in profits and losses and the right of control is fixed by agreement. Unlike a partnership, a joint venture is of limited scope and duration.

judge: Public official with the authority to preside and administer the law in a court of justice.

judge advocate corps: Staff of Judge Advocate General.

Judge Advocate General: The senior legal officer and the principal legal advisor of each branch of the United States Armed Services.

judge pro tempore: Person appointed for the term or portion thereof, during which time he performs the duties of the regular judge.
judgment: The decision of a court; the final determination of a court on a matter submitted to it.
judgment creditor: A person who has obtained a judgment against a debtor under which he can obtain the sum due him.
judgment debtor: A person against whom judgment has been awarded to a creditor, and the debt remains unpaid.
judgment in rem: A decision by a court which affects the status of a specific item or matter, as opposed to the person owning the item.
judgment note: A promissory note that authorizes an attorney or some other designated person to enter an appearance for the maker of the note and confess a judgment against him for a sum therein named, upon default on payment of the note.
judgment on the merits: Decision by a court based on an analysis of the factual issues presented in a case rather than on some technical issue.
judgment proof: Status of all persons against whom judgments for money recoveries are of no consequence, *e.g.*, persons who are insolvent.
judicial: Relating or pertaining to legal proceedings or the administration of justice.
judicial notice: Decision by a court recognizing the validity of certain facts without the need for proof, thereby relieving one party of the burden of producing evidence to prove these facts. *E.g.*, a court can take judicial notice that Thanksgiving is a legal holiday.
judicial sale: The sale of property made under the authority or supervision of a court, such as, the sale of property ordered by a court to satisfy a tax lien.
judiciary: The courts of justice; the branch of government entrusted with judicial power and the administration of the courts in the federal system.
judicis est jus dicere, non dare: Lat. It is for a judge to declare the law and not to make it.
jura publica anteferenda privatis: Lat. Public rights are to be preferred over private ones.
jurat: Certificate of appropriate person that confirms a writing has been sworn to by the person who signed it; the certificate states when, where, and before whom the writing was sworn.
juridical: Relating or pertaining to a legal proceeding. That which is done in compliance with the laws of a country or a particular jurisdiction.
juridical day: Day on which court is in session.
jurisdiction: Authority by which courts and judicial officers hear and determine cases. The geographic region over which a court's power to hear and determine cases extends.
juris doctor: Doctor of laws. Basic professional degree in legal education; J.D.
jurisprudence: The science or philosophy of law. A system or body of laws, such as case law.
jurist: A legal scholar; a person proficient and accomplished in law.
juror: Member of a jury; one who serves on a jury. *See* jury.
jury: A group of persons chosen from the eligible public that are convened and sworn at a trial to determine the facts in dispute.
jury box: The area in a courtroom where the jury sits during a trial.
jury list: Roster of jurors selected to hear a case. Roster of prospective jurors summoned to attend court for purposes of jury selection.
jury wheel: Device that stores and randomly selects the names of prospective jurors.
jus: Lat. Law; a legal system. A right; a recognized privilege.
just: Legally proper; lawful; that which conforms to the law.
just compensation: Consideration that adequately indemnifies a person whose property has been taken for public use through the government's power of eminent domain.
jus tertii: Lat. The right of a third person.
justice: Title given to judges, particularly those that sit on the United States and State Supreme Courts. A standard of conduct that requires persons to fulfill their social, legal, and moral obligations to society. To do that which is right or equitable.
justice of the peace: A judicial officer of lesser rank having jurisdiction as set forth by statute over civil matters and minor criminal offenses.
justiciable: Matter suitable for review by a court.
justifiable homicide: The killing of a person which the law sanctions or permits. *E.g.*, the killing of a person in self-defense is permitted under the law.
justification: Rationale; lawful excuse or reason offered for a person's conduct.
juvenile court: A court having jurisdiction over minors, especially juvenile delinquents. (*See* juvenile delinquent) An adversarial system is avoided in favor of a paternal concern for the minor's well-being.
juvenile delinquent: Minor who has committed an offense punishable by criminal penalties but who is under the age, set by statute, for criminal responsibility.

K

kangaroo court: Spurious legal proceeding; proceeding where a person's rights and liberties are ignored and the result is a foregone conclusion.

keep: To maintain; to conduct; to manage, *e.g.*, to "keep" a house in good repair. To record; to maintain for purposes of documentation, *e.g.*, to "keep" financial records for a business.

kickback: A payment back of a portion of the purchase price of a property by the seller to the buyer to bring about the purchase or future purchases; a bribe.

kidnapping: To unlawfully seize and detain a person by force against his will whereby the person is taken away from the place where he was found.

kin, kindred: Relationship by blood or consanguinity.

King's (Queen's) Bench: The highest English common law court that hears both civil and criminal actions, so called because the King or Queen formerly sat there in person.

kiting: The practice of writing checks against an account where the funds are insufficient to cover them, in the hope that before they are cashed the necessary funds will be deposited in the account.

kleptomania: An obsessive impulse to steal.

knowingly: Consciously; with knowledge; scienter. *See* scienter.

knowledge: Comprehension of the truth; understanding of facts; perception of the truth. Learning acquired by education.

L

labor: Work; to provide a service or perform a job.

labor dispute: Expression that covers any controversy concerning the terms of employment, such as, wages, fringe benefits, duration of employment or conditions in the work place; more specifically, any dispute concerning an association of persons that negotiate or seek to arrange the terms of employment with an employer.

labor union: An alliance or association of workers formed to bargain and negotiate with employers the terms and conditions of employment.

laches: An equitable defense doctrine which prevents enforcement of a claim or right which, because of neglect, lapse of time, and other circumstances, has resulted in some change in the condition or relationship of the property or parties that is prejudicial to the adverse party.

Landrum-Griffin Act: Federal statute enacted for purposes of curbing union corruption and restraining undemocratic management of internal union affairs as well as eliminating some types of secondary boycotts.

lapse: To cease; to end; the termination of a right or privilege through failure to act within a certain time period, or through failure of some contingency.

larceny: The unlawful taking and carrying away of another's personal property with intent to deprive the rightful owner of possession.

lascivious: Lewd; lecherous; salacious; indecent; obscene.

last clear chance: Doctrine under which a defendant may be liable for injuries he caused, even though the plaintiff caused himself to be placed in a dangerous situation or was contributorily negligent, if the defendant could have avoided injury to plaintiff by exercising ordinary care.

last resort: A court from which no further appeal is allowed is known as a "court of last resort."

last will and testament: Legal instrument which determines the disposition of a person's real and personal property upon his death.

latent: Hidden; concealed.

latent defect: A hidden or concealed flaw, such as, a deficiency in a product that cannot be discovered upon casual inspection or examination.

lateral support: The right of a landowner to the natural support of his land by the adjoining land or the soil beneath.

law: A body of rules or standards of conduct promulgated or established by some authority, *e.g.*, those standards of conduct adopted by the legislative authority of a government.

lawful: That permitted or authorized by the law.

law merchant: The general body of commercial practices and customs which over time have become an established part of the law, unless displaced or modified by statute, and which relate principally to transactions involving those engaged in trade or commerce.

law of the case: Doctrine whereby courts will refuse to reconsider those matters of law in a proceeding that have been previously settled in a prior appeal, assuming that the facts in the case have not changed. *See* stare decisis, res judicata, and collateral estoppel.

law of the land: Those basic principles of justice that constitute due process of law which cannot be abolished or significantly restricted; more specifically the law as developed by the courts or statute in complaisance with those principles.

lawsuit: An action between two or more persons instituted in a civil court; an action or proceeding in a civil court.

lawyer: An attorney; a person licensed by an appropriate authority to practice law; a person trained and educated in the law.

layman: A person not a member of a religious or ecclesiastical order. A person who is not a member of a particular profession, *e.g.*, one who is not a lawyer.

leading case: Decision which because of its legal analysis or scholarship, or the notoriety of the facts in dispute, is viewed as having settled or resolved the law on a particular subject, and as a consequence is relied on by courts.

leading question: Query which suggests to a witness the answer that is desired by the inquiring party or directs a witness towards the desired response. At trial, leading questions are permitted on cross-examination and when a hostile witness or an adverse party is being questioned.
lease: Agreement between two parties whereby one party, the lessor, yields his right of possession and use of some real or personal property for a specified period of time to a lessee in return for consideration.
leasehold: A lessee's estate or interest in real property that is created by a lease.
leave and license: A defense to an action of trespass that asserts the consent of the plaintiff to the trespass alleged.
legacy: A bequest; a disposition or distribution of personal property by will.
legal: That which is lawful; permitted by the law; established or mandated by the law. Relating or pertaining to the law.
legal ethics: Customs and norms among members of the legal profession that relate to their professional and moral responsibilities to their profession, toward one another, to their clients and toward the courts.
legal fiction: A fact or situation assumed or created by a court so it can settle a matter before it, *e.g.*, the fiction that an unsigned agreement was properly signed so a court could enforce a contract.
legalize: To make lawful.
legal representative: A person who oversees and represents the legal affairs and interests of another, *e.g.*, a court appointed guardian of a minor.
legal tender: Lawful currency that may be used for the satisfaction of any and all debts or claims; all coins and currencies of the United States, regardless of when issued, may be used to settle all debts or claims, public and private. The act of making or offering to make payment on a debt or claim.
legatee: The person to whom a legacy or bequest in a will is given.
leges posteriores priores contrarias abrogant: Lat. Later laws abrogate prior laws that are inconsistent with them. Provisions of later laws take precedent over provisions of earlier laws that conflict with their terms.
legislation: Laws made by a legislative body; regulations adopted by a lawmaking body. The act of making or enacting laws.
legislator: A member of a lawmaking body; a person who enacts laws; a representative.
legitimate: That which is lawful; proper; acceptable. To make lawful, *e.g.*, to make an illegal alien a legal alien. A child born in wedlock, in contrast to a child born outside a marriage.
Legum Doctor: Lat. Doctor of Laws; legal degree that is customarily awarded as an honorary degree.
lesion: Injury; wound; diseased tissue. An injury suffered by a party to an agreement where he does not receive what he is entitled to receive for what he contributes to the contract.
lessee: One who rents property; one who holds an estate in real or personal property by virtue of a lease agreement; a tenant.
lesser included offense: A crime that is necessarily proven by proof of a greater or more serious crime; a crime that has many elements of a greater crime and which does not have any element not included in the greater crime; *e.g.*, the crime of larceny is necessarily proven by proof of the crime of robbery.
lessor: One who rents property to another; one who grants to another an estate in real or personal property for a specified duration under terms of a lease agreement; landlord.
let: Conveyance: To lease or rent property to another. Contracts: To award a contract to one of several parties that have entered a bid for the contract. Judicial order: It is hereby ordered, *e.g.*, it is hereby ordered that the property be sold at public sale.
letter: A communication in writing from one party to another; a written communication that is usually delivered via the postal system. A written instrument that grants some authority, privilege or right.
letter of credit: A written instrument whereby one party requests that another party advance a certain sum of money or give credit to a third party, and in return guarantees repayment of the money advanced.
letter of safe conduct: Written instrument that guarantees a person or a vessel protection and unhindered movement in a war zone, thereby preventing the person or the vessel from being seized.
letters testamentary: The formal document of authority and appointment issued by a court to an executor, thereby allowing him to fulfill his duties as executor of an estate.
levy: To impose; assess; tax; collect. A seizure; *e.g.*, to satisfy a debt, money is raised by use of legal proceedings through seizure and sale of property.
lewd: Indecent; obscene; lascivious.
lex: Lat. A collection, system, or body of laws.
lex communis: Lat. The common law.
lex domicilii: Lat. The law of the domicile. The law of a given jurisdiction.
lex est dictamen rationis: Lat. Law is the dictate of reason. The common law will judge according to the laws of nature and the public welfare.
lex fori: The law of the forum or court. The law of the jurisdiction where an action is brought and the law which governs the remedies that are allowed in the jurisdiction.

lex loci: Lat. The law of the place. The substantive rights of parties to an action are governed by the law of the place.

lex loci contractus: Lat. The law of the place that governs a contract. The proper law applicable in determining the rights and liabilities of parties to a contract.

lex loci delictus: Lat. The law of the place where the offense or wrong took place.

lex neminem cogit ad vana seu inutilia peragenda: Lat. The law will not compel one to do useless things.

lex non scripta: Lat. The unwritten, or common law. The common law which includes customs and usages, and particular local laws.

lex scripta: Lat. Written law. Law deriving its power from statute or legislative enactment.

lex semper dabit remedium: Lat. Law always provides a remedy.

lex terrae: Lat. Law of the land.

liability: Any type of obligation or debt, fixed or contingent; an indebtedness owed to another party; a duty to pay another monies on funds owed. An obligation or mandate to do or refrain from doing something.

liable: Responsible; to be obligated; accountable; to be bound by law.

libel: Any false and malicious written publication printed for the purpose of defaming another's character or reputation; any written defamation of character, not privileged, which is false and malicious and which "tends to expose a person to public scorn, hatred, contempt or ridicule." *Bowie v. Evening News, 148 Md. 569, 574 (1925).* The appropriate libel standard for a public person is different than one for a private person. *See New York Times Co. v. Sullivan, 376 U.S. 254 (1964).*

libera batella: Lat. The liberty of free fishery in certain waters.

liberty: Freedom; lack of restraint; freedom from arbitrary control; the right to exercise one's free will, except as limited by law.

license: A right granted to a person to do something which he otherwise could not legally do, *e.g.*, the right to operate a motor vehicle on public streets, as granted by a state. To grant permission to do that which would be illegal if permission was not granted; to authorize conduct that would otherwise be improper.

licensee: The person who receives or acquires a license.

licensor: The person who grants or bestows a license.

licentiousness: Lasciviousness; lewdness; the state of acting or functioning without moral or legal restraints.

lien: A claim on another's property asserted in order to secure payment upon a debt; to assert an interest in another's property until an indebtedness is discharged.

lieu: Place; situation; locale. *Note*: "in lieu of" means in place of.

life annuity: A fixed sum of money paid yearly during one's life or the life of another.

life estate: An ownerhsip interest in property granted to a person for as long as he or another person lives; upon the end of the measuring life, the land will either revert to the grantor of the life estate or will go to a person holding a remainder interest in the property.

life tenant: A person granted a life estate; a person who has an ownership interest in property for as long as he lives.

limitation: Restriction; restraint; qualification; such as, to place a limitation on the amount of unemployment benefits any one person may receive.

limited partnership: A business venture in which one group of persons (called the general partners) with unlimited liability manages the venture, while another group (called the limited partners) only contribute capital and have no right to participate in the management of the venture.

Lindbergh Act: Federal statute which punishes kidnapping that involves the interstate movement of kidnapping victims, that is, the taking of a victim from one state to another or to a foreign country.

lineal: Direct; unbroken chain; such as, being in the direct line of succession from one's ancestor, *e.g.*, lineal descent.

line of credit: The maximum amount of credit that a financial institution is willing to extend to a business or a person at any one time. *E.g.*, if a bank has lent a business the full amount of its "line of credit" it will not make any more loans to the business until some of the debt is paid off, and then only in amounts that will not exceed the business' line of credit.

liquidate: To resolve; to settle; to discharge; such as, to discharge a debt or obligation. To convert assets or property to cash. To close down the affairs of a business; to settle all liabilities and obligations of an entity; to wind up the affairs of a business.

liquidated: Settled; fixed; resolved; specified.

liquidated damages: An amount of money specified in a contract to compensate a party for injuries suffered because of a breach of contract by the other party to the agreement; the amount agreed to in advance of a breach of contract to serve as compensation for any injury or damage suffered, thereby precluding any liability in excess of the amount stipulated in the contract.

liquidation: The act of settling or resolving an obligation, *e.g.*, the settling of a debt. The act of converting assets and property to cash. The procedure whereby the financial affairs of a company are resolved. The company's liabilities and obligations are paid off and any remaining assets are divided between those persons authorized to receive them. Usually payments are made in the form of cash.

lis pendens: Lat. A suit pending in court. Notice of lis pendens filed with a public records office is said to put the whole world on notice that the status of the property or matter being litigated is unsettled and therefore one should proceed with caution in entering into agreements concerning said property or matter.

litigant: A person involved in a lawsuit; a party to a legal proceeding.

litigation: Legal dispute or controversy; lawsuit; any civil action, as opposed to criminal proceeding, before a court.

litigious: Prone to legal dispute; inclined to file a lawsuit or initiate legal proceedings about a matter in dispute.

littoral rights: Rights and privileges that pertain to the use and enjoyment of coastal property; rights that pertain to property that abuts or borders on an ocean or a lake.

livery: The act of conveying legal possession of property to a party. Uniform or distinctive dress of a particular profession or occupation, *e.g.*, the uniform a doorman wears. The business of hiring or leasing out horses and carriages.

livery of seisin: English common law ceremony whereby real property is transferred from grantor to grantee.

living trust: A trust whose provisions are in effect during the lifetime of the seisin who established the trust. Also called an "inter vivos trust."

loan: The lending of funds, under an express or implied agreement, whereby the party receiving the funds will repay the sum lent plus interest on the sum at some future date; a debt that is to be repaid. To give or lend personal property for temporary use by another party. Frequently, no charge is involved for the temporary use of the property.

lobbying: The act of seeking to sway, influence, or manipulate the beliefs and opinions of legislators; any attempt to influence the status of proposed or existing legislation.

lobbyist: A person who attempts to influence the members of a legislative body or the status of any legislation pending before that body.

lockout: The practice used by an employer in a labor dispute whereby workers are denied an opportunity to work or even enter the place of work so as to give the employer a stronger bargaining position.

locus: Place; the site where some event has or will take place.

locus contractus: Lat. The place of a contract. The place where a contract is made or entered into.

locus delicti: Lat. The place where an offense takes place. The scene or site of a crime.

locus sigilli: Lat. The place in a written instrument where a seal is affixed.

loiter: To be dilatory; to stand idle; to loaf; to meander; to wander about aimlessly. Most jurisdictions prohibit a person from loitering in public areas, *e.g.*, it is usually illegal to loiter on the grounds of a school.

long arm statutes: State legislative acts which allow local courts to obtain jurisdiction over nonresident defendants to a lawsuit where the cause of action is local in origin or has an effect in the state. *E.g.*, a nonresident corporation could be a party to a lawsuit in a jurisdiction other than its own if its goods injured residents of that jurisdiction.

loss: Injury; forfeiture; deprivation; damage; deficiency. In its most common usage it means any reduction in value of an asset or a group of assets.

lucid interval: Temporary period of sanity; that period of time in which a normally insane or mentally unbalanced person is in control of his faculties and can think rationally.

lump-sum settlement: A one-time payment of funds to discharge or settle a liability or an obligation. The payment covers the entire amount of any sum due.

lynch law: Action or conduct done without sanction or approval of law; the actions of a mob that seek to punish an alleged wrongdoer without benefit of a trial, protection of the accused's civil rights, and without legal authority; vigilante justice.

M

magistrate: A public officer with specific, delegated executive or judicial powers; usually a local judicial officer who conducts preliminary hearings or has limited powers to try minor criminal or civil offenses.

Magna Charta: Lat. Great Charter. Document of English liberties granted to the barons by King John in 1215 at Runnymede, which formed the basis of many English and American constitutional liberties, including limits on taxation, the right to own property, the right to a jury trial, and the proper administration of justice.

maiming: The wrongful and intentional act which results in the loss of a limb or bodily organ of the person attacked, which is disfiguring or disabling. *See* mayhem, mutilation.

maintenance: Financial or other support to a spouse or children during marital separation, usually under court order. Meddling in a legal suit by a nonparty by providing financial or other support to either party.

majority: Full age; the age when a person attains full citizenship, the right to vote, power to make a will, and the right to manage personal affairs. Any number greater than half the total, usually in elections.

maker: One who signs and becomes responsible for a promissory note, *e.g.*, the maker of a check.

mala fides: Lat. Bad faith, the opposite of bona fides.

mala in se: Lat. Wrong in themselves. *See* malum in se.

malfeasance: Wrongful and unlawful conduct, especially conduct by public officials which interferes with their public duties. *Contrast* with misfeasance and nonfeasance.

malice: Mental disposition to commit a wrongful act or injury without legal justification. "Express malice" is deliberate and actual ill will against a person. "Implied malice" is reckless disregard of the consequences of wrongful acts.

malice aforethought: Mental determination to commit a wrongful act or injury without legal justification, before committing the act; usually part of the charge of murder. At common law, intent to kill, willful, wanton, reckless disregard, intent to cause great bodily harm, intent to commit a felony.

malicious: Having wrongful and wicked intentions without legal justification.

malicious arrest: Wrongful arrest, without grounds to believe the person has committed a crime.

malicious mischief: Destruction of personal property out of ill will against the owner.

malicious prosecution: Wrongful prosecution of a criminal action without grounds to believe the person has committed a crime; wrongfully instituting a civil action without probable cause and for motives other than adjudication of a legal claim. If the prosecution terminates in favor of the accused defendant, there is a right to recover damages.

malinger: To pretend sickness or insanity in order to avoid labor or military duty, or for financial gain.

malpractice: Misconduct of a doctor, attorney, accountant or other professional in the performance of professional services, through negligence or unreasonable lack of skill, prudence, or diligence.

malum in se: Lat. A wrong in itself. An inherently evil or morally wrong act, whether prohibited by law or not, *e.g.*, murder.

malum prohibitum: Lat. A prohibited wrong. An act or offense which is not inherently immoral, but is prohibited by law, *e.g.*, speeding.

manager: A person who controls the business affairs of another or of a corporation.

mandamus: Lat. We command. A writ or order, issued by courts only in extreme necessity, to a public official or corporation, commanding the performance of some public duty required by statute.

mandate: Order of a court directing some specific action or enforcement of a judgment. Bailment of property, when the bailee agrees to do some act without pay.

mandatory: Having an obligation or command which must be obeyed.

mandatory injunction: Order of a court which compels the defendant to perform a particular act or restrain from performing an act.
manifest: Document which indicates the quantity, description, origin, and destination of a ship's entire cargo, shown to United States Customs officials. That which is obvious to the understanding, evident to the senses, especially to sight.
Mann Act: Federal statute prohibiting transportation in interstate or foreign commerce of women and girls for prostitution or any immoral purpose. *18 U.S.C. §§2421-2423.*
manslaughter: Negligent or unlawful killing of a person without malice, premeditation, or deliberation. "Voluntary manslaughter" is an unlawful killing without malice, upon sudden provocation in the heat of passion. "Involuntary manslaughter" is a negligent killing with no intention to take life or to commit an unlawful act.
margin: Method of stock purchasing where the stockbroker purchases on the customer's account and requires only a fraction of the purchase price (or margin) to be paid by the customer, as security against losses due to price fluctuations. The edge or boundary, particularly of property.
marine insurance: Insurance against losses to ships, freight, and cargo in navigation during a certain period or voyage.
marital: Relating to marriage; the reciprocal rights and duties of spouses.
maritime contract: A contract having anything to do with navigation, *e.g.*, marine insurance, seaman's wages.
maritime law: Law of the sea, concerning commerce and navigation, ships, seamen, contracts made at sea, and salvage. In the United States, maritime is included in the admiralty jurisdiction of the federal courts.
marketable title: Title to property which is free from reasonable objections from a reasonably well-informed purchaser exercising ordinary business prudence. Courts may force a purchaser, who has contracted to purchase the property, to accept a marketable title, even if it is not perfect.
market value: The price of property or goods sold in the ordinary public market of willing buyers and willing sellers.
marriage: Relationship established by law between one man and one woman united for life to perform the duties of husband and wife. The ceremony creating the relationship.
marshal: Federal officer responsible for executing the process of the United States courts, *e.g.*, delivering summons and subpoenas. In some states, a local police officer similar to a sheriff.
marshaling: Process whereby the court arranges, ranks, and disposes of competing claims to obtain the largest amount of satisfaction for all claimants. If there are two competing claims against one fund, and one of the claimants has a claim against another fund, that claimant may be ordered by the court to resort to his exclusive claim, so as to obtain the largest amount of satisfaction for both claimants, *e.g.*, marshaling of assets, marshaling of liens.
martial law: Temporary control over civilians by a military commander, usually in wartime and possible only in extreme emergency and utter necessity, during which all civil law and authority is suspended.
master: One who employs another to perform services with the right to control the performance of those services. "Special master": Officer appointed by courts to assist the court in taking testimony, computing damages, or performing a sale.
material breach: A breach which affords the nonbreaching party remedies of damages and rescission. It also discharges all of the nonbreaching party's remaining duties to perform.
material fact: A fact, the consideration of which would substantially determine the ultimate decision, *e.g.*, whether to make a contract, to approve a loan, or to choose a verdict in a trial.
material witness: A trial witness whose testimony tends to prove or disprove a significant issue being considered.
matter of fact: A purely factual dispute for the consideration of the jury or fact finder.
matter of law: A legal dispute for the judge's consideration of various statutes and legal rules; the legal consequences of a particular act.
matter of record: Any fact which may be proved by reference to court records.
maturity: The time a legal obligation reaches full development. In commercial law, the time a bill or note becomes payable.
maxim: General principle of law, traditionally and universally accepted, often used to support general legal conclusions, *e.g.*, "no one is above the law."
mayhem: The unlawful and malicious deprivation of a limb or bodily organ of another which is disfiguring or disabling. *See* maiming.
mayor: Chief executive officer of a city, town, or municipality, whose powers are defined by state law or municipal charter.
measure of damages: Test for determining compensation for losses occurring in a tort or breach of contract.
mechanic's lien: A claim against buildings and real property, created by statute, to secure payment to those who provide labor and materials in constructing

or repairing a building. Also applies to automobiles and other goods as well as to structures.
mediation: Intervention; settlement of disputes by an objective third person who attempts to work a compromise.
medical jurisprudence: Principles of medicine used to determine scientific or medical evidence in legal cases (*e.g.*, the cause of death, the extent of disability, the presence of poisons); forensic medicine.
meeting: A gathering of interested persons for the discussion and resolution of matters of mutual concern, *e.g.*, shareholders' meeting.
meeting of minds: In contract law, a rule of decision limiting the effect of the contract to the stated purposes and intentions of both parties, mutually agreed upon; mutual assent.
memorandum: An informal note or record of some agreement or transaction. A written argument to a court without the formal style of a brief, often requested by the judge during a trial. In a law office, an informal report of the legal issues in a pending case.
mens rea: Lat. A guilty mind. Criminal intent; the mental state of a person committing an act which constitutes a crime.
mensa et thoro: Lat. From bed and board. A partial divorce or separation, not a dissolution of the marriage, where the husband and wife no longer live together.
mental anguish: The mental suffering resulting from grief, distress, fright, indignation, or shock connected with a physical injury; sometimes part of the damages in a tort action.
mental cruelty: Action by one spouse towards the other which is so cruel or harmful as to cause mental or physical damage and makes the marriage intolerable.
mercantile: Concerning the business of buying and selling merchandise; trade; commerce.
merchantable, merchantability: A "merchantable" good must be fit for the ordinary purposes of sale, of good and ordinary quality, and salable at the current, regular market price. "Merchantability" is the state of being merchantable.
merger: Joining of two estates or contract rights into one when the new owner acquires both; *e.g.*, when a bank forecloses a mortgage, it achieves a merger of the mortgage right and the property. In corporations, a consolidation of two or more corporations into one under the same governing organization. At common law, inchoate offenses merged into the substantive offenses committed.
merits: Evidence and arguments relating to the substance of the legal claim, rather than the technicalities of jurisdiction, process, waiver, etc.
mesne: Lat. The middle. Intermediate. In common law procedure, "mesne process" refers to writs or court orders which come between the original complaint and the judgment.
metes and bounds: The boundary lines of property, including lengths and angles.
middleman: Person who brings together the parties to make a contract.
military law: Body of law governing members of the military services, distinguished from "martial law." In the United States, military law cases are heard by the Court of Military Appeals.
minatur innocentibus qui parcit nocentibus: Lat. He threatens the innocent who spares the guilty.
mineral estate, mineral rights: A property interest in minerals; the right to take minerals or to receive a royalty for minerals taken.
ministerial: Concerning official, nondiscretionary duties or functions of a government official.
minor: A person who has not attained full age and citizenship.
minor breach: A partial breach; a breach which gives the nonbreaching party a claim for damages stemming from the breach but which does not discharge the nonbreaching party's remaining duties to perform.
minority: The condition of a minor. A number less than half the total, especially in elections. *See* "majority."
minutes: In corporations, official notes or records of meetings or transactions. Memorandum or record of courtroom proceedings, authorized by the judge.
***Miranda* warning:** Statement of constitutional rights which must be read by law enforcement officers when a person is arrested or taken into custody. These include the suspect's right to remain silent, that any statement made may be used against him in court, that he has a right to an attorney, and that if he cannot afford an attorney, one will be appointed for him. *See Miranda v. Arizona, 384 U.S. 436 (1966).*
misappropriation: Wrongful or unauthorized use of property or funds, *e.g.*, using trust funds other than for the beneficiary of the trust.
misbehavior: Wrongful, improper, or unlawful conduct.
miscarriage of justice: Prejudice to the rights of a party at a legal proceeding, contrary to the ends of justice, which requires reversal of the outcome or another trial.
miscegenation: Marriage between persons of two different races, at one time a crime against state law.
misdemeanor: A crime punishable by a fine or imprisonment for less than one year; less serious than a felony.

misdirection: Error in the legal reasoning of a judge's instructions to the jury.
misfeasance: The improper or wrongful performance of some lawful act. *Contrast* malfeasance, nonfeasance.
misjoinder: The improper joining of parties or claims in one lawsuit.
misnomer: Using the wrong name in legal documents or legal proceedings.
misprision: In old common law, represents several separate offenses not signified by a name, including contempt of court, sedition, disloyalty to the government, public neglect, and failure to report a crime.
misprision of felony: The offense of concealing a felony or failing to report a felony. Today this is being "an accessory after the fact."
misrepresentation: A false and misleading statement about a material fact, which may be grounds for rescinding a contract or for the recovery of damages in contract or tort.
mistake: An act or omission done out of ignorance or faulty judgment which would not have been done without an erroneous belief.
mistake of fact: An incorrect belief or ignorance of a fact, usually a reason for voiding a contract or for a criminal defense.
mistake of law: An incorrect judgment of the legal consequences of known facts, usually not a reason for a criminal defense, due to the maxim "ignorance of the law is no excuse."
mistrial: Termination of a trial due to some misconduct or extraordinary circumstance, *e.g.*, tampering with the jury, violation of ethics, or death of the judge.
mitigating circumstances: Circumstances surrounding the criminal act which can reduce the penalty to the defendant, in the discretion of judge and jury; *e.g.*, homicide can be reduced from murder to manslaughter if committed in a sudden heat of passion. Also includes attributes or acts of the defendant which may reduce the sentence of the crime, in the judge's discretion, *e.g.*, a first offense, good faith, good character.
mitigation: Lessening of the damages or punishment imposed by law.
mitigation of damages: Any lessening of the damages caused by tort or breach of contract; legal requirement that the injured person, in the exercise of ordinary care, use reasonable efforts to minimize the damages arising out of the injury.
mittimus: Court order to sheriff or prison warden directing him to deliver, receive, or keep a prisoner in custody. Form of court order used to transfer records from one court to another.
M'Naghten Rule: Common law test of criminal responsibility of the insane, first introduced in England in 1843 and accepted by many American courts. Under this test, insanity is grounds for acquittal if the suspect, while committing the act, was laboring under such a defect of reason from disease of the mind as not to know the nature and quality of the act he was doing, or if he did know it, that he did not know what he was doing was wrong. *M'Naghten's Case, 8 Eng. Rep. 718 (1843).*
modification, modify: A change which alters the terms and conditions of a contract but leaves the basic purpose intact; to change part of a contract.
modus operandi: Lat. Method of operating. The particular way an act is carried out, *e.g.*, murder by poisoning the victim's dinner with cyanide.
moiety: Half of something, usually half of an estate in property; *e.g.*, a joint tenant holds half an estate, or by moiety.
molestation: The offense of disturbing another and violating his or her freedom; particularly the offense of using a child for sexual gratification.
money: Standard means of exchange and valuation, adopted by national governments.
monogamy: Marriage to one person, contrasted with polygamy or bigamy. *See* polygamy, bigamy.
monopoly: Exclusive privilege of manufacturing, using, or controlling the sale of a particular market commodity. Business combination to fix prices of a commodity or otherwise dominate the market in restraint of free trade. In antitrust, possession of a monopoly power in the market along with acquisition or maintenance of that power is illegal under the Sherman Act. *15 U.S.C. §§1-7.*
moot: A matter for argument, never decided by a court. A case is moot when it presents a pretended controversy or when a judgment by the court would have no effect upon the controversy.
moral certainty: Certainty beyond any reasonable doubts; an assurance that excludes all reasonable doubts that a contrary conclusion may exist.
moral obligation: A duty which is not recognized by law but rests on good conscience and notions of natural justice; a moral obligation may be created by contract.
moral turpitude: Intentional acts or behavior involving dishonesty, wickedness, depravity, or grave infringement of the good moral sentiment of the community.
moratorium: Delay or suspension in the obligation to perform some legal duty or in the right to have some legal duty performed, when ordered by a court or enacted by the legislature; *e.g.*, a moratorium in suits against debtors during a period of financial upheaval.

mortgage: Security for a loan; an interest in property given by the debtor (the mortgagor) to the creditor, loan company, or bank (the mortgagee) to secure payment of the loan. At common law, the mortgagee had the legal right to possession. Today, in most states a mortgage is a lien, therefore, the mortgagee may only have the legal right to possession after a foreclosure hearing with proof of default in payments by the debtor.
mortis causa: Lat. In contemplation of death. A gift may be given mortis causa by a dying person but is void if the person recovers and survives; sometimes used as "causa mortis."
mortmain: "Dead hand." In the old common law, represented property in perpetual ownership of the church or some corporations. Parliament enacted the "mortmain acts" to limit the creation of perpetual ownership of property.
mortuary: A place for embalming, undertaking, or burial.
most favored nations clause: In international law, a clause in treaties which guarantees to the citizens of the participating countries the same rights and privileges given by each participating country to the most favored nations of that country.
motion: A request by a party to the court, made orally or in writing, for a favorable order, rule, or remedy, concerning a question within the judge's discretion, *e.g.*, motion to dismiss the action, motion for retrial.
motive: The reason or inducement that causes a person to act in a certain manner, contrasted to "intent," which is the purpose a person has when acting.
movable: In property, articles which can be transported away, contrasted to "fixtures" which are attached to the land.
move: To make a "motion" to the court for a particular order, ruling, or remedy.
multifarious: The improper joining of independent and distinct issues in one suit or of several unrelated defendants in one action. Also called "misjoinder." Under the Federal Rules of Civil Procedure, broad joinder of separate claims and defendants is encouraged.
multiplicity of suits (or actions): Grounds for the court to unite numerous separate actions or suits into one court in equity jurisdiction, where the actions are against the same defendant and concern the same right, and separate actions would be unnecessarily wasteful for the defendant.
multitudo imperitorum perdit curiam: Lat. A great number of unskilled practitioners ruins a court.
municipal: Concerning a city, town, or other local governmental or public unit. In a broader sense, referring to the public and political functions of a government, *e.g.*, the "municipal purposes" of the flood relief act.
municipal corporation: Local institution of government, created by state charter for a particular geographic area, which exercises local powers delegated by the state, such as controlling transfers of property, building and maintaining roads, establishing local ordinances, and other local functions.
municipal court: Local court of limited jurisdiction to consider traffic and city ordinance violations and other minor criminal or civil offenses.
muniments: Document by which rights and privileges are proved, *e.g.*, deed, charter.
murder: An unlawful killing of another person with malice aforethought, committed either purposely or recklessly with disregard of the value of human life.

Murder is commonly divided by statute into different degrees for purposes of punishment: "First-degree murder," punishable by death or life imprisonment, is the unlawful killing of another by poison, by lying in wait, through a willful, deliberate premeditation, or during the commission or attempted commission of a felony. "Second-degree murder" is the unlawful killing of another with malice aforethought but without premeditation. "Felony murder" is the unlawful killing of another during the commission or attempted commission of a felony. *See* manslaughter.
mutatis mutandis: Lat. With the necessary changes in detail to be made in compliance with one major change, *e.g.*, in renewal of a contract, details of time and delivery will be revised to comply with the new order.
mute: Unable or unwilling to speak. In criminal law, "standing mute" is the refusal to plead guilty or not guilty at the trial, which is technically construed as a plea of not guilty.
mutilation: In criminal law, the deprivation of another person's use of limbs or other essential parts of the body. (*See* mayhem, maiming) An alteration in a written document by cutting, tearing, erasing, or burning, without destroying the whole.
mutiny: To revolt against or to resist lawful authority, especially on a ship at sea or in the naval forces; the act constituting the revolt.
mutual: Common to both parties; giving and receiving in a reciprocal way; agreed to by both parties.
mutual fund: An investment fund of many public contributors, operated by a financial group which invests the contributions in securities, with the value of the fund fluctuating with the success of the investments.
mutual insurance company: A company which sells insurance only to its members, with the profits and losses being divided among all the members.

mutuality of contract: Principle which requires that each party to a contract have some obligation to the other party, for the contract to be enforced against that party; neither party is bound unless the other is bound.

mutuality of estoppel: Principle by which a court will not consider a judgment conclusive against one party to a lawsuit unless it is conclusive against the other party to the lawsuit.

mutual mistake: In contracts, a misconception or ignorance shared by both contracting parties, regarding a material fact, so that the contract does not express the parties' true intentions. Mutual mistake is grounds for the court to alter the contract.

N

naked: Bare; incomplete; insignificant. *E.g.*, a "naked contract" is one without consideration; a "naked trust" is one without duties for the trustee; a "naked possession" is one without proper title.
N.A.S.A.: *See* National Aeronautics and Space Administration.
National Aeronautics and Space Administration (N.A.S.A.): Established in 1958 to promote space travel and technology.
nationality: Relationship of belonging to one nation; citizenship; involving the duty of allegiance to the nation and the reciprocal duty of the nation to protect its citizens.
National Labor Relations Board (N.L.R.B.): Created by the National Labor Relations Act of 1935 to prevent unfair labor practices and to oversee union elections.
National Science Foundation: Created in 1950 for the development and advancement of the sciences.
natural: Arising under the ordinary operation of physical laws; likely to occur in the ordinary course of things; distinguished from "artificial" (those things requiring human action) and "legal" (those things based on legal enactments).
natural child: A child of one's body, in contrast to an adopted child. The child may or may not be legitimate.
naturalization: The act of granting citizenship and its privileges to a foreigner. In the United States, naturalization requires that the person be a lawful resident of the United States for five years, speak and write the English language, know the fundamentals of American government, adhere to the Constitution, be of good moral character, and take the oath of allegiance. *See 8 U.S.C. §1421.*
natural law: The moral or ethical law, formulated in accordance with reason, natural justice, and the original state of nature.
natural person: A human being, rather than an "artificial" being such as a corporation.
navigable: Used or capable of being used for commerce by ships and other vessels. Interstate commerce in navigable waters is subject to federal regulation and federal maritime law.
N.B.: Lat. "Nota bene," note well. Used to call the reader's attention to a significant part of the text.
necessaries: Those articles which are actually needed for the sustenance of life, *e.g.*, food, drink, clothing, shelter, medical care. Necessaries are not limited but vary with the circumstances of age, rank, position, earning capacity, and way of living.
necessity: A defense to an unlawful act, where the act is compulsory and unavoidable, *e.g.*, breaking and entering to save a dying man, or shooting in self-defense. In property law, a reasonable need for the use of a certain parcel of land, *e.g.*, when the only access to a public road is over another's property.
ne exeat: Lat. No exit. A writ or order of the court to restrain a person from leaving the country, state, or jurisdiction of the court, or to restrain a person from taking property out of the jurisdiction.
negative pregnant: A denial implying an affirmative which is beneficial to an opponent. *E.g.*, a denial that the value of goods is more than $1000 implies that the goods are worth $1000.
neglect: Failure to do something which one is legally, contractually, or morally required to do.
negligence: The inadvertent or unintentional failure to exercise that care which a reasonable, prudent, and careful person would exercise; conduct which violates certain legal standards of due care. Negligence constitutes grounds for recovery in a tort action if it is the proximate cause of injury to the plaintiff.

"Contributory negligence" is the negligence of the injured person which contributes to the injury and precludes his recovery in a tort action.

"Comparative negligence" is a proportional division of the damages between the plaintiff and the defendant in a tort action according to their respective shares of fault contributing to the injury.

"Gross negligence" is the failure to exercise even a minimal amount of care.

"Criminal negligence" is reckless, unintentional disregard for the rights of others.

"Slight negligence" is the failure to exercise a great amount of care.
negotiable instrument: A writing signed by the maker, or drawer, which contains an unconditional promise to pay on demand or at some future time a fixed sum of money to "bearer" or to "order" and containing no other promise, order, obligation, or power. *E.g.*, a check for $100, signed by the drawer and payable to the bearer. *See U.C.C. §3-104.*
negotiation, negotiate: To meet and bargain over the terms and conditions of some future transaction or agreement; the meeting itself is the "negotiation."
nemo agit in seipsum: Lat. No man acts against himself.
nemo dat qui (quod) non habet: Lat. He who has not cannot give. *E.g.*, a person with restrictions on his title to property cannot sell the property with a perfect title.
nemo debet bis puniri pro uno delicto: Lat. No one should be punished twice for the same crime.
nemo debet esse judex in propria causa: Lat. No one should be a judge in his own cause.
nemo est supra leges: Lat. No one is above the law.
nemo praesumitur malus: Lat. No one is presumed to be evil.
nemo tenetur ad impossibile: Lat. The law requires no one to perform an impossibility.
net: The balance remaining after all deductions, including taxes, expenses, discounts, etc.
newly discovered evidence: Evidence which constitutes grounds for a new trial if it is discovered in all due diligence only after the first trial, is material, is not merely cumulative or minor, and would probably result in a decision contrary to that of the first trial.
new matter: Issue or substantial fact raised at the time of trial or hearing which had not been raised by either party in the pleadings. Under *Federal Rule of Civil Procedure 15*, parties must amend or supplement the pleadings to include the new issue or fact in the litigation.
new trial: A rehearing of a case after its dismissal during or at the close of the first hearing. Grounds for a new trial include misconduct of the jury, misconduct of counsel, error in the judge's charge to the jury, or newly discovered evidence not available previously.
next friend: A person who represents an infant or other legally incompetent person in litigation, not an officially appointed guardian. The next friend, often a close relative, does not become a party to the suit.
next of kin: In wills and trusts, the nearest blood relatives to the decedent. More specifically, "next of kin" describes those entitled to inherit or acquire property under statutory distribution.
nihil: Lat. Nothing.
nil: Lat. Nothing. Contracted form of "nihil."
nil debet: Lat. He owes nothing. The common law defense to an action for the recovery of debt.
nisi: Lat. Unless. A "rule nisi" or "decree nisi" will take effect unless the party against whom the rule is directed successfully appeals. A "decree nisi" is the opposite of an "absolute" rule, which absolutely takes effect.
nisi prius: Lat. Unless before. A "nisi prius court" is any court of original jurisdiction, where the facts of a case are first heard by a jury with judge presiding. *See* original jurisdiction.
N.L.R.B.: National Labor Relations Board. Administrative body of the United States government responsible for enforcing the National Labor Relations Act governing private employment practices.
no fault: A type of automobile insurance, required in several states, which covers all automobile damages or injuries to the insured up to a certain amount, without requiring fault on the part of the insured.
A type of divorce, allowed in some states, which dissolves the marriage due to "irreconcilable" differences, rather than by requiring fault on the part of either spouse.
nolle prosequi: Lat. Unwilling to prosecute. A formal entry on the record by the prosecutor in a criminal action or by the plaintiff in a civil action, stating that he will not further prosecute the case.
nolo contendere: Lat. No contest. A plea in a criminal action, similar to a plea of guilty, in which the defendant does not admit the charges but will not deny the charges. If the court accepts the plea as voluntary and proper, it has the same effect as a plea of guilty (with the same punishment), but it cannot be used against the defendant in any other action. *E.g.*, a corporation's plea of nolo contendere in a criminal charge of antitrust may not be used against the corporation in a civil antitrust suit by its competitors or buyers.
nominal: Not real; not actual; merely named; so small or insignificant that it is barely entitled to the name given.
nominal damages: A small and insignificant sum awarded the plaintiff as recognition of a legal injury where damages are nonexistent, or where the plaintiff has not established a recoverable loss.
nominal party: A party joined to an action, not because of any claim or liability in damages, but because of technical rules of pleading.
nomination: Appointment of a person or candidate for a certain office or duty.
non-access: A defense by the alleged father in a paternity action, arguing the absence of intercourse or opportunities for intercourse with the mother.
non-age: The legal status of a minor.

non assumpsit: Defense to the common law action of "assumpsit," in which the defendant maintains he made no promise as the plaintiff alleged.

non compos mentis: Lat. Not sound of mind. Insane or mentally incompetent.

nonconforming use: In property law, use of property which was once lawful but does not conform to newly-enacted zoning use restrictions. The use and the structures may be continued as actually used before the restriction but may not be enlarged or extended.

non culpabilis: Lat. Not guilty. Abbreviated as "non cul."

non damnificatus: Lat. Not injured. Common law defense in an action of debt on a bond, which alleges that the plaintiff has suffered no injury under the terms of the bond.

non decipitur qui scit se decipi: Lat. He is not deceived who knows himself to be deceived.

nondisclosure: Failure to reveal information to a certain party, even if it has not been deliberately concealed from that party.

non est factum: Lat. It is not his deed. Common law defense which alleges that the defendant did not execute the deed or contract sued upon.

non est regula quin fallet: Lat. There is no rule without an exception.

nonfeasance: Failure to perform a duty which one is obliged to perform. (*Contrast* malfeasance and misfeasance.) In agency law, failure of an agent to perform a duty he contracted with his principal to perform.

non possessori incumbit necessitas probandi possessiones ad se pertinere: Lat. A person in possession is not required to prove that the possessions belong to him.

non pros: Abbreviation of "non prosequitur."

non prosequitur: Lat. He does not pursue. The defendant is entitled to judgment of "non pros" against the plaintiff if the plaintiff does not properly pursue or follow up the case. In modern practice, the plaintiff's failure to pursue the case results in a default judgment for the defendant or a dismissal.

nonresidence, nonresident: A person who resides outside of a particular jurisdiction is a "nonresident" of the jurisdiction or forum. The residence outside the jurisdiction is called "nonresidence" with respect to the jurisdiction.

non sequitur: Lat. It does not follow.

non sui juris: Lat. Not his own master. Lacking legal capacity to act for oneself, *e.g.*, a minor or insane person.

nonsuit: Judgment against a plaintiff who does not proceed to court or prove the case; a judgment without a decision on the merits or substantive issues of the case. In modern practice this is called a "dismissal."

Norris-LaGuardia Act of 1932: Federal statute restricting the federal courts' power to issue injunctions in labor disputes.

notary, notary public: A person who is licensed as a public officer to administer oaths, certify certain documents or signatures, take depositions, or perform other specified official acts.

note: To make a brief statement for the record. An informal statement or memorandum. A document which contains an absolute promise by the maker (or signer) to pay to the bearer a specific sum of money at a specific time. *See* negotiable instrument.

not guilty: Defendant's plea in answer to a criminal charge; verdict by which the jury acquits the defendant.

notice: Communication to a person of some significant information, either by another person who has a duty to give notice, or by another proper source. *E.g.*, notice of arrest is given by the arresting officer who has the duty to give notice of arrest; notice to a defendant that an action has been filed against him is given by service of the complaint. Notice may be "actual" or "constructive" (where the person deliberately avoids inquiring or communicating about information he would have discovered otherwise).

notice of motion: Notice in writing to all parties in a cause of action, stating that one of the parties will make some motion to the court on some specified date.

notice to quit: Notice in writing from the landlord to the tenant stating that the tenant must quit the premises and remove himself and his belongings, at some future time after the expiration of the lease.

notorious possession: Publicly known, open, and conspicuous occupation of real property. If possession of another's property is notorious, it will constitute notice to the true owner of the property that another person is in adverse possession. *See* adverse possession.

N.O.V. (non obstante veredicto): Lat. Notwithstanding the verdict. A judgment by the court in favor of one party notwithstanding the jury's verdict in favor of the other party.

novation: In contract law, the substitution of a new contract or party to a contract for an existing contract or party. A valid novation requires a valid existing contract which is extinguished and replaced by a new, valid contract with the agreement of all the parties.

N.R.C.: See Nuclear Regulatory Commission.

Nuclear Regulatory Commission (N.R.C.): Created in 1974 to regulate the uses of nuclear energy.

nudum pactum: Lat. Naked contract. A contract which is no more than a bare promise; made without any consideration other than goodwill or natural affection. A naked contract, one without any obligation by one party, is unenforceable.

nuisance: Anything which, in the unreasonable or unlawful use of one's property, disturbs another in the lawful and productive use of his property, endangers the health and safety of others, or violates the standards of decency. Nuisance is grounds for a tort action against the offender.

Nuisance is distinguished as "public" (that which affects the property or health of many persons or an entire community), "private" (that which affects the property of one person), and "mixed" (that which affects many, with varied consequences). Further, nuisance may be categorized as "nuisance per se" (always producing injurious effects, no matter what the circumstances) and "nuisance in fact" (producing injurious effects due to local conditions or factual circumstances).

null: Invalid; void.

nullity: An act or proceeding that has absolutely no legal effect; one that becomes totally null and void.

nunc pro tunc: Lat. Now for then. When the court allows acts to be done after time for their performance has expired, it will issue a "nunc pro tunc order" which gives the act the same effect as if it had been performed before expiration, or as if it had been recorded at the earlier date. *E.g.*, if a party files a late appeal, a "nunc pro tunc order" by the court will treat the appeal as if it had been recorded on time.

nuncupative will: A will declared or dictated orally shortly before death in the presence of several witnesses. Proof of such a will thus depends on the testimony of these witnesses. Some states render a noncupative will invalid.

O

oath: Pledge. To fulfill a duty or obligation; profession of one's intent to carry out a responsibility entrusted to one.

obiter dicta (dictum): Lat. Remarks made in passing. Language in a judicial opinion that does not pertain to those legal issues that are dispositive in the case; that part of a judicial opinion which does not address the central legal issues in the case.

object: (Verb) To dispute a ruling by a court; to disagree or challenge a decision made by the court in the course of legal proceedings. (Noun) Goal; purpose. Tangible item or thing.

objection: The act of objecting. The reason or rationale offered by a party at trial in opposing or challenging a judge's decision or an opponent's tactics.

obligation: A duty owed to another; a responsibility that requires a person to act in a certain manner, such as, to perform a service or discharge a debt. A debt; an indebtedness; a liability.

obligee: A person to whom an obligation is owed, *e.g.*, the person to whom a debt is owed.

obligor: A person who owes an obligation to another, *e.g.*, a person who owes a debt to another.

obliterate: To purposely remove a clause or a provision of a written instrument from a document. Destroy; devastate; demolish.

obscene: Lewd; indecent; lascivious.

obscenity: Behavior which is so indecent and improper that it is an affront to accepted standards of decency.

obstructing justice: To hinder, impede, or prevent the efforts of those who seek to exercise their legal rights in court or those whose duties involve the administration of justice, *e.g.*, to seek to prevent a person from testifying at a trial.

obvious: Readily understood; manifest; clear; apparent.

occupation: Tenancy; possession; use and enjoyment of property, *e.g.*, to have possession of a house and its surrounding property. Profession; career; how a person makes his livelihood.

Occupational Safety and Health Administration (O.S.H.A.): Created in 1970 to enact and enforce employment safety standards.

odium: Ill feelings toward a person; hatred or dislike. The situation where a party to a judicial proceeding is so hated or loathed in a particular area that it cannot receive a fair trial in that venue.

offense: A violation of the criminal laws; a felony or misdemeanor.

offer: (Noun) A proposal to do or to abstain from doing something in the future that is binding upon the offeror upon the offeree's acceptance of the proposal. *Restatement (Second) of Contracts §24* defines offer as: "The manifestation of willingness to enter into a bargain, so made as to justify another person in understanding that his assent to that bargain is invited and will conclude it." (Verb) To propose; to tender; to make a proposal.

office: A position of trust and authority that is conferred by election or appointment.

officer: A person holding a position of authority, control, and influence in government, a corporation, or some other organization.

official: (Noun) A person endowed with the authority and powers of the office that he holds. (Adj.) Authoritative; authorized by an officer of an organization.

offset: A reduction or cancellation of a claim; a counterclaim; a claim which counterbalances another claim.

olograph: A legal document totally written by the person who transmits the document to another.

omission: Failure to act in the way that the law mandates, *e.g.*, the failure to report a crime to the authorities.

omnibus: Including many different things at once. *E.g.*, a legislative act that deals with two or more independent matters is said to be an omnibus bill.

on demand: When desired; upon request, *e.g.*, a promissory note that is payable upon request by the holder of the note.

onus probandi: Lat. The burden of proof.
open court: A court that permits the general public to view its proceedings.
open-end contract: Agreement which allows the buyer to acquire goods over a period of time without a change in the provisions of the agreement by the seller. A requirements contract is a type of open-end contract.
opening statement: Presentation made by counsel at beginning of trial in which she summarizes her client's case and the evidence which she will present on the client's behalf.
open shop: Commercial enterprise in which membership in a union or a similar organization is not a condition of employment.
operation of law: Process by which legal rights and obligations are transmitted to a person upon the application of established legal principles which are activated by the occurrence of a particular transaction and not by the purposeful efforts of the person.
operative part: That part of a legal instrument which creates or transfers rights from one party to another and thereby fulfills the purpose of the instrument.
opinion: Judicial decision which states the court's reasons for deciding a case as it did. Legal advice given by an attorney to his client, in the form of a letter or other document, which states the attorney's understanding of the law with respect to a specific set of facts submitted to him for the purpose of his rendering legal advice.
opinion evidence: Testimony by a witness that is not based on his personal knowledge of facts but rather what he thinks or surmises with respect to the facts in dispute.
oppression: The wrongful punishment of a person through bodily harm, incarceration, or other injury by a public official in the exercise of his duties. Any act of brutality or unfair hardship imposed on another person.
option: A privilege obtained by the payment of money or other consideration which allows a person to buy real or personal property at a stipulated price and fixed terms at any time within a specified period. Under the U.C.C., an option contract does not need consideration.
oral contract: An agreement which has not been totally reduced to writing, but rather all or some of its terms depend on spoken words. Also called a "parol contract."
order: Decision of a court made in writing with regards to a matter that is not part of the case's final judgment. Directive; request, *e.g.*, a request by a person made to his broker that he sell the client's stock portfolio. A designation of a grouping of persons that are organized by position or class.
ordinance: Law; statute; legislative act of a municipal government; *e.g.*, a law setting zoning standards for a community.
ordinary: Typical; common; usual; regular.
organization: Any entity where a group of persons is united for some common purpose or in some common interest, such as, a corporation, a partnership, a government agency, an association.
original jurisdiction: Authority of a court to recognize a suit at its beginning, act as trier of fact, and pass judgment on the case.
orphan: A person whose parents are both deceased.
O.S.H.A.: *See* Occupational Safety and Health Administration.
ostensible: Apparent; supposed; seeming; outwardly evident.
ostensible authority: Apparent power; the authority a principal induces a person to believe that the principal's agent enjoys.
ouster: The improper removal of a person or a group of persons from real property that they are legally entitled to possess.
output contract: A contract in which one party agrees to purchase all that the other party is able to produce, in good faith.
overdraft: A check drawn in an amount that exceeds the balance of funds present in the checking account.
overdraw: The act of seeking to obtain from a financial institution an amount of funds in excess of the balance that one has remaining in one's favor in an account with the financial institution.
overdue: Beyond an agreed time; past a fixed date; past a scheduled time, *e.g.*, a mortgage payment not paid until after the date it was originally owed.
overhead: The fixed costs of a business enterprise; the costs of a commercial enterprise that do not vary with respect to the goods produced, bought, or sold.
overreaching: Taking fraudulent advantage of someone through cheating, lying, or cunning. Situation where one party by reason of his position or relationship with the other gains for himself any unjust or unfair advantage. The practice in a commercial setting of obtaining an unfair advantage with respect to a competitor or business associate through fraud, deception or other improper action.
overrule: Overturn; set aside; reverse; annul, *e.g.*, to reverse a judicial decision handed down by a prior court.
overt: Open; public; evident; conspicuous; not hidden.
oyer: To hear; to ask or demand a hearing. A copy of a written instrument that is given to a party that requests it, in lieu of it being read aloud.

oyer and terminer: To hear and determine. A grant or commission of power given to judges under the English common law to hear and determine criminal cases. The name given to a senior criminal court in certain jurisdictions of the United States.

oyez: Hear ye (English term). A command given to secure a group's attention and silence, *e.g.*, the command issued by a bailiff to bring a courtroom to order before a judge begins the proceedings before the court.

P

pactum; pact: Lat. A contract; an agreement. In civil law: A pact; an agreement without a title and without consideration which may, however, produce a civil obligation by its very nature. A "nudum pactum," a bare agreement, is an agreement without consideration and is therefore unenforceable.

pais: Fr. Country or district. It refers to acts done outside the court and not made as part of the record, *i.e.*, "in pais." Trial "per pais" indicates trial "by the country" or by jury. A "matter of pais" is a matter of fact, since matters of fact are usually determined by the "country" or jury. "Estoppels in pais" are estoppels by conduct, and distinguished from estoppels by deed or record.

palpable: Obvious; plain; easily noticeable. Easily perceptible either intellectually or through the senses.

pander: To pimp; to procure a female for the purposes of prostitution. To exploit or cater to the lusts or prurient interests of others. "Pandering" is the crime of influencing a woman to become a prostitute. In obscenity, pandering may also refer to promoting obscene material appealing to people's prurient interests and is not protected by the first amendment.

paper, papers: A written or printed document, instrument, or book which may be relevant to a suit, as in "papers in the case" or "papers on appeal." Any writing or printed document which the Constitution protects against unreasonable searches and seizures in regard to one's "papers." A negotiable instrument or an evidence of debt as in "commercial paper."

par: Lat. Of equal value. In negotiable instruments, par denotes the face value of the instrument as opposed to its market value. If a share of stock has a face value equal to its market value, then the share is "at par." If the share can be sold for more than its face value, it is "above par," and if the share can only be sold for less than its face value, it is "below par."

In mercantile law: "Par" is the established exchange value of the currency of one country in terms of the currency of another country, *e.g.*, a dollar is equal to five francs. The exchange rate may shift depending on the demand in one country for the currency of another.

paralegal: An assistant to a lawyer or a judge who is not an attorney in his own right. A paralegal is not licensed to practice law, but is trained to perform many of the functions of an attorney.

paramount title: A superior title. In real property, a title which is superior to that with which it is compared, meaning that the latter title is derived from the former. A title which is stronger than another or which would prevail over another title which challenges it. A paramount title indicates an immediate right of possession, and is used as a basis for the eviction of a tenant by one whose rights of possession are superior to those of a tenant. The term also applies to chattels. *E.g.*, one who purchases a car has paramount title to it unless the car was stolen from its original owner.

parcel: A small package or bundle. In land: A contiguous portion of land in possession of, owned by, or recorded as the property of one person, claimant or company.

parcenary: The condition of holding title to lands jointly by parceners, joint heirs, before the common inheritance has been divided. A parcenary arises when several persons inherit as one heir from an ancestor.

parcener: A joint heir; one who holds an estate with others in a parcenary.

pardon: An act of release or exemption by the executive authority (a president in federal cases and a governor in state cases) of a punishment which a person convicted of a crime has been sentenced to undergo. An act by the governing power which lessens the punishment demanded by law for the crime and restores rights and privileges lost due to the commission of the crime.

parens patriae: Lat. Parent of the country. In the United States: the State, as sovereign, referring to its sovereign power of guardianship over persons under a disability like minors and insane and incompetent persons.

parent: The lawful father or mother of a child. The term is distinguished from ancestors, which refers to remote relatives as well as to immediate ones.
parent corporation: A corporation which owns all or a majority of the stock of another corporation so that the second corporation becomes a subsidiary of the first.
parenticide: The crime of murdering a parent. The person who murders his/her parent.
pari delicto: Lat. In equal fault; in a similar offense or crime. Used when one who has participated in a wrong sues to recover in contract or tort based on that wrong, as in a suit to recover on a gambling debt. The "pari delicto" doctrine is that courts will not enforce an invalid contract and no party can recover based on an illegal claim.
pari materia: Lat. On the same matter; on the same subject. Statutes "in pari materia" deal with the same subject and must be interpreted with reference to each other.
pari passu: Lat. By equal steps. Equally and to the same degree; without preference. Used to refer to creditors who are equally entitled to receive payment from the same fund, without precedence over one another.
parish: In English ecclesiastical law, a territory administered by a parson, vicar, or other priest who tends to the religious needs of people therein. Hence, an ecclesiastical division of a town, city, or district under the administration of one minister or priest. The members of the congregation of any church. In Louisiana, a territorial governmental division of a state, corresponding to a county in other states.
parliamentary law, parliamentary rules: The generally accepted rules and usages which determine the procedure of legislative assemblies (*e.g.*, the Senate) and other deliberative bodies such as board meetings or town meetings.
parol: A word, speech; hence, oral or verbal. That which is expressed or evidenced by speech alone, and not by writing.
parole: In criminal law, a conditional release from prison of a prisoner who has served part of his sentence, allowing the prisoner to complete his term of punishment outside the prison if he satisfactorily complies with the terms of the parole. A parole board will grant parole where there is a reasonable probability that the parolee will not violate laws while at liberty. A release from jail or confinement after one has served part of his sentence.
parol evidence: Oral or verbal evidence. The kind of evidence given by a witness in a court.
parol evidence rule: Rule of substantive law which states that once an agreement is reduced to writing and both parties have acknowledged this writing as the final expression of their agreement, then parol (oral) evidence of any prior or present understanding of the parties as to the terms of the agreement is inadmissible if it alters or contradicts the meaning of the written document. The basis of the rule is that a clear and unambiguous writing is the best evidence of the intent of the parties and the terms of the agreement. Agreements made subsequent to the writing, whether written or oral, are not subject to the rule. Furthermore, all evidence (whether written or oral) concerning the finality of the agreement is admissible as is evidence of fraud, duress, mistake, misrepresentation, or illegality or evidence offered to rescind or reform the contract.
parricide: The crime of killing one's father; patricide. The person who kills his father.
particular average: In maritime law, a loss occurring to a ship, freight, or cargo which is borne exclusively by the owner who suffers the loss and is not shared proportionately by all interested parties. "Particular average" contrasts with "general average" which is a loss to one which is compensated by the other interested parties.
particulars: The details of a claim or the individual items of an account. A "bill of particulars" states the specific occurrences to be investigated in a criminal proceeding and details the offenses charged so that the defendant will be informed of the evidence that he faces. "Particulars of sale" is the document describing fairly and accurately all property to be sold during an auction. Copies are distributed among the bidders.
partition: A judicial or voluntary separation of land held by joint tenants, coparceners, or tenants-in-common so that the parties may hold their estates severally and not in union with others. When partition is not an available option, the court may order a sale of the property and distribute the income proportionate to the interest held in the property. Any division of real or personal property between co-owners which leads to each owner individually possessing his interests.
partner, partnership: A partner is a member of a partnership. A partnership is a voluntary agreement between two or more competent persons to place their money, effects, labor and skill, or some or all of them, in lawful commerce or business, with an understanding that any profit or loss shall be divided in certain proportions.

An association of two or more persons to carry-on as co-owners a business for profit. A general partner has unlimited liability for the debts of the partnership, but also has input in the management of the partnership. A general partner is individually liable for the debts of the partnership and his personal assets may be used to pay a debt when the partnership has insufficient assets. Partnerships are regarded as a conduit and are not taxed. The individual partners report any gains or losses on their personal income tax returns where they are subject to taxation. *See* limited partnership.

partus sequitur ventrem: Lat. The offspring follows the mother; the offspring of a slave belongs to the owner of the mother. A maxim of civil law, which the law of England has accepted for animals, but never accepted for humans.

party: A person officially designated as a litigant (plaintiff or defendant) in a judicial proceeding. A person directly interested in the subject matter of a trial and, who, therefore, has the right to control proceedings, make a defense, assert a claim, cross-examine witnesses and appeal a judgment.

"Indispensable party": One whose interest in the controversy is so essential to an equitable resolution that, in his absence, the suit cannot proceed. *Federal Rule of Civil Procedure 19(b).*

"Necessary party": One whose interest will be affected by the suit or without whom a complete relief cannot be granted, but who need not be joined if his joinder will deprive the court of jurisdiction in the case. *Federal Rules of Civil Procedure 19(a).*

"Party aggrieved": Any party having an interest recognized by law in a judicial proceeding and whose interest is adversely affected by a judgment is a "party aggrieved" and is entitled to appeal.

"Third party": Someone other than the parties directly involved in the suit or agreement.

A person or entity which enters into a contract, lease, etc. A political party is a group united by common political goals specifically including the nomination and election of its candidates for office.

party wall: A wall erected on a property boundary partly on the land of each owner as a mutual support to structures on both sides which are under different ownership. A division wall between two adjacent properties belonging to two different persons and used for the mutual benefit of both parties. The wall may stand on part of the land of each owner or may stand wholly upon one lot. A wall of which two neighboring owners are tenants-in-common.

pass: (Verb) To transfer or to be transferred as in "property passing." To enact or approve as in "to pass a law." In negotiable instruments: To deliver or circulate. (Noun) Permission or license to go or come. An authorized document allowing a designated individual to travel beyond certain boundaries which without such permission, he could not lawfully pass. A ticket issued by a railroad or other transportation company allowing a designated individual to travel free on certain routes or for a limited time.

passage: The act of passing; transit. A way over land or water or through the air; a route. An easement giving the right to pass over a privately-owned body of water. Enactment; the emergence of a bill as a law or a motion as a resolution, either when a bill has passed one or both houses of the legislature or when it has been signed by the President or Governor.

passion: In voluntary manslaughter cases, a state of mind incapable of premeditation. Passion includes any emotion such as rage, anger, or fear which leaves the mind incapable of cool reflection and is enough to lessen a murder charge to manslaughter.

passive: Inactive; permissive. Consisting in endurance or submission rather than in action. Subjected to a burden or charge. Passive negligence is the failure to do something required by law and which failure amounts to a breach of the duty of care.

passive trust: A trust which gives the trustee no responsibilities or discretionary duties to perform; it may be terminated by a court of equity.

passport: Document issued by the government to citizens who travel to foreign countries. The passport identifies the citizen, requests foreign governments to allow the citizen to pass freely and safely, and entitles the citizen to the protection of his government's diplomatic and consular offices. In international law during wartime, the passport grants the citizen the right to remove himself from a belligerent country without being detained on account of the war.

patent: A grant issued by the government to an inventor, giving him the exclusive right to make, use, or sell the invention for a specified number of years, constituting a legitimate monopoly.

patent defect: A defect in personal property which is plainly visible or would be discovered in the exercise of ordinary care and prudence. *See U.C.C. §2-605(1).*

paternity suit: A lawsuit brought to determine the father of an illegitimate child and to provide for paternal support of the child.

patricide: Murder of one's father; parricide.

pauper: A person in poverty, who is allowed to sue and defend cases without paying court costs, or who is represented by the public defender in a criminal case.

pawn: To give goods or property to another (usually a pawnbroker) as security for a loan or existing debt. The action of pawning goods as security. The goods or property pawned.

pawnbroker: A person in the business of lending money to those who pawn goods or personal property to him as security for the loan.

payable: The amount of money which a person is under a legal obligation to pay.

payee: The person to whom money, checks, orders, promissory notes, or bills of exchange are paid.

peace: State of international relations opposite of war. Public safety, comfort, and happiness represented by good order, obedience to the law, and public tranquility.
peculation: Fraudulent misappropriation of money or property for one's own use by one who was legally entrusted to care for it.
pecuniary: Monetary; related to money and finances. A "pecuniary loss" is one which can be valued entirely in monetary amounts.
peer: In old English law, the ranks of the nobility, *e.g.,* duke, marquis, earl, baron. Those in each rank sat in court as judges of those of equal rank being tried. A "jury of his peers" in America means a jury of citizens, all citizens in America being equal.
penal: Having to do with punishment or penalties.
penal action: Broadly speaking, any criminal prosecution. Also refers to civil actions brought to enforce a penalty arbitrarily created by statute for some act or omission of the defendant, *e.g.*, a fine or penalty payable to the aggrieved party.
penal law, penal code, penal statute: Generally, state and federal laws which define criminal offenses and create punishment of fines or imprisonment. A "penal code" is a collection of all the state's criminal laws. Also refers to laws which proscribe certain public conduct and create penalties for violation of that conduct. Laws which provide the injured party with a "right of action" for damages are called "remedial"; laws which impose penalties are "penal."
penalty: Payment of a sum of money or other punishment imposed by the law for the commission of an offense or the neglect of a duty. Provision in a contract or bond setting forth a sum of money as punishment for default or as security for actual damages occurring in case of default.
pendente lite: Lat. Pending the suit. Contingent upon the determination of the lawsuit; *e.g.*, in an action to determine the ownership of property, the property itself is "pendente lite."
pending, pendency: During the occurrence of something; before the completion. A suit is said to be "pending" or in its "pendency" from its beginning until judgment is given.
pension: Systematic payments made to retired persons, based on length of service and the level of past salary.
Pension Benefit Guaranty Corporation: Created in 1974 by the Employee Retirement Income Security Act of 1974 (ERISA) to guaranty pension benefits in covered private plans if they terminate with insufficient assets.
pensioner: The person who receives pension payments.
per: Lat. By or through.
per annum: Lat. By the year; *e.g.,* salaries, interest rates, and business growth statistics are measured "per annum."
per capita: Lat. By the head. Equally divided among all the people. Used in the old law of inheritance, "per capita" means an equal division of the estate among those who stand in equal rank to the deceased; the opposite of "per stirpes." Used in statistics, "per capita income" is the average income per person in a society, calculated by dividing the total income by the number of people.
per curiam: Lat. By the court. Term used to distinguish an opinion of the whole court from that written by any one judge; often used in brief or unimportant decisions.
per diem: Lat. By the day. Term used to signify an allowance or expense account with a specific "per diem" amount allocated for each day of service.
peremptory: Absolute; final; conclusive of the matter. *E.g.*, the "peremptory challenge" in jury selection is the means by which each side may conclusively reject a certain number of potential jury members in a trial without giving a reason for the challenge.
perfect: Complete and executed. *E.g.*, a security interest is "perfected" when collateral is taken, notice is filed, or a purchase money interest in the goods (in consumer credit sales) is retained. A creditor holding a perfected security interest has priority against other creditors. To create a perfected security interest; to "perfect."
performance: The complete fulfillment of one's obligations according to the contract. "Part performance" is the fulfilling of only some of the contract obligations. "Substantial performance" is performance of the essential purpose of the contract, although insignificant deviations from the strict obligations of the contract may remain.
peril: The risk or cause of loss which is covered by an insurance policy.
perjury: The criminal offense of making a false statement under oath in a legal proceeding with no sincere belief in its truth, when it is relevant to a material issue in the proceeding. Some states have broadened the reach of perjury by statute, to include any false statement made under oath in a legal instrument or legal setting, *e.g.*, in the pleadings, affidavits, interrogations, or license applications.
permanent disability: A physical disability which causes loss of earning power and which will last or is expected to last for the rest of the disabled person's life.
permission: Formal consent, authorization, or license without which an act would be unlawful.
permissive: Allowed; endured.

permissive waste: Waste or damage to a building caused by a tenant's failure to make necessary repairs. *See* waste.
permit: (Noun) A license which allows some act, such as the building of a house. (Verb) To give permission.
perpetuity: Something lasting forever. Real property: The limitation of the disposition of property for longer than the life of a person then living, plus 21 years. *See* Rule Against Perpetuities.
per quod: Lat. Whereby. *E.g.,* a libel or slander action is either "actionable per se" or "actionable per quod." "Per se" means the words themselves constitute the injury; "per quod" means that special circumstances caused the injury or that special damages resulted, whereby the defendant should be liable.
per se: Lat. By itself. Considered alone; unconnected with other matters.
person: An existence capable of having rights and duties, be it a human being (natural person) or a corporation (artificial person). Partnerships, associations, foreign governments, and municipalities are persons. Related to the body.
personal: Pertaining to a human being; limited to an individual person.
personal injury: Injury to the body. A violation of a personal right, *e.g.,* injury to a person's reputation.
personal property: All property not real estate. The two categories of personal property are "corporeal," consisting of movable objects such as furniture or jewelry, and "incorporeal," consisting of the interest one has in something, such as in a corporation by the ownership of stock. *See* chose in action, personalty.
personal representative: An executor or administrator who handles the estate of a deceased person, though, according to the intent of the user, it may also include heirs, assignees, grantees, receivers, and trustees.
personalty: Personal property; movable property; property which is not real estate. If personalty is affixed to real estate, it becomes part of the real estate if removing it would damage the realty.
per stirpes: Lat. By the roots. In the law of inheritance, "per stirpes" means division of the property by representation according to the relative number of heirs in each class; the opposite of "per capita." *E.g.,* under "per stirpes," grandchildren would inherit only their parents share; under "per capita," all grandchildren would inherit equally.
pertinent: Relevant; significant; applicable. Evidence is pertinent if it tends to prove or disprove an allegation.
petition: A formal written request for something to be done. *E.g.,* a petition to a court is a request to find relief for some wrong committed against one, or for authority to do something, such as sell trust property. A petition in bankruptcy is a request by a creditor or debtor to the bankruptcy court to find that a debtor is unable to pay his debts and is entitled to the provisions of the Bankruptcy Act.

petit jury: A common trial jury of usually 12 persons which renders a verdict in civil and criminal cases, as opposed to a grand jury which has a greater number of persons and whose role is not to render a verdict but to determine whether an indictment is justified. Also called "petty jury."

petit larceny: Unlawful taking and carrying away of personal property valued below an amount set by statute (*e.g.,* $200), with the intent to deprive its owner of its use. Also called "petty larceny." *Compare* grand larceny.

petty jury: *See* petit jury.
petty larceny: *See* petit larceny.
physical fact: A fact perceived by the senses.
picket: The practice of attempting to influence someone by patrolling a location, usually with signs or placards. This is often done by labor in disputes with management to publicize grievances, to promote a strike, or to promote union membership by employees. The right to picket is constitutionally protected when done peaceably, but may be unlawful when it is not a truthful representation of the facts, or if it is dangerous to the public safety.

pickpocket: One who secretly steals money or other valuable property from the person of another.

pilferage: Stealing something of small value; petty larceny; stealing a small part of something rather than the whole.

pimp: Person who procures customers for prostitutes; a panderer.

piracy: Act of robbery and violence committed on the high seas or in the air. Infringement of copyright.

plagiarism: Copying and publishing as one's own work all or part of the copyrighted writing of another. Plagiarism does not exist if work alleged to be copied is arrived at independently. Certain uses of copyrighted material are allowed under the "fair use doctrine" of the Copyright Act without the consent of the copyright owner.

plaintiff: Person who brings a lawsuit; the complainant; the prosecution in a criminal case.

plea: In common law pleading, a defendant's formal response to a criminal charge or a civil suit. Pleas in equity are either "dilatory" or "peremptory." Dilatory pleas seek to defeat the plaintiff's case based on a matter not connected with the merits of the case. Peremptory pleas are based on the merits of the action. These equity pleas are now obsolete with the adoption

of the Rules of Civil Procedure. Criminal pleas are guilty, not guilty, and "nolo contendere."
plea bargaining: Process by which a defendant's attorney and a prosecutor bargain for a mutually satisfactory disposition of a criminal case. Often this involves the defendant's pleading guilty to a lesser offense or to only some counts in a multi-count indictment in exchange for a lighter sentence. The plea bargain arrangement is subject to court approval.
plead: To formally answer a criminal charge or a plaintiff's complaint in a civil action; to make a pleading.
pleading: A written statement by a plaintiff or defendant setting forth the material facts on which he bases his case. Under the Federal Rules of Civil Procedure the pleadings consist of a complaint, an answer, a reply to a counterclaim, an answer to a cross-claim, a third-party complaint, and a third-party answer. *See Federal Rule of Civil Procedure 7(a).* Pleadings consist of simple, concise and direct averments of claims for relief, defenses, and denials. *See Federal Rule of Civil Procedure 8.*
pledge: Act of delivering personal property to a creditor to be held as security for payment of a debt or performance of an obligation. The property so delivered.
plenary: Absolute; complete, full. *E.g,* a "plenary action" is a complete, formal action heard on the merits, where a "summary proceeding" is a shortened, simplified process used to expedite the disposition of a case.
plurality: A greater number. A plurality of votes received by a winning candidate in an election with more than two candidates is greater than the number received by any other candidate. A plurality opinion of an appellate court is that opinion held by the greatest number of judges while not being a majority, *i.e.,* more than half.
point: A proposition or question of law raised in a suit. Real estate: A charge for lending money, collected at the time the loan is made, equal to one percent of the principal amount of the loan. In the stock market, a point means $1; in the bond market, it means $10.
police court: A local or municipal court; an inferior court with jurisdiction over minor offenses.
police power: A broad, flexible term for the authority possessed by the state to regulate private actions in order to promote and maintain the public health, safety, welfare, and order.
policy: The principles which guide a government's actions; the course of action taken, *e.g.,* foreign policy, domestic policy. The intention or objective of a statute or law as distinguished from the letter of the law. "Public policy" means the public good. An insurance policy is a contract for insurance. A lottery; a numbers game.
political: Related to government. Political rights or liberties are those which a citizen has to participate in government. A political crime is a crime against the government.
political party: An association of individuals united to pursue political goals, such as the nomination and election of a candidate, whose members usually possess certain common beliefs about governmental policy.
poll: (Verb) To question each juror individually as to his verdict. To question the electorate for the purpose of forecasting the result of an election. To vote or to receive a vote. (Noun) A head; an individual; a list of individuals, as of jurors or of persons who may vote in an election.
poll tax: A tax levied on certain classes of people as a prerequisite to voting. Illegal in all federal and state elections.
polyandry: The condition of a woman who has more than one living husband.
polygamy: The condition of a man or woman who has several living spouses. It is illegal in all states.
positive evidence: Direct evidence which can prove a fact without any presumption, *e.g.,* eyewitness testimony. It is distinguished from "circumstantial evidence."
positive law: Law specifically created and enforced by a proper authority for the government of society. Also, those laws established by tacit approval of society.
posse: Lat. A possibility. A thing "in posse" may possibly exist. "In esse" means it actually exists. A group of persons that assists a sheriff with his duties, such as the arrest of a suspect. Same as "posse comitatus."
posse comitatus: Lat. The power of the country. This includes all able-bodied men who may be called to assist a sheriff with his duties. Such persons have the same protection of the law that the sheriff has when they act under the sheriff's orders. Same as "posse."
possession: Exclusive dominion and control over property. Possession is more than actual physical custody, which is mere keeping and caring, but it involves an assertion of a *right* to exercise dominion and control. The two kinds of possession are "actual" and "constructive." Someone who has direct physical control over something has actual possession of it. Constructive possession is where someone has the power and intention of exercising control over something while it is not in his actual possession. A tenant who occupies an apartment is in actual possession of

it while the owner of it is in constructive possession of it.
possessory action: A lawsuit to obtain actual possession of property, as distinguished from a "petitory action" in which a plaintiff seeks to establish title. An eviction is a possessory action. *See* eviction.
possibility of reverter: Reverter or reversion is a future interest kept by someone who transfers property. "Possibility of reverter" is such an interest remaining only as a possibility because it is dependent on the occurrence of a future contingency. Thus when a grantor or testator conveys an estate by conditional or determinable fee, there remains only the possibility of reverter because the estate does not "revert" back to him until a specified condition is breached or an event occurs.
Postal Rate Commission: Created in 1970 to regulate and determine postage rates.
post date: To date an instrument, such as a check, later than the actual date on which it is signed. This does not affect the negotiability of the instrument. *U.C.C. §3-114.*
post mortem: Lat. After death. Term usually refers to an autopsy; an examination of a dead body.
potentia non est nisi ad bonum: Lat. Power does not exist, except for the public good.
power: The right, ability, or authority to do something, such as to change a legal relation or to dispose of property. Powers are classified as "naked" and "coupled with an interest." *E.g.*, when authority is granted to a stranger to dispose of property in which the stranger had and continues to have no interest, the authority is called "naked power." Authority granted to a person who has a present or future interest in property is called power "coupled with an interest."
power of appointment: Authority given to a person (donee) by deed or will to dispose of property, or interest therein, vested in someone other than himself. A donee with "*general* power of appointment" is unrestricted as to whom he may appoint to receive the property. "*Special* power of appointment" limits the donee's choice of beneficiaries. *See* power.
power of attorney: Document by which a person (principal) grants authority to another (agent) to perform specified acts on his (principal's) behalf. Also called "letter of attorney" and "warrant of attorney."
practice: Custom; habit; usual procedure. Court procedure, *i.e.*, the formal steps of a judicial proceeding. (Verb) To engage in a profession, such as medicine or law.
praecipe: A command; an order; a written note ordering a person to do something or show cause why he should not. A note stating the particulars of a writ one wishes to be issued by a court officer, *e.g.*, for summons.
prayer (for relief): The request made by a person seeking relief, or redress of an alleged wrong; the part of a pleading in which such a request is made.
preamble: A clause at the beginning of a constitution, statute, document, or ordinance which states the purpose for its enactment. A preamble is explanatory and is not an essential part of a document.
precatory words: Words expressing advice, recommendation, wish, or request, rather than those that command. Term is used to describe certain language in a trust or will. A "precatory trust" is one that uses such language. It can be interpreted as being unenforceable due to its mild, nonobligatory language; or it can be held as a valid, enforceable trust if the language on the whole might be construed as imperative and the subject of the request and the person(s) intended to benefit from it are clear.
precedent: A previously decided case which is used as an example or authority for similar cases which subsequently arise. (*See* stare decisis.) A rule of law established for a certain type of case. A "precedent condition" or "condition precedent" is a condition that must exist before something, such as a contract or an estate, can take effect.
precept: An order, command, or writ given by one in authority to another to perform a duty within his power; a warrant; a process. *E.g.*, a precept is given by a judge to the police to bring a person to court.
precinct: A police or election district.
predecessor: One who goes or has gone before another; correlative of "successor."
preemption: A doctrine based on the Supremacy Clause of the U.S. Constitution (article VI, clause 2) which holds that federal legislation overrides state legislation when both deal with the same subject matter. Act of buying something, such as stock, before all others.
preference: Act of preferring one over another, especially as in an insolvent's payment of some of his creditors over others.
preferred stock: Type of capital stock of a corporation that gives its holder priority over common stockholders in the distribution of dividends, or of company assets upon dissolution. Shares of this stock are called "preferred shares."
prejudice: Bias; preconceived opinion; a leaning in the mind toward one side of an issue without justification. Prejudice in a judge refers to a mental dispositon he has toward a party to the litigation and not toward its subject matter. It renders him unable to make an impartial decision. Detriment; deprivation of a right or interest, as in a change of position for the worse after relying on another's promise.

prejudicial error: Error by a court which detrimentally affects the legal rights of a party and which, if uncorrected, would result in a miscarriage of justice. This may be grounds for a new trial or for a reversal of a decision of a lower court. Same as "reversible error."
preliminary hearing: An initial hearing conducted to determine whether probable cause exists to justify holding a person for trial. In felony cases, it is a hearing conducted before an indictment. Same as "preliminary examination."
premeditation: Thinking about and deciding to do something before doing it; plotting. The thought may be for any length of time. It is one of the elements of first-degree murder. *See* malice aforethought.
premises: Land, building, and the surrounding environs; *e.g.,* in criminal law, a search warrant covers the "premises" owned by the suspect. In insurance law, insurance covers the "premises." Workers' Compensation: "Premises" is wherever business activity occurs. The statements or clauses put before; *e.g.,* in pleading, the "premises" are the earlier clauses in the pleading.
premium: The amount paid by the insured for an insurance policy. The excess of the market price of stock over its par value. A reward; bonus.
preponderance: In civil litigation, when all the evidence more clearly and more probably favors one side than the other, that side has established a "preponderance of the evidence" which satisfies its burden of proof.
prerogative: An exclusive power or privilege, exhibited by an official or branch of government. *E.g.*, the power to veto legislation is the president's prerogative.
prerogative writ: In the old common law, discretionary writs of the court issued not as a matter of right but for good cause, *e.g.*, writs of mandamus, certiorari, procedendo, quo warranto, and habeus corpus. Today, many of these writs are specifically established and regulated by statute, and the old discretionary prerogative writs are abolished.
prescription: Remedy for disease; drugs and medicine. The process of acquiring an easement (the right to use part of another's property, water, or light) by continuous use, rather than by asking the owner of the property. "Prescription" applies to easements as "adverse possession" applies to real property.
present: Now existing; now occurring. *E.g.*, a "present estate" is one in which the owner now possesses the estate; a "present sale" is one in which the property exchanges hands when the contract is made.
presents: Term used in a legal document to designate that document, *e.g.*, "By these presents the parties agree . . ."
president: Chief officer or executive of an organization or corporation who presides at meetings, administers the business of the organization, and supervises employees. Chief executive of a nation or state, usually elected by the citizens, *e.g.*, President of the United States.
presumption: In litigation, an assumption of fact based on a rule of law, created by statute or by the courts. The presumption is a rule of evidence which shifts the burden of proof or the burden of producing evidence to the party against whom the presumption is made, to prove that the fact assumed is not true. *E.g.*, in a criminal trial, the defendant is entitled to the presumption of innocence (based on a rule of law) and the prosecutor must prove him guilty.

Presumptions are either "conclusive" or "rebuttable." Conclusive presumptions are, as a matter of law, final against the parties and the opposing party may introduce no evidence on the matter. Rebuttable presumptions may be attacked by the opposing party, who may introduce evidence on the matter.
pretermitted heir: Offspring of the testator omitted in the testator's will or born after the will was made. Some states provide by statute that the pretermitted heir be included in the distribution of the testator's property.
price: The amount a seller charges for his goods or a buyer pays for goods purchased; consideration given for goods received.
price discrimination: The practice of selling the same product to different buyers at different prices. Price discrimination is prohibited under the Clayton Act where it interferes with fair competition, unless costs of production are different between the buyers, the products are obsolete, or the price was lowered in good faith to meet the competition.
prima facie: Lat. On its face. Describing a fact convincing on its face, without any further proof of validity.
prima facie case: A case in which the plaintiff has presented sufficient evidence to entitle him to a decision by the judge or jury; a case which compels a favorable decision when no contrary or rebutting evidence is presented.
primary: First in time or importance.
primary evidence: Original or "best evidence" which is the most satisfactory way of proving a point in issue, *i.e.,* the real gun in a murder case, the eyewitness's testimony, or the original contract.
primogeniture: Ancient common-law rule of inheritance in which the eldest son of the deceased would inherit all the property. By contrast, "gavelkind" inheritance gave all sons an equal share.
principal: Most important or highest in rank. In agency law, one who directs or allows another to act

for his benefit, subject to his direction and control. The principal may be "disclosed" (known to third parties); "partially disclosed" (when third parties know only that the agent is acting for some principal); or "undisclosed" (when third parties do not know that the agent is acting for any principal). In criminal law, one who commits a crime, as opposed to an "accessory," who may aid the crime but is not present at the commission of the crime. In commercial law, the amount of the loan or investment, not including any interest. In trust law, the money and property in the trust, not including any profit. In the law of guaranty and surety, the one who is obligated to perform a contract which the surety guarantees.

principle: A rule or doctrine of law which guides judicial decisions.

priority: A legal preference; a right to go first. *E.g.*, in a bankruptcy action, creditors with "priority" are entitled to the first proceeds of the assets.

privacy: The right to be let alone, protected by law. The various rights of privacy include the confidentiality of private communications and letters, the freedom to make personal decisions (*e.g.*, marriage and abortion), the right to enjoy private property, and the interest against false publicity. Some states provide for penalties and civil remedies for breach of privacy.

private nuisance: Interference with one's use and enjoyment of his own property, through unreasonable or unlawful means.

privies: Those joined together in interest or in relation to a thing, *e.g.*, privies to contract (those who signed the contract), privies to estate (lessor and lessee), or privies of blood (blood relatives).

privilege: Some advantage or benefit enjoyed by one person or a particular group of persons; a benefit which all citizens do not share.

privileged communication: Statements made by one person or another which may be withheld as confidential by that other person when he is a witness in court regarding the conversation. *E.g.*, patient-physician, client-attorney, penitent-priest, or husband-wife communications are protected.

privity: A relationship of common interests or common legal rights. *E.g.*, a privity of contract is required in a breach of contract action; the defendant must be a party to be the plaintiff's contract.

privy: One person who has privity with another.

pro: Lat. For.

probable cause: The existence of certain facts which would lead a person of reasonable intelligence and prudence to believe that a crime has been committed. Probable cause is required before an arrest or search warrant is issued by the judge.

probate: The legal procedure necessary to prove that a will was legally made; more generally, the whole legal process having to do with legal administration of wills and estates.

probation: In criminal law, the sentence imposed by the judge when the defendant is not imprisoned but instead is required to report periodically to the "probation officer" who supervises the probation, ensuring that the person on probation is productively employed and out of trouble with the law. "Parole," in contrast, is release of the defendant after he has served part of his prison sentence.

pro bono publico: Lat. For the public good. *E.g.*, a lawyer engaged in "pro bono publico" activities represents, without charge, those who cannot afford legal services.

procedure: The process by which lawsuits are resolved; the rules regulating the pleadings, service of process, trial practice, evidence, and appeal. In contrast, "substantive" rules create and define legal rights and duties.

proceedings: The events which take place in court connected with a lawsuit. More generally, all the actions of legal officials (judges, clerks, magistrates, officers) from the commencement of a lawsuit until the enforcement of the final judgment.

process: The formal papers used to notify a defendant in a civil suit that he must appear at trial; the method by which a court exercises its jurisdiction over persons or property connected with the action.

proclamation: An official announcement, usually made by a high government official, *e.g.*, president, governor. The document containing such a public declaration. A bailiff's declaration that something is about to be done.

proctor: Person appointed to manage another's affairs or to represent him in court; a procurator, attorney, or proxy. Originally, an officer who performed the duties of an attorney in ecclesiastical or admiralty courts.

procuration: Act by which one person gives another authority to act in his behalf; agency; proxy. Act of procuring women for sexual purposes.

procurator: An agent; attorney; proctor; anyone who, under power of attorney, acts in another's behalf. *See* proctor, procuration.

produce: (Verb) To show; to bring forth; to furnish, such as to produce evidence. To yield, as in to produce dividends. (Noun) Something that grows or is found in the earth, *e.g.*, fruits, vegetables, gas, oil.

product liability: Responsibility which manufacturers and sellers of merchandise have to persons injured or damaged due to defects in their products. The manufacturer or seller is liable even though he has not been negligent, *i.e.*, he is "strictly liable." *See* strict liability.

proffer: To offer or present, as in to produce and offer a document to support a cause of action.

profit: Gain, benefit, or advantage realized in money or money's worth. In business transactions, it is the difference between income and expenditures. "Gross profit" is the money made from the sale of goods minus the cost of the goods to the seller, excluding expenses and taxes. "Net profit" is money made from the sale of goods minus all costs to the seller.

profit a prendre: Fr. A right to enter another's land and to profit from the removal of designated products it yields, such as minerals, trees, or game.

profiteering: Practice of acquiring excessive profits. This is usually done by taking advantage of unusual circumstances, and thus the term carries a derogatory connotation.

pro forma: Lat. As a matter of form, or for the sake of form. Term is used to mean a decree or judgment was rendered to facilitate further proceedings, not because it was necessarily right. It is also used to describe financial statements that are based on assumed or anticipated facts.

prohibition: Short for a "writ of prohibition." An order issued by a court of superior jurisdiction to an inferior court or quasi-judicial tribunal preventing the latter from dealing with matters outside its jurisdiction.

prolixity: The use of unnecessary words; the state of being verbose. Applied especially to wordiness in pleadings and affidavits. Adj. is "prolix."

promise: An expression of an intention to do or not do something. A promise binds a person in honor, conscience, or law, and it may be written or oral. A promise made by deed is called a "covenant." A reciprocal exchange of promises, or a promise made in exchange for consideration, is called an "agreement."

promissory estoppel: Doctrine in equity that states that a promise is binding if the person who made it (promisor) could reasonably expect another (promisee) to rely upon it in a substantial way, and that the promisee did indeed rely upon it. The promisor is "estopped," or barred, from denying his promise created a contract, even though one has not been made in the normal way. *See* estoppel.

promissory note: A negotiable instrument by which the maker promises to pay a sum of money. It may be made out "to the order of" a person named on it or simply to "bearer," and it may be payable on demand or by a specified date.

promoter: Person who takes the initial steps in the formation of a corporation. These steps include issuing a prospectus, writing a charter, and selling stock.

promulgation: Publication; act of officially announcing.

proof: The result of evidence; that evidence which establishes the existence of a fact, *i.e.*, that which is required to convince a judge or jury as to the truth of something. (For distinction between proof and evidence, *see* evidence.) Summary of the oral testimony a witness is expected to give at trial. This testimony is given to the witness's counsel before trial to guide counsel during the trial.

property: The exclusive right one has to possess, use, enjoy, and dispose of anything he owns. Anything that is owned, be it land, personalty, or an incorporeal right. In criminal law, property means anything that has value. When used in reference to trusts, it means an interest in something and not the thing itself. *See* personal property, real property, community property, chattel.

proposal: An offer; an expression of intention to do something. A proposal is not always an offer, but may only be an initial statement made for consideration by another. When this is the case, a proposal does not ripen into a contract as an offer does.

propound: To propose; to offer; to put something forth for consideration. *E.g.*, to propound a will is to offer it to the probate court with the request it be declared valid.

pro rata: Lat. According to the rate; in proportion to some rate or standard; proportionately. *E.g.*, an insolvent may have his assets divided among his creditors on a "pro rata" basis, meaning each would receive payment in equal proportion (*e.g.*, 20%) to what he is owed.

pro rate: To divide, distribute, or assess proportionately. *See* pro rata.

prorogation: Act of putting off something to another day, especially a legislative or court session. (*See* continuance.) Civil law: An agreement to extend time beyond which was previously allowed.

pro se: Lat. For himself; in his own behalf. A person who appears in court "pro se" does not have a lawyer and represents himself.

prosecution: The process of initiating and proceeding with a criminal or civil lawsuit; process of trying formal charges against an alleged offender. Verb is "prosecute." The government's side of a criminal suit. *See* prosecutor.

prosecutor: Public official who prosecutes a person accused of a crime. A prosecutor acts as the trial lawyer on behalf of the government and may be elected or appointed. A prosecutor for the state is called a District Attorney, County Attorney, or States Attorney depending on the jurisdiction. A federal prosecutor is called a U.S. Attorney.

prospective: Concerned with or related to the future. A prospective law applies to situations in the fu-

ture, as opposed to a retrospective or retroactive law which encompasses the past.
prospectus: A document published by a company which describes the company and the securities it offers for sale to the public. By law, a prospectus must be furnished to a potential buyer before he purchases any securities. More broadly, prospectus means any communication, either printed or broadcast, that offers securities for sale or confirms the sale of securities.
prostitute: One who engages in indiscriminate sexual intercourse for pay.
prostitution: Act of offering, agreeing to, or actually engaging in sexual intercourse, or any unlawful sex act, for pay.
pro tanto: Lat. For so much; to such an extent. Commonly used to describe the government's partial payment for property taken under right of eminent domain.
pro tem: Lat. Short for "pro tempore," for the time being; temporarily. A mayor who serves "pro tem" serves on a provisional basis until he, or someone else, is officially elected.
protest: Written expression of disagreement with the legality or justice of a payment, or the amount of a payment, made to protect oneself against the effects one's payment would imply. *E.g.*, taxes are sometimes paid in full but under protest, protecting the taxpayer's right to have his taxes readjusted. Statement written by a notary public at the request of a holder of a negotiable instrument, that states the instrument was presented for payment or acceptance, and that same was refused. In the statement, the notary "protests" against all parties to the instrument, and declares them liable for losses or damage due to their "refusal of payment or acceptance." A statement written by an importer contesting the amount of the duty charged on his goods. Maritime law: A written statement by the master of a vessel stating the weather-related or natural causes of damage to his ship or cargo.
prothonotary: Title sometimes given to a chief clerk or registrar of a court.
protocols: First or original drafts of an agreement between countries or records of preliminary negotiations. Accepted methods of procedure among diplomats or heads of state; ceremonial rules and procedures; formalities.
province: A colony or geographical division of a country, *e.g.*, the Canadian province of Quebec. Duty, function, power, responsibility, or sphere of activity of a profession.
provisional: Temporary; preliminary; made or existing for a time or until something further is done; tentative; *e.g.*, provisional remedy is a court order which helps to enforce the law on a temporary basis.
proviso: "It being provided"; condition or stipulation; qualification; limitation. Usually a clause in a contract, statute, deed, or lease which imposes a condition which must be met in order for the instrument to be valid.
provocation: An act by one person that incites or influences a second person to perform a particular act, usually an illegal one. An act by one person that so enrages a second person that he loses self-control and commits an act he would not ordinarily commit. Provocation may reduce the severity of a crime, such as reducing murder to manslaughter.
proximate cause: Something that produces a result in the natural sequence of events and without which the result could not have occurred. One's liability is generally limited to results "proximately caused" by his actions. Real cause; direct cause; legal cause.
proxy: Person who is authorized by another person to act for him, usually to vote for him at a meeting, *e.g.*, one permitted to vote for a shareholder of a corporation. Written authorization given by one person to another so that the second can act for the first.
public: All of the citizens of a state, nation, city, or community. That which belongs to the people at large. That which affects, or is open to or related to all persons, as distinguished from private. The body politic.
publication: Making public; the offering of anything to the public at large. In libel and slander law, the communication of defamatory material to someone other than the person defamed. A printed book, circular, magazine, or newspaper. The acknowledgment by a testator in the presence of witnesses that an instrument is his last will.
public domain: Land owned by the government, as opposed to private property. Free for anyone to use; not protected by patent or copyright.
public policy: Flexible, vague term often meaning "what is good for (or will not harm) the general public"; principle of law holding that no person can do that which has a tendency to harm the general public.
publish: To make or effect a publication; to give publicity to; to print for general circulation; to print a manuscript.
puffing: Statement made by a seller which is not a representation of fact, but rather an exaggeration concerning the quality of goods; generally bragging about the product rather than a legally binding representation.
punitive damages: Award of damages not related to actual harm caused to plaintiff, but instead intended to punish the defendant and deter future wrongdoing. Usually awarded when a tort is aggravated by evil

motives, actual malice, deliberate violence or oppression. Also called "exemplary damages" or "vindictive damages."

pur autre vie: Fr. For or during the life of another. Also "per autre vie." An "estate pur autre vie" is an estate held for the life of a third person.

purchase: To acquire title to property by voluntary act and agreement and for valuable consideration; to buy.

Acquisition of property by any means other than by descent.

"Purchase" includes taking by sale, discount, negotiation, mortgage, pledge, lien, issue or reissue, gift or any other voluntary transaction creating an interest in property. *U.C.C. §1-201(32).*

purge: To cleanse; clear. To exonerate from some criminal charge or imputation of guilt or from a contempt.

purloin: To pilfer, steal, filch, commit larceny.

purport: (Verb) To imply; claim; mean; convey; give the impression. (Noun) The meaning, intent, purpose, or objective of something.

purview: The purpose, scope, and design of a statute or other enacted law. The enacting part of an act, as distinguished from other parts such as the preamble.

putative: Reputed; supposed; commonly esteemed; believed; assumed. *E.g.*, a putative father is the man believed to be the father of a child born out of wedlock.

Q

qua: Lat. In the character or capacity of.
quaere: Lat. A question, query, doubt. Indicates that the proposition is open to question.
qualification: Possessing the qualities, property, or other circumstances which make a person eligible to fill a public office or profession. Limitation or restriction.
qualified endorsement (indorsement): An endorsement on the back of a negotiable instrument by which the endorser excludes his liability, usually by adding the words "without recourse" after the signature. *U.C.C. §3-414(1).*
qualify: To prepare or make oneself fit to exercise a right, franchise, or office. To restrict, limit, modify.
quantum damnificatus: Lat. How much damnified? How much was he damaged? The issue for determining the amount of compensation to be awarded to the plaintiff.
quantum meruit: Lat. As much as he deserves. An equitable doctrine which allows a party to recover for the value of his labor and materials furnished to another even though there was no actual contract so that the other party will not be unjustly enriched. The suit is based on an implied promise.
quantum valebant: Lat. As much as they are worth. Form of pleading for payment for goods sold and delivered, based on implied promise by the buyer to pay the seller as much as the goods are reasonably worth.
quarantine: Enforced isolation for the purpose of preventing the spread of contagious or infectious diseases. Forty-day period during which persons, goods, or animals on a ship where there is a contagious disease must wait before being allowed to land. Privilege of a widow to use a portion of her husband's estate before the estate is settled.
quare: Lat. Wherefore; why; on what account; because.
quare clausum fregit: Lat. Wherefore he broke the close. Action for trespass to recover damages for the unlawful entry upon land of another.
quash: Vacate; set aside; annul; suppress; make void, *e.g.*, to quash an indictment.

quasi: Lat. As it were; as if; having the qualities of; related to. Frequently used to show similarities between two subjects, but indicating that there are differences, *e.g.*, quasi-contract.

quasi-contract: Contract created by law based on relationship of parties or their actions. An implied contract. Quasi-contract is used to prevent unjust enrichment. Based on theory of quantum meruit.

quasi-judicial: Function like that of a judge. Term is applied to the case-deciding functions of an administrative agency or an authority which are not really courts of law. The action may include investigating facts, holding hearings and drawing conclusions from them by exercising discretion and judgment of a judicial nature.

queen's bench: Superior English common law court, so called because the king or queen formerly sat there in person. It was called queen's bench during the reign of a queen.

question: Problem; the issue to be decided in a court of law; matter about which opposing parties in a suit disagree; point in controversy. An interrogatory or query put to a witness.

"Question of fact": Disputed factual contention; question of the truth to be decided usually by a jury after hearing evidence on both sides of a case.

"Question of law": Disputed legal contention; matter for the court to decide based on interpretation or application of existing laws.

quia timet: Lat. Because he fears or apprehends. Technical name of a bill in equity practice filed by a party seeking an injunction "because he fears" injury to his rights or property in a pending case.

quid pro quo: Lat. What for what; something for something. Synonymous with consideration, as in the mutual consideration in a contract which makes the contract binding and valid.

quiet enjoyment: Covenant in a lease or conveyance by which the lessor or grantor warrants that the lessee or grantee shall enjoy the possession of the prem-

ises in peace and without disturbance. It is not a warranty of title.
quitclaim deed: Deed by which the grantor releases all his interest in property by passing any interest, claim, or title in the property which he has. The grantor makes no warranties or covenants for title in a quitclaim deed. The deed only purports to convey such title as the grantor has.
quittance: Lat. Abbreviation of "acquittance"; release.
quo animo: Lat. With what mind, intent, motive.
quorum: Majority of the entire body; minimum number of persons required to be present in order for a deliberative body, such as a committee, board of directors, or shareholders to legally transact business.
quotation: In commercial usage, the stated price of an item. Word-for-word repetition of a statement from some authority, case, law or statute.
quo warranto: Lat. By what authority. A writ by which the court inquires into the right of a person or corporation to hold an office or to exercise a franchise.

R

rape: Unlawful sexual intercourse by a man with a woman committed without her consent and through the use of fear or force by the man against the woman. "Statutory rape," in modern usage, is unlawful sexual intercourse with a female under a certain statutory age, with or without her consent.
rate: Proportional or relative amount. *E.g.*, the "rate of interest" is the percentage of the whole which will be paid in interest; the "price rate" is the price amount relating to each specific unit or quantity.
ratification: The acceptance or confirmation of a prior act done by oneself or another for one's benefit, which authorizes the prior act as if it had been originally authorized. The approval by state legislatures or popular conventions of proposed constitutional amendments.
ratio decidendi: Lat. The reason for decision. The grounds or rationale in a case which determine and support the court's decision.
ratio legis est anima legis: Lat. The reason of law is the soul of law.
ravish: To rape. To have carnal knowledge of a woman against her will and with force.
real: In civil law, referring to a "thing," as distinguished from a "person." In evidence, referring to the actual, physical objects used by the parties or witnesses. In property law, referring to land, buildings, and estates, as distinguished from "personal" property such as jewelry, objects, etc.
real estate: Land and permanent attachments to the land, including buildings, fences, and all the permanent attachments to the buildings, including heating, plumbing, lighting, masonry, etc.
real evidence: Evidence submitted during a trial which represents the actual, physical thing sought to be proved, *e.g.*, the murder weapon, the stolen goods, the heroin, the scar on the victim's body. Real evidence is distinguished from "demonstrative evidence" which can only demonstrate conclusions made from the real thing, *e.g.*, maps, charts, diagrams, scale models.
real party in interest: The party with the legal right under the applicable substantive law to prosecute or defend the contemplated legal action; the party who is actually interested in the outcome of the action.
real property: Land (including buildings and other permanent attachments to the land) and the rights arising out of land. Real property is distinguished from "personal property," which is temporary and moveable in nature. A "leasehold interest," the right to rent land for a particular time, is characterized as personal property because it is thought to be temporary.
realty: Another term for real estate or real property.
reasonable doubt: In a criminal trial, that doubt which is direct and reasonable in light of all the evidence presented at the trial, which would justify the jury in reaching a verdict of "not guilty." Where the evidence presents a case of guilt beyond all reasonable doubt, the evidence justifies the jury in reaching a verdict of "guilty." A reasonable doubt is more than a mere skepticism but does not need to be represented by clear evidence; it need only be that doubt which reasonable people would consider.
reasonable time: In contract law, when contracting parties do not set a time for "acceptance" or for "performance," it must be done within a reasonable amount of time, that time which is not unreasonable depending on the nature and circumstances of each case.
rebate: A discount or refund of money given for purchases, prompt payment, overpaid taxes, or rate charges, given back to the payer after he has already paid the full, original sum.
rebut: To defeat, refute, or prove the contrary of an assumption or inference made at trial. *E.g.*, if a plaintiff introduces evidence which raises the presumption that the defendant had notice of a particular fact, the defendant may rebut that presumption with evidence that he had no such notice.
rebuttal, rebutting evidence: Evidence which defeats, refutes, or proves the contrary of facts or presumptions offered in evidence by the opposing party.

Rebuttal evidence may be offered at the close of the opponent's case.

recall: Procedure in which a public official, including a judge, may be removed from office through popular vote or through a circulating petition. Procedure in which purchasers of a particular product are notified to take the product back to the seller for adjustments or examinations, usually when the seller or manufacturer believes the product is defective or dangerous.

recaption: At common law, the peaceful recovery of one's property when one is legally entitled to it and when one finds it in another's wrongful possession.

receipt: Written and signed document, showing the taking or receiving of money or goods. A receipt is not conclusive evidence at court of the taking or receiving and it may be supplemented in court with oral evidence.

receiver: A court-appointed custodian of assets which are subject to litigation or to a bankruptcy action. The receiver will hold and preserve property of the parties or of the bankrupt while awaiting the court's ruling. In the case of corporations, a receiver may not only manage the assets but will sometimes, upon the court's order, manage the operation of the business.

receivership: A remedy where the court appoints a receiver to hold, preserve, or manage property subject to litigation or to a bankruptcy action. The property or corporation controlled by a receiver is said to be "in receivership."

receiving stolen goods (or stolen property): The criminal offense of receiving property which has been unlawfully stolen by another, when the person who receives the property knows it to be stolen and acts with fraudulent intent.

recess: The time when a trial or hearing is suspended for a short period, for meals, overnight, over the weekend, or for a short investigation. Any period longer than three days is generally called a "continuance." The time between court sessions or between legislative sessions, without a final adjournment of the body.

recidivist: A habitual criminal; a repeat offender. Many states have "recidivist statutes" which subject the repeat offender to longer sentences.

reciprocity: A relationship between corporations, persons, or nations, where privileges and benefits are granted by each entity to the other. *E.g.*, "trade reciprocity" is where one country will sell a commodity to another country and that country will sell another commodity of equal worth to the first country.

recitals: Specific statements in a document, deed, or statute, listing the reasons or basis for enacting the document, usually beginning with the word "whereas."

reckless: Careless; inattentive; indifferent. The meaning of "reckless" varies, depending on the circumstances, from merely negligent or careless action to willful disregard of the consequences of an act. "Reckless" conduct indicates a conscious disregard of the substantial risks of certain conduct which a reasonable person would recognize.

reckless driving: Recklessness in operating a motor vehicle, with the knowledge that one's acts will result in probable injury to others, or with wanton disregard of the safety of others.

reclaim: To demand the return of one's property.

recognition: Acceptance or acknowledgment of another's act by one who has given him the authority to perform that act.

recognizance: Formal obligation entered into at court by which a person agrees to perform some act in the future. Courts may or may not require the person to post a bond. In a criminal case, the defendant may be released if he promises to appear for a future hearing. (*See* release on recognizance.) "Personal recognizance" occurs when the court does not require a bond.

reconciliation: The reuniting of husband and wife with the resumption of marital duties and the cessation of enmity and discord. In accounting, the process of adjusting the records to conform with each other, to correct possible errors.

reconveyance: The transfer or sale of real property back to its previous owner.

record: The precise history of a lawsuit from its commencement to its termination, including all pleadings, evidence, testimony, and judicial decisions. This history is also known as the "record of appeal" and the appellants are usually restricted to those facts in the record.

The writing, the memorandum, the item which holds the information preserved, *e.g.*, the sales slip, the transcript, the letter. A "public record" is one prepared and used by a public agency as required by law, *e.g.*, birth and death records, etc. A corporation's records include its charter, bylaws, meeting minutes, contracts, and other accounts of the official business of the corporation which are kept in the regular course of business.

(Verb) To record; to preserve information in a writing, *e.g.*, to record a deed.

recoupment: Defendant's right to recover part of the plaintiff's award of damages by reducing the plaintiff's claim due to previous payment by the defendant or plaintiff's own wrongful or defective performance of the contract.

recourse: The right of the person who holds a negotiable instrument to recover against someone who is secondarily liable, *e.g.*, the endorser or cosigner of the instrument.

recover: To gain back that which is lost, *e.g.*, to recover one's property. More specifically, to collect the amount of the court's judgment against the other party.

recrimination: In a divorce case, a charge made by the defendant against the plaintiff that alleges the same or similar marital misconduct, *e.g.*, adultery or cruelty. Recrimination traditionally blocked the divorce; *e.g.*, if the husband sued the wife for a divorce on grounds of adultery and the wife alleged that the husband also committed adultery, he would not be entitled to a divorce. Many states have abolished this doctrine in "no-fault divorce" statutes.

reddendum: In old English law, rendering; yielding. The clause in the conveyance used by a grantor to denote that he is reserving something for himself, such as rents from the land.

redeem: To buy back; to repurchase; to pay the debts. To redeem a mortgage means to pay the outstanding value of the mortgage and hence achieve full control over the property. A corporation may redeem stock held by shareholders by purchasing it with cash.

redemption: The repurchase of property or the cancellation of debt, *e.g.*, the purchase of a loan or of a corporation's own shares of stock, or the payment of the outstanding balance of a mortgage. The "right of redemption" is the right of the mortgagor to buy back the property after a "foreclosure" or forced sale, which is a limited right created and regulated by state statute.

redress: Payment or compensation for damages or injuries.

reductio ad absurdum: Lat. Reduced to the absurd. An argument showing that the logical consequences of another argument would be absurd.

reentry (right of): The right of the grantor to resume possession of land granted to another, due to some condition reserved in the lease, *e.g.*, death of the tenant, nonpayment of rent, or expiration of the lease. In the old common law, reentry was always allowed for nonpayment of rent, but today it must be reserved in the lease. Also, the old common law allowed the grantor to enforce his right of reentry but today he must initiate legal proceedings to do so.

reexamination: The examination of a witness which immediately follows cross-examination, also known as redirect examination.

referee: Quasi-judicial officer appointed by the court for a specific purpose, who may hear testimony, decide factual disputes, and report his findings.

referee in bankrupty: Before the 1978 Bankruptcy Act, the officer appointed by the courts who administered bankruptcy proceedings. Today their functions are performed by judges of the Bankruptcy Court.

reference: The act of referring a legal case to a "referee" or "master" for resolution. The agreement between parties to a contract to submit their disputes to arbitration. A person who will provide information regarding another's character, credit, or abilities.

referendum: A popular election held for consideration of a law passed by the state legislature or of a proposed constitutional amendment. A report by an ambassador to his country concerning matters which he cannot decide without further orders.

reformation of contract: An equitable remedy used to change a written contract so that it conforms to the actual agreement of the parties, when either by mistake of both parties or by mistake of one party with fraud by the other party, the writing does not conform to the contract as actually made.

refreshing memory: A witness who once had knowledge about some act or transaction, but has insufficient recollection to be able to testify fully, may consult his own records or memoranda made near the time of the act or transaction, to refresh his memory. *See Federal Rule of Evidence 803(5).*

register: To formally record a matter, as on a list. The public record of facts, *e.g.*, births and deaths, patent filings, wills, deeds. The public officials who keep public records.

registrar: Private officer who keeps a register or registry; *e.g.*, at a school, a list of students; or at a hospital, a list of patients; or at a corporation, a list of shareholders.

registry: The book containing the recording of facts and documents, authorized and maintained in accordance with the law, *e.g.*, registry of deeds, or registry of ships at a customs house.

regulation: A rule or order of the executive branch of government which has the same force of law as if issued by the legislative branch, *e.g.*, a tax regulation issued by the Internal Revenue Service which dictates the proper payment of specific tax receipts.

rehabilitation, rehabilitate: The restoring or reinstatement of something or someone to its former capacity or position; to restore or reinstate, *e.g.*, in corporation law, to administer the assets of an insolvent corporation and to continue the business in hopes of its eventual return to solvency. In litigation, a witness may be "rehabilitated" after a cross-examination, through redirect examination, to improve his standing, credibility, or integrity.

rehearing: A retrial or reconsideration of the issues of a case by the same court in which the suit was originally heard, *e.g.*, when a party alleges oversight in the first hearing, or when new evidence is discovered.

reimburse: To pay another person for costs and expenses incurred on one's behalf.

reinstate, reinstatement: To restore someone or something to its former position; the restoration, *e.g.*, in insurance, a restoration of the insured person's rights and benefits under a policy which had expired or been cancelled.

reinsurance: An insurance contract between two insurers (or insurance companies) to insure one of them against risk of loss in insurance policies with its insured persons; or the substitution of another insurer for the original insurer on an insurance policy, with the consent of the insured person.

rejoinder: In common law pleadings, the defendant's second formal pleading, in answer to the plaintiff's replication to the defendant's first pleading.

relation: A relative or kinsman, by blood or marriage. In a restrictive sense, it means only blood relatives. When used in a will, it means only those who would inherit the estate under the state statute of distributions. Generally, the connection between two persons, *e.g.*, the "marital relation" between husband and wife, the "agency relation" between master and servant. A narrative, given by the "relator." Doctrine of legal fiction whereby some act is considered to have taken place at some time earlier than it actually did occur, sometimes called "relation back."

relator: An informer; an interested person who complains and instigates litigation against a defendant in the name of the state; *e.g.*, in *State ex rel. Jones v. Smith*, Jones is the relator and Smith is the defendant.

release: The giving up of some claim, right, or interest, before the court or in writing between the parties; *e.g.*, a person injured by another may sign a release which is his promise not to sue in court for damages. In property law, the owner of property or an interest in property may release his interest to another, usually a person who has a different interest in the same property.

release on recognizance (ROR): Release of a criminal suspect from custody on his promise to appear at a later hearing. The court will decide whether to release the suspect upon an examination of the nature of the charge, the suspect's family ties, employment, character, past criminal record, etc.

relevant, relevant evidence: Something is relevant if it tends to prove or disprove an issue in controversy. "Relevant evidence" is any evidence having any tendency to make the existence of any fact that is of consequence to a final determination more or less probable than it would be without the evidence. *See Federal Rule of Evidence 40.*

reliance: Confidence or belief which causes a person to act to his detriment on the promises, acts, or representations of another. Reliance is often an element in legal actions, *e.g.*, in an action for fraud, the plaintiff must prove he relied on the defendant's fraudulent misrepresentation, which caused injury.

relict: A widower or widow; technically, the relict of the marriage is the one who survives the union after the other is deceased.

relief: The assistance or redress which a person seeks of the court, *e.g.*, an "injunction" against wrongs, or "specific performance" on the contract. In feudal property law, the sum paid to the lord by a deceased tenant's heirs for the right to inherit the tenant's lands. Public assistance given to the poor or indigent.

religious freedom, religious liberty: Guarantee in the first amendment to the United States Constitution, of the right to worship God according to the dictates of one's conscience, including the right to do or not do any act of religious observance which is not inconsistent with the peace and order of society.

relinquish, relinquishment: To abandon or surrender; the act of abandoning or surrendering. Relinqishment will occur when a federal court refuses to hear certain cases which it will "relinquish" to the state courts. *See* abstention.

remainder: In property, an interest or estate in land which will take effect when the immediately preceding estate terminates. Thus, if *A* grants Greenacre to *B* for ten years with the "remainder" to *C*, *C*'s estate will begin ten years after the original grant, on the condition that *C* is existing and ascertained at the time his estate is due to commence. A remainder can only be valid when the previous estate is less than a "fee simple," when the previous estate terminates regularly, when the remainder is created in the same grant as the previous estate, and when the remainder "vests" (or becomes ascertained) during the previous estate.

A "contingent remainder" is one that is subject to a condition precedent, *e.g.*, a remainder "to the children of *D*" when *D* has no children at the time of the grant, or a remainder "to *E* if *E* marries" when *E* is unmarried. The remainder is said to "vest" when the condition occurs, *e.g.*, when *D* has children, or when *E* marries.

A "vested remainder" is one to a person in existence who is certain to take immediate possession of the estate when the immediately preceding estate terminates.

remainderman: One who is entitled, by grant of the original owner, to a future estate in a remainder of land at the termination of the previous estate.

remand: To send a case from a higher court back to a lower court for a new hearing consistent with the higher court's decision.
remedial statute: A law passed by the legislature which creates or expands the methods and legal measures which private parties can use to obtain relief or compensation for damages.
remedy: The methods used by a court to redress an injury or protect a right. *E.g.*, the court may order the defendant to pay money to the injured party. Or, the court may issue an "injunction," which orders a party to cease some activity which violates the plaintiff's rights.

Remedies may be "legal" or "equitable." Equitable remedies, *e.g.*, an injunction or specific performance on a contract, are available only in "courts of equity." "Provisional remedies" are those employed by the court during the cause of action and before a final decision in the case, *e.g.*, a preliminary injunction or a restraining order.
remission: The release of a debt. The forgiving of an offense or injury.
remit: To send or send back; to relinquish, *e.g.*, to remit money borrowed.
remittance: Money one person sends to another.
remittit damna: Lat. Entry in the record that the plaintiff has remitted or given up part of the damages awarded by the jury.
remittitur: The power of the judge to order the plaintiff to remit, or accept a reduction in the amount of the damages awarded in the jury's verdict, when the judge believes the verdict is excessively high as a matter of law. The judge may order a retrial if the plaintiff does not accept the reduction.
removal: Generally, the transfer of a person or thing to another state. In federal civil procedure, a case may be "removed" on the defendant's request from a state court to the federal district court if the case could have been originally brought in the federal court. *See 28 U.S.C. §1441.*
render: To announce or declare, *e.g.*, to render the verdict of the jury. To return, surrender, or yield.
renewal: The revival of a right that has expired; the substitution of a new right or obligation for an old one, which extends the time for performance of the right or obligation. *E.g.*, the renewal of a debt means the rewriting of the original debt to extend the deadline to repay.
rent: Payment to the owner for the possession by the tenant of land, buildings, or tenements.
rent strike: An organized movement by tenants to not pay the rent until their disputes with the owner are settled.
renunciation, renounce: The abandonment of a contract right of one party, often without payment or other consideration. In criminal law, voluntary abandonment of the intention to commit a crime, prior to the actual commission of the crime. Renunciation is usually an affirmative defense to the charges of attempt, conspiracy, solicitation, and accessory. Renunciation is not valid as a defense if it is motivated by a possible failure of the crime, an increased risk of detection, or a mere desire to postpone the crime. *See* affirmative defense.
renvoi: Fr. A dismissal; a sending back. Method used by the courts in cases involving potential conflict of laws between two or more jurisdictions. The courts must determine whether to utilize the law of the forum (where the court is located), the law of the domicile (where the party resides), or the law of the place where the act or injury occurred. "Doctrine of renvoi" refers to doctrine under which a court is referred in a particular matter to the rules of foreign law as to conflict of laws which in turn refers court back to the law of the forum.
reorganization: In corporation law, reorganization is achieved by transferring all the assets of an insolvent corporation to a newly-formed corporation with substantially the same stockholders as the old corporation.
reparable injury: An injury that may be cured sufficiently through payment of damages or other relief.
reparation: Aid in relief of injuries, given by the one who caused the injuries.
repatriation: Achieving nationality after abandoning it earlier. *See* expatriation.
repeal: The complete rescinding of a statute by a subsequent statute of the legislature. An "express repeal" is one which specifically revokes a statute. An "implied repeal" is caused by creating a statute which conflicts with and overrides a previous statute.
replevin: An action to recover the possession of personal property which has been unlawfully taken from the plaintiff. *Compare* trover.
replevy: To deliver goods or personal property back to the rightful owner, usually in connection with a "replevin" action.
replication: In common law pleading, the plaintiff's pleading following the defendant's first pleading. In modern practice this is called the "reply."
reply: In modern civil procedure, the plaintiff's pleading following the defendant's answer. The reply may respond only to the defendant's counterclaims unless the court orders the plaintiff to respond to the defendant's answer or a third-party answer. *See Federal Rule of Civil Procedure 7(a).*
reporter: The person who officially reports, or publishes a court's decisions. The unofficial or commercially printed volumes of the cases decided by a court, sometimes also called "reports."

reports: Printed volumes of cases decided by a court, *e.g.*, Supreme Court Reports, Pennsylvania Superior Court Reports. Also includes volumes of administrative agency decisions. Formal statement of activities or facts, *e.g.*, annual report, credit report.
repossession: The process of taking back items (by the seller) because the purchaser fails to pay. Before actually taking the items back, the seller must follow, in most states, requirements to give notice, identify the goods, and meet timing deadlines.
represent: To exhibit; to appear in the character of; impersonate, *e.g.*, "the diagram represents the scene of the crime." To speak or act with authority on behalf of another, *e.g.*, the speaker "represents" General Motors Corporation. *See* agent.
representation: Any statement of fact or conduct which implies a particular fact. In an action for fraud, a statement or conduct designed to mislead others. In contract law, an express or implied statement made before the signing of the contract regarding some fact influential in the decision to sign the contract. A representation is "material" when the parties would not have made the contract without the representation. (*See* misrepresentation.) The act of representing another.
representative: One who represents another. (*See* agent.) A representative may be an agent, an executor, an administrator, a receiver, a trustee, a director, an officer, etc. A person elected by the voters to serve in a legislative body.
representative action: Method for a large group of interested persons to be represented in an action by one or more of its members who will represent the entire group or class. Also called "class action." The class must be ascertainable, must have similar interests, must be too numerous to be heard in one court, and must be adequately represented by one named member. *See Federal Rule of Civil Procedure 23.*
reprieve: In criminal law, a delay in the execution of a sentence. A "reprieve" merely postpones the sentence, while a "pardon" totally abrogates it.
reprisal: The taking or doing of one thing, in satisfaction for another. One nation's deprivation of another nation's rights or property in retaliation for an injury committed by the other nation. Reprisals may be "positive" (actual seizing of property) or "negative" (refusing to honor a valid contract right).
republic: A nation with the sovereign power in the people, or citizens, who elect representatives to a national legislature to govern the nation.
republication: The second publication or establishment of a will by a testator who earlier revoked it.
repudiate, repudiation: To reject or deny a claim, right, or privilege; the rejection or denial. In contract law, "repudiation of a contract" is the unequivocal declaration before performance is due that performance will not be made.
repugnancy, repugnant: An inconsistency or opposition between a clause in a contract, deed, statute, or other writing, and a previous clause in the same writing. In pleadings, the affirmation of a cause of action in one count and the denial of same in another. Inconsistent claims or defenses are permitted under *Federal Rule of Civil Procedure 8.*
requirements contract: A contract where the buyer agrees to purchase all his requirements of a particular item for use in his business over a period of time. The uncertainty of a requirements contract does not destroy its validity. *See U.C.C. 2-306.*
requisition: Seizure of property by government. Demand of one government for a fugitive criminal located within the bounds of another government. Generally, any formal request.
res: Lat. A thing. The object of an action "in rem" (brought to determine the legal status of the object or "thing"). *E.g.*, in an action of title, the res is the land; in an action to determine ownership of tangible personal property, the res is the property. The purpose of the res is to establish the jurisdiction of the action; the action must be brought in a court in the jurisdiction where the res is located.
rescind: To abrogate, annul, avoid, or cancel a contract, and in so doing, to restore the parties to the position they occupied before the contract was made.
rescission: The abrogation or voiding of a contract, removing all obligations of the parties, and restoring them to their original positions.
rescue: In common law, to free a prisoner, using force, from lawful custody without his aid; or to unlawfully or forcibly retrieve goods lawfully taken in securing rent payment or cure for damages.
rescue doctrine: In tort law, doctrine that one who imperils the life of another through negligence is also liable for injuries of a third party who attempts to rescue the victim if such a rescue is not rash or extremely reckless.
reservation: A clause in a deed retaining some right or interest for the grantor, *e.g.*, the right of reentry. Land area set aside for a specific purpose, *e.g.*, wildlife conservation, Indian tribal lands, etc.
res gestae: Lat. Things done. The events which form the litigated act. Statements made as part of the "res gestae" are admissible in evidence under an exception to the hearsay rule, when the statement accompanies an event which is otherwise admissible and explains the event. *See Federal Rule of Evidence 803(1), 803(2). E.g.*, a driver states, during an automobile accident, "My gas pedal is stuck."
residence: A person's dwelling place. "Residence" differs from "domicile" in that the domicile is a per-

son's legal home for tax and voting purposes, and the residence is where the person lives.
residuary: Making up the surplus of an estate after all debts, devises, and costs are taken out. The surplus, or "residue," includes devises which are invalid or impossible to take effect.
residuary bequest: A bequest which disposes of the entire contents of the estate after all debts, devises, and costs are taken out.
residuary clause: Clause of a will which disposes of the residue of the estate after all debts, devises, and costs are taken out.
residuary devise (devisee): A devise of the residue of the estate after all debts, other devises, and costs are taken out. The "residuary devisee" is the person who receives the residuary devise.
residuary legacy (legatee): The legacy of the residue of the estate after all debts, devises, and costs are taken out. The "residuary legatee" is the person who receives the residuary legacy.
residuum: In general, what is left after a separation. In wills, the residuum is the content of the estate after all grants, debts, and devises are taken out.
res ipsa loquitur: Lat. The thing speaks for itself. Doctrine in tort cases which creates a permissible inference of negligence unless the defendant can prove otherwise when (a) the defendant had exclusive control of the thing producing injury and (b) the injury would not normally occur without negligence. *E.g.*, a baby exhibits clear dog bite marks and the defendant owns the only dog in the neighborhood.
res judicata: Lat. A thing already judged. Doctrine that a final judgment of a court is conclusive against the same parties in any further, identical cause of action between the parties.
resolution: Formal statement expressing the opinion of a legislative body. A resolution differs from a law or ordinance because it expresses only an opinion and does not permanently control or direct the citizens.
resort: To seek help; a person or thing from which help is sought. *E.g.*, a "court of last resort" is a court whose decision is final and without further appeal. To frequent; a place frequented by persons, usually for illegal or illicit activities.
respite: A delay in the execution of a sentence. (*See* reprieve.) A delay in the payment of debts, granted by the court or by the creditor to a debtor. It is "voluntary" if granted by the creditor and "forced" if granted by the court.
respondeat superior: Lat. Let the superior answer. Doctrine that a principal (master or employer) is liable for injuries proximately resulting from the negligent acts of his agent (servant or employee) when the acts are committed within the scope of the agent's authority or apparent authority of employment. The principal, who is deemed to act through his agents, maintains a duty to conduct his affairs so as not to injure others, and is thus liable for the negligent acts of his agents.
respondent: One who argues against an appeal by the petitioner. Also, one who answers a bill or pleading in equity.
responsive: Answering the allegations directly and completely without introducing new allegations; *e.g.*, in an answer to a complaint, pleading new matters is nonresponsive to the complaint.
rest: When the party has no more witnesses to present at a trial, he will "rest" his case, and may offer only rebutting evidence afterward. Lapse of activity; repose. The "residue" of an estate.
restitution: A common law remedy by which the court can, in its discretion, restore the injured party to a previous position, return something to the rightful owner, or restore the status quo.

In contracts, restitution occurs when a party recovers monetary payments already made or when a party is ordered to pay the value of performance already rendered. In torts, restitution is used to prevent unjust enrichment at the expense of others. In criminal law, restitution may be part of the sentence, when the offender is required to pay the victim in some way.
restrain: To impede, hinder, or repress.
restraining order: An order of the court, after an application for injunction is filed, forbidding the defendant from doing some particular act until the court holds a hearing on the propriety of issuing the injunction sought.
restraint of trade: In antitrust law, contracts or combinations designed to thwart business or commercial competition, achieve a monopoly, affect prices, or in any other way obstruct free trade as it would occur in a natural economy, are illegal under the Sherman Antitrust Act. *See 15 U.S.C. §§1-7.*
restrictive covenant: In a deed, a promise to restrict the use of real property, which is a covenant said to "run with the land." Racially restrictive covenants are unenforceable by the courts under the Due Process Clause of the fourteenth amendment.

In a contract, a promise by the employee or partner to refrain from performing similar work after the contract terminates, which is valid if limited to a reasonable geographical area and period of time.
restrictive indorsement: An indorsement which restricts the negotiability of an instrument, by creating a condition, restricting transferability, including restrictive words (*e.g.*, "for deposit only"), or limiting the use of the instrument (*e.g.*, "for accounts payable only").
resulting trust: Occurs when a trust must be created to fulfill the apparent intentions of the parties, who

dispose of property for another's benefit without expressly creating a trust. A "resulting trust" differs from a "constructive trust" which is created contrary to the parties' intentions, often in the presence of fraud.

retainer: Advance deposit paid to an attorney for representing a client, including full or partial fees, expenses, and the agreement not to represent the client's adversary.

retire, retirement: To redeem, to pay off, or to cash in, *e.g.*, to retire a bond is to turn it in for cash. To withdraw voluntarily from employment. In a trial, after the parties present their cases and the judge instructs the jury, the jury will then retire to deliberate its verdict.

retraction: To withdraw a statement made earlier, *e.g.*, to withdraw an offer before acceptance, or to correct a defamatory statement.

retroactive: Refers to a law which affects rights or acts which were fully legal in the past. Retroactive includes both "retrospective" and "ex post facto" laws. Retrospective technically applies only to civil laws which impair vested rights or create new duties. Ex post facto applies to criminal laws which make illegal something which was legal when the act occurred. Ex post facto laws are unconstitutional under the U.S. Constitution (article I, section 10).

retrospective: Refers to a civil law which affects rights which were fully legal in the past. A retrospective law impairs vested rights, creates new obligations, imposes new duties, or applies a new disability to a valid transaction.

return: Report of a sheriff or other official stating whether or not he was able to carry out a court order. A "false return" is one in which the official falsely reports that he has carried out the order when in fact he has not. A report of information filed with the government, *e.g.*, tax return.

return day: The day, noted in a writ or process, when the officer must make a "return" of the writ or process.

revenue: Income from property, commerce, or investment, *e.g.*, rents from land, proceeds from the sale of merchandise, or interest on savings accounts. "Public revenue" is the government's income from taxes, duties, customs, or fines.

reversal: The appellate court's changing or annulling a lower court's decision. Distinguished from "remand," where the appellate court returns the case to the lower court for further proceedings.

reverse: To change or annul a lower court's decision, by ruling against the winning party in the lower court.

reversion: In property law, the residue of an estate returns to the grantor by operation of law upon the termination of the estate granted. The reversion takes effect when the owner grants an estate less than his own; the grantor or his heirs take possession upon the natural termination of the estate granted. *E.g.*, if *A* grants to *B* a life estate, when *B* dies, *A* or his heirs will take possession by operation of law. *See* remainder.

revert: To return to the original owner. In property law, the residue of an estate will "revert" to the grantor, under operation of law, upon the termination of the estate granted if it is less than the grantor's whole estate. *See* reversion.

reverter: "Possibility of reverter" exists in a grantor when he conveys a defeasible estate subject to a special limitation. Reversions exist in a grantor when he conveys a lesser estate and does not dispose of the remaining interest. Similar to "reversion."

review: A reexamination by the court or administrative body of its previous decision in a case; the examination of an appellate court of the decision of a lower court or administrative body.

revival: The renewal of an unexecuted judgment of a court when that judgment may not be executed without a new process or court order; the renewal of an expired contract obligation by giving a new promise or acknowledgment of the contract.

revocation: The cancellation or rescinding of power or authority granted to another; *e.g.*, revocation of an offer to contract, valid if made before the acceptance of the contract; revocation of a will; revocation of a deed or instrument.

revoke: To cancel or rescind a power or authority granted to another; to rescind privileges formerly granted. *E.g.*, the state board of examination may revoke a medical practitioner's license, for good cause.

rex: Lat. The king. Used in the names of English criminal prosecutions, *e.g., Rex v. Smith.*

rex non potest peccare: Lat. The king can do no wrong. Old English legal maxim that parties could not sue the king or his government in a tort or breach of contract action.

rider: An addition to a statute or contract which is annexed to the document and considered a part of the document, without having to rewrite the entire document, *e.g.*, a clause added to an insurance policy which specifically modifies the policy but does not necessitate revising the entire policy.

right: Inherent power or privilege to freely act; an inherent privilege or interest which is recognized and protected by the power of law. *E.g.*, in the United States, the "Bill of Rights" guarantees the right to worship freely and the right against self-incrimination, etc.; "civil rights," which belong to all American citizens, include the right to vote, the right to own property, the right to sue in court.

A legally enforceable claim of one person against another, *e.g.*, the right to exclude others from one's property, the right to have a contract performance, the right to receive damages for injuries received by another.

An interest in real or personal property, including the rights to freely use or convey the property.

right of action: The legal right to sue another which arises out of certain facts or conditions. *E.g.*, a breach of contract gives rise to a right of action to sue for performance on the contract.

right of entry: The right to possess or to regain possession of real property by peacefully entering the property upon breach of a condition created in the conveyance of certain defeasible estates.

right of first publication: In copyright law, the rule which protects against unauthorized publication of a work before it is published by the author. This is also called the "common law copyright" because the statutory copyright only protects works after publication.

right of way: The right of one to pass over or use the land of another. (*See* easement.) The strip of land upon which one exercises his right of way. In highway safety law, the right of one driver to proceed without stopping at an intersection when another driver approaches from a different direction.

right to work laws: Statutes which eliminate as a condition of employment the requirement that the employees join or pay dues to a labor union. Such statutes are permissible under section 14(b) of the National Labor Relations Act, and exist in about twenty states.

riot: A public disturbance involving the disorderly behavior of three or more people, threatening violence or acting in violence, which produces an injury to life or property or has the clear and present danger of producing injury to life or property.

riparian rights: The legal rights of owner of land adjacent to a stream or river to use the natural flow of the stream for reasonable purposes which do not obstruct another's use of the stream. The right includes land beneath the stream; it is limited to waterways, not including oceans or seas.

risk: Uncertainty about the future; the degree of danger or hazard associated with loss of life or property.

robbery: The taking of property from the person or presence of another by the use of force or by threatening the imminent use of force.

rogatory letters: A formal request from one judge to a second judge within another jurisdiction to take the testimony of a witness located within that jurisdiction.

roll: List of persons or property for a particular purpose, *e.g.*, "tax roll" of those subject to a particular tax. Record of the actions of a court, *e.g.*, "judgment roll," which includes the pleadings, admissions, orders, and judgment of every case decided by a court.

royalty: Payments to the owner of property for the business use of that property, expressed as a percentage of the profits or gross product, *e.g.*, payments to an author for the right to publish and distribute his copyrighted work or payments to the owner of mineral lands for the right to extract minerals.

rule: To decide the law; to require a certain action. A principle or standard established by authority; *e.g.*, the Supreme Court established the rights of a criminal defendant in *Miranda v. Arizona*.

Rule Against Perpetuities: In property law, the ancient rule that a future (or contingent) interest which, by any possibility, may not vest within twenty-one years after a life or lives in being at the time of its creation is void from the time it is created. The rule was introduced to promote the free transfer of land and to restrict tying up the land indefinitely for some unknown claimant.

rule nisi: A proposed rule, introduced by one party, which will be made absolute and final unless the other party, against whom the rule is directed, shows cause why it should not be made final.

running with the land: An obligation or right "runs with the land" when it passes to all future owners and assignees of the land. A covenant or easement running with the land is valid if it affects the use or value of the land and is intended by the parties who form the covenant or easement.

S

sabotage: To purposely destroy or ruin property, *e.g.*, the destruction of a manufacturer's equipment by employees during a labor dispute.
said: Already referred to; aforementioned.
sale: Transaction between buyer and seller in which real or personal property is transferred from the seller to the buyer in exchange for some form of consideration.
salvage: To save property from loss or destruction. Personal property or goods that survive some destructive event, such as a flood.
sanction: To approve; to confirm; to ratify. To punish; to rebuke; to censure. A criminal penalty; a measure adopted by one nation against another in order to punish the latter for a violation of international law.
sane: Rational; reasonable; of sound mind.
satisfaction: The fulfillment of an obligation; the elimination of a debt owed.
saving: An act of fiscal economy that seeks to prevent waste or financial loss; preservation from forfeiture.
saving clause: A provision in a legislative act which maintains the validity of the act even though certain clauses of the act may be held invalid by a court. A provision in a legislative act which excepts a specific item or concern from the general body of things mentioned in an act, *e.g.*, a clause that preserves legal remedies at common law from an act that repeals a prior statute and its statutory remedies.
S.B.A.: *See* Small Business Administration.
schedule: A listing; a roster; a timetable. A writing attached to a legal document which lists in detail the items referred to in the document, *e.g.*, a listing of the prior owners of a parcel of property referred to in a deed.
scienter: Lat. Knowingly. Intentionally; purposely; with knowledge.
scintilla: Lat. A spark; a trifle. The "scintilla doctrine" holds that if there is any evidence at all in a case that tends to support a material issue the case should not be taken from the jury, but left to their decision.
scire facias: Lat. You have cause to know. A judicial writ that requires a person bound by a judgment to show cause why the person bringing the writ should not have advantage of the judgment.
scope of employment: The duties or conduct of an employee that fall within the parameters of his job or position.
scrip: Paper currency issued for temporary use. A writing which entitles the bearer to receive something of value, *e.g.*, the right to exchange the scrip for shares of stock.
scrivener: A writer; one who prepares and writes out legal instruments, such as, contracts of sale.
scroll: A rolled-up parchment which contains writing, frequently a formal legal document. Mark made with a pen, intended to take the place of a seal.
seal: Any symbol or mark that indicates a legal document has been formally executed.
search: An investigation of property or person with the purpose of seeking to find prohibited articles.
search and seizure: In a criminal investigation by law enforcement officials, the practice of searching persons or property and confiscating any items found during the search that are relevant to the investigation.
search warrant: Written court order issued by a judge to a law enforcement official granting permission for the official to search and confiscate any property that is material evidence with respect to a criminal investigation.
seaworthiness: Word that describes a ship's ability to sail and to engage in those activities that it was designed to engage in.
S.E.C.: *See* Securities Exchange Commission.
secondary boycott: Any association of two or more persons formed to exert pressure on the customers of a business with the purpose of causing the customers or the suppliers of the business not to deal with it.

secondary evidence: Evidence that is not original or first-hand evidence, *e.g.*, a photocopy of an agreement.
Secretary of State: The principal appointed official in the federal government charged with carrying out American foreign policy. In most state governments, the elected official charged with registering corporations and other formal duties with respect to licensing and recording.
secundum: Lat. According to.
secured creditor: A creditor who holds pecuniary assurance of payment of his debt, such as by a lien on property, a mortgage, or collateral.
securities: Written certificates indicating obligations owed or ownership of property and assets.
Securities Exchange Commission (S.E.C.): Established in 1934 to regulate the trading and sale of stocks, bonds and other securities.
security: A written certificate that indicates an indebtedness is owed or ownership in property, *e.g.*, a share of stock or a debenture. Collateral; assurance of payment; deposit.
security deposit: Funds given by a lessee to a lessor to guarantee his compliance with the terms of the lease.
sedition: Any communication which advocates treasonous conduct or the illegal overthrow of any lawfully constituted government.
seduction: The act of one person inducing another to engage in sexual intercourse without the use of force.
seisin: Ownership and possession of real property under lawful title.
seizure: Confiscation of property; the taking of property by a law enforcement official, *e.g.*, the taking of a person's property to satisfy a judgment against him.
Selective Service System: Created in 1980 to organize a system for conscription.
self-dealing: Situation where a fiduciary or trustee uses confidential information obtained from his position of trust for his own personal enrichment; insider trading.
self-defense: Right of a person to take any action necessary to protect himself or his family from harm by another.
self-incrimination: Any action or admission made by a person that implicates that person in the commission of a crime, either before trial or at trial.
seller: Person who exchanges goods or property in return for money or its equivalent; vendor.
Senate: The upper chamber in a bicameral state legislature. The upper chamber in the United States Congress, comprised of two elected representatives from each state.
sentence: A court judgment that imposes a penalty upon a person convicted of a crime, *e.g.*, a prison term imposed on a person found guilty of bribery.
separate estate: The real or personal property solely owned by a person who also owns other property jointly with another person in a marital or business relationship.
separate maintenance: Funds paid by one married person to another for support and financial assistance if they are no longer living together as a married couple.
separate property: Those assets solely owned by a married person and which are not jointly owned by both partners in the marriage.
separation: A division; a split. Situation where a married couple lives apart from each other though they do not divorce.
separation agreement: Compact between a married couple that is about to divorce or separate that divides up property, allocates income and determines who has custody of the children.
separation of powers: Division of authority between the various branches of government. One branch of government is not permitted to impinge on the duties of another; *e.g.*, the judiciary is not permitted to legislate and enact laws, which is the domain of the legislature.
sequester: To isolate; to quarantine; to keep from the public, *e.g.*, to keep members of a jury from the public while a trial is in progress.
sergeant at arms: Person appointed by a legislative body or other organization to keep order while the legislative body is in session or while the organization is meeting.
seriatim: Lat. Severally. Individually; one by one; in order.
servant: Employee; a person who works for another person; a person in the employ of another; an agent.
service: To perform a job; to render labor for the benefit of another. A department or agency of government, *e.g.*, the armed services. The delivery of any communication.
service of process: The delivery of a summons, a complaint, or any notice of a legal proceeding to a person.
servient: Subject to a servitude; encumbered by an obligation; *e.g.*, a servient estate is an estate that is obligated to provide a benefit for another estate.
servitude: A burden or an obligation imposed upon one estate for the benefit of another estate, *e.g.*, an estate that must provide water to another estate free of charge. State or condition in which a person willingly or unwillingly is a servant for another.

session: A meeting of a legislative or judicial body for a specific period of time, *e.g.*, a court's daily sitting.
set aside: To reverse a judgment; to vacate a prior court's decision. To reserve funds for a specific purpose.
set-off: A counterclaim demand brought by a defendant, extrinsic to the cause of action, to reduce the amount of the plaintiff's recovery; *e.g.*, a counterclaim demand based on breach of contract brought by a defendant in a tort action for the purpose of reducing plaintiff's possible recovery.
settle: To resolve a dispute; to agree to terms; to reach agreement.
settlement: An agreement which resolves conclusively a dispute or conflict between two or more persons, with judicial approval usually not required.
settlor: A person who creates a trust. The person who furnishes the corpus for a trust.
sever: To separate; divide; bifurcate; *e.g.*, to separate a cause of action into a trial to determine liability and a trial to fix damages.
severable: Capable of being divided or separated, *e.g.*, an estate that can be divided into smaller estates.
severalty: To have individual or sole control over something. *E.g.*, severalty in estate means that a person owns an estate exclusively and not with any other person.
severance: The state of being divided or separated.
sham: Without merit; spurious; bogus; false. *E.g.*, a sham pleading is a pleading that is spurious and has no legal basis.
share: A person's interest in the ownership of some asset or entity; the portion of some benefit or liability that is allotted to a person. A single unit of stock that represents ownership in a business entity.
Shelley's Case, Rule in: Early English common law rule that holds that conveyance of an estate for life to a person, and with the remainder to the grantee's heirs, in fact gives the grantee title in fee simple absolute and the heirs get nothing. *E.g.*, Red, owner in fee simple of Blackacre, conveys Blackacre to Blue for life and the remainder to the heirs of Blue. Under Shelley's Rule, Blue takes Blackacre in fee simple absolute, getting both the life estate and the remainder.
sheriff: Chief law enforcement official of a county.
Sherman Antitrust Act: Federal statute which prohibits any contract, combination, or conspiracy in restraint of interstate or foreign trade or commerce and which also prohibits any monopoly or attempt to monopolize interstate or foreign trade or commerce.
short sale: A sale of shares of stock which the seller does not own or control at the time the sale is negotiated but which he acquires prior to the time the delivery of the shares to the buyer is required.
show cause: Give proof; provide a reason.
shyster: A deceitful person; an unethical individual; most commonly used to refer to an unethical and unscrupulous lawyer.
sic: Lat. Thus; in such manner; as it appears. The word is used in written texts to indicate that a misspelling of a word or a grammatical error found in a quotation can also be found in the original text and is to be read as it appears.
signature: A person's name as written by himself, *e.g.*, the name of an individual as written by himself and affixed to a contract.
simple negligence: The failure to exercise the needed degree of care in a particular situation as would be exercised by the typical careful person in the same situation.
simplex commendatio non obligat: Lat. Mere recommendation does not bind. Used with respect to sellers' representations: A recommendation of a good by a vendor does not create an obligation like a warranty.
sine: Lat. Without.
sine die: Lat. Without day. Without assigning a day for holding the next meeting, *e.g.*, when the United States Senate adjourns without fixing the date on which it will next meet.
sine qua non: Lat. Without which not. An essential qualification or requirement. *E.g.*, a person must be thirty-five years of age to be elected President of the United States.
slander: Oral defamation; spoken words that defame a person in front of others and that cause harm or some damage.
slander of title: An erroneous and malicious statement that asperses a person's legal title to and ownership of real or personal property.
slip decision: A separate and early printing of a court's opinion before it is printed in the court reporters.
Small Business Administration: A federal agency whose mission is to encourage, promote and protect the interests of American small business.
Small Claims Court: Court established to deal solely with civil suits involving small amounts of money.
smart money: Punitive damages awarded a plaintiff in a civil action because of the defendant's extremely improper behavior.
Smith Act: Federal statute which prohibits any seditious activity, including the advocating of the overthrow of the government by violence or other unlawful means.
smuggling: The crime of bringing goods in or out of a country that are either prohibited or where there has been a failure to pay custom charges owed on the goods.

socage: Under medieval English law, land occupied by a person who rendered certain services to the owner in fee simple of the property for the right to occupy and enjoy the property.
Social Security Act: Federal statute which provides supplemental income to the retired, the disabled, or the survivors of a person who was covered by the act. The social insurance programs that fall within the act's guidelines are funded by mandatory contributions from employees and employers at a rate established by Congress.
sodomy: Copulation by a person with a person of the same sex, an animal, or unnatural copulation with a member of the opposite sex.
solatium: Compensation; damages awarded; payment made to a person who has suffered an injury, *e.g.*, compensation paid to a person whose feelings have been hurt.
Soldiers' and Sailors' Civil Relief Act: Federal statute that alters, or even defers, the civil liabilities of a person who is in the military and that sets forth specific procedures for persons who want to enforce their claims against persons in the military.
sole: Only; exclusive; one; single; individual.
solicitation: To entreat a person to engage in a specific type of behavior; to importune; to implore; to ask a person to do something; to request something of a person, *e.g.*, to implore a person to make a statement in court with respect to his opinion of a person's reputation.
Solicitor General: A federal official whose duty it is to represent the United States Government before the Supreme Court.
solvency: Capacity to pay debts as they are due; ability to meet financial obligations.
solvent: Capable of meeting the financial obligations one owes. *E.g.*, a person who can pay his debts as they come due is solvent.
sound: Valid; reliable; whole; true solvent; in good condition. Noise; utterance.
sovereign immunity: Theory that holds that a government or sovereign is immune or exempt from tort liability because of its status in society.
special agent: A person engaged by another to execute or conclude a particular deal or transaction, such as, a person hired by a corporation to sell a particular factory. A law enforcement officer assigned to a specific area or project.
special appearance: The presence of a person, a party to a legal proceeding by judicial summons before a court for the sole purpose of denying the jurisdiction of the court over his person with respect to the legal proceeding in question.
special damages: Damages which are the direct result of defendant's actions but are not the necessary or typical result of such conduct and therefore must be specifically pleaded by plaintiff in his cause of action.
special demurrer: A demurrer filed by a defendant in opposition to a plaintiff's cause of action which attacks with specifics the flaws in the composition or form of the plaintiff's pleading.
special indorsement: An indorsement that states to whose benefit a financial instrument is payable and therefore requires his signature for it to be exchanged for cash or other assets.
specialty: A legal instrument or agreement that is under seal; such as, a contract that is under seal. An area of expertise or proficiency, *e.g.*, a lawyer who has an area of expertise in the practice of admiralty law.
special verdict: Special finding by the jury on each material issue of the case, leaving the application of the law to the court; *e.g.*, in a negligence case, the jury finds that defendant was driving too fast under the circumstances.
special warranty deed: A deed in which the grantor of real property agrees to defend and protect the grantee's interest in and title to the property against all claims that arise out of the grantor's interest in the property.
specification: A detailed description or statement of some matter or item, *e.g.*, the provisions of a contract detailed in a separate schedule.
specific bequest: The giving of a gift of a specific item of personal property to a person as set forth in the provisions of a will.
specific performance: Equitable remedy granted by a court where there has been a breach of contract and where damages would be inadequate to compensate the injured party so that the court requires the breaching party to fulfill his obligations under the contract. The fulfillment or achievement of one's obligations under a contract.
speedy trial: The constitutional right of a person accused of a crime to a swift and expeditious trial.
spendthrift trust: A trust established for the benefit of a person that has restrictions attached to it so as to guard against that person's misuse or wasting of the trust's proceeds.
spite fence: A fence constructed for the sole purpose of annoying the owners of adjoining property.
splitting a cause of action: The separation of a cause of action into several different parts, claims, or actions.
spoliation: The destruction or severe modification of evidence.
spoliatus debet ante omnia restitui: Lat. A party despoiled ought first of all to be restored. A person un-

justly dispossessed of his property should be restored to possession.
squatter: A person who occupies and takes possession of real property without title or legal authority to do so.
stakeholder: A third party selected by two or more parties to hold money or some property until one of the parties can establish their legal right to it.
stale check: A check whose date of issue is so much earlier than the date on which it is presented for satisfaction that it will not be accepted.
stamp tax: The charge for getting legal documents certified or approved by a government official, *e.g.*, the cost of getting a contract certified by a county clerk.
stand: To remain valid; to be viable; to be in force. To present oneself; to submit oneself, *e.g.*, to present oneself as a candidate for public office. To remain upright; to be still; to remain motionless.
standing: To have the right to bring a suit or other legal action before a court of justice (*i.e.*, having a stake in the outcome); to be eligible to bring a cause of action against another party in a court of justice. A person's status, rank, or position within society, an organization or government.
standing mute: Where a defendant refuses to respond to the charge or charges brought against him.
Star Chamber: A medieval English court that principally heard criminal cases without the use of a jury and it could fix any penalty but death. It was eventually abolished because of abuses perpetrated on defendants.
stare decisis: Lat. To abide by decided cases. Judicial doctrine that holds that legal precedent will not be set aside unless there is good cause to do so.
state: A geographic region with its own government; a nation; a country; a commonwealth, *e.g.*, the United States of America or the State of Illinois. To assert; allege; express; aver.
state secret: Concealed, nonpublic information that is vital to the welfare and well-being of a country.
state's evidence: Testimony presented to a court by a party to a crime that incriminates others in the commission of a crime for the purpose of his receiving immunity from prosecution or a lesser sentence for his criminal conduct.
status: Condition; position; situation; rank.
status quo: The existing state of affairs; the condition of things at a certain time.
statute: A law; legislative enactment; codified rule of law.
statute of frauds: Law that holds that certain contracts may not be enforced unless there is some writing signed by the defendant to the dispute indicating that there was an agreement.
statute of limitations: Law that prohibits the bringing of any civil action or criminal prosecution after a specified period of time has elapsed from when the right to bring the action or prosecute the crime started.
statute of wills: Medieval English law that set forth the manner in which property could be bequeathed by a person to others upon his death.
statutes at large: The official listing of legislative enactments passed by Congress in a particular session.
statutory: Based on law; derived from or referring to a legislative enactment.
statutory rape: The crime of engaging in sexual intercourse with a female who is under the age of consent.
stay: The stopping of legal proceedings for a temporary period by court order.
stay of execution: The stopping or suspending of the performance of a court judgment for a temporary period, *e.g.*, the stopping of the performance of the death penalty upon a convicted murderer.
stealing: Theft; the felonious appropriation of another's personal property; the crime of taking another's property.
sterility: Inability to reproduce and have offspring.
stipendiary estate: Estate or real property given to a person for services rendered, generally of a military kind.
stipulation: Assumed fact; admission, or agreement between opposing parties in a judicial proceeding. A condition, term or proviso of an agreement.
stirpes: Lat. Descents, root; the base or stock of a tree. Used in reference to the descendants of a particular person or family. *See* per stirpes.
stock: Capital invested in a corporation; the equity interest in a business enterprise. A person's equity and ownership interest in a corporation. Merchandise; goods; inventory.
stockbroker: A person who acts as an agent for another in the selling and buying of stock and other securities.
stock dividend: Dividend distributed by a company to its stockholders in the form of the company's stock and which involves a transfer from the surplus capital to the stock account on the corporation's balance sheet in an amount equal to the dividend distributed.
stockholder: A person who owns shares of stock of a corporation and therefore has an ownership interest in the corporation.
stockholder's derivative action: A suit brought by a stockholder on behalf of his corporation against a third party to recover for injuries suffered by the corporation, the stockholder initiates the suit because

the corporation refuses to file suit against the third party.

stop order: A directive given by a stockholder to his stockbroker to buy shares of stock or other securities at a specified price above or to sell such securities at a specified price below their current market price.

stoppage in transitu: The right of a person who sells goods on credit to stop the transfer and transport of the goods to the buyer and to regain possession and control of the goods until he receives payment or suitable guarantee from the buyer.

stranding: The running aground and stopping of a ship on a shore, sandbar or other barrier.

stranger: An outsider; a person who has no privity to a relationship, transaction, or agreement.

straw man: A person who secretly acts on behalf of others while at the same time he represents himself to third parties as acting in his own behalf, *e.g.*, a person who buys a building in his own name from a third party but who is in fact purchasing the building on behalf of someone else.

strictissimi juris: Lat. Of the most strict law. To strictly and literally apply the law to a situation or person.

strict liability: Legal doctrine that holds a manufacturer or a seller liable for all the defects and injuries caused by his products regardless of the degree of care that he exercised.

strike: Work stoppage engaged in by employees as a means to get better terms of employment from their employer. To remove; delete; expunge. To hit; beat; *e.g.*, to hit a person repeatedly about their face.

struck jury: A jury convened to hear an important, profound or complex legal question.

sua sponte: Lat. Of his own will. To take a course of action without the suggestion of another, *e.g.*, a court may raise an issue sua sponte, *i.e.*, on its own.

sub: Lat. Under; upon.

subcontractor: A person who enters into an agreement with a contractor to perform part, or all, of the work the contractor has undertaken, *e.g.*, a person who handles the electrical wiring in a building that is being constructed.

subject matter: The topic or issue that is being considered; the issue in dispute before a court, legislature or an administrative body.

sublease: Agreement whereby a lessee grants his rights and interest in a lease to a third person for a period of time less than the lease.

submission: Agreement between two or more persons to submit a dispute to a court for judicial resolution. The acquiescing and giving in to the power or authority of another person or a government, *e.g.*, an escaped convict who turns himself into law enforcement officials.

sub modo: Lat. Subject to a condition or under a restriction.

sub nom/sub nomine: Under the name.

subordinate: To make subservient; to place at an inferior rank; to put in an inferior class, *e.g.*, to place a mortgage in a junior position to another mortgage loan.

subornation of perjury: The crime of inducing another person to make a false oath before a court.

subpoena: A judicial order requiring a person to appear in court and to give testimony with respect to a dispute before the court.

subpoena duces tecum: A judicial order requiring a person to bring all documents in his possession that pertain to the matter in dispute to the court.

subrogation: The placement of one person in the place of another so that he succeeds to that person's rights and obligations with respect to a third person.

subscribe: To sign a legal document or other agreement. To agree to buy a portion of the initial stock offering of a corporation. To pledge or contribute money to a cause.

subsidiary: Secondary in importance; subordinate in position or influence. A company having more than 50% of its stock owned by another company.

subsidy: Financial aid and assistance given to a business enterprise or other organization by government.

substance: The material aspect or part of something, *e.g.*, the essence of a legal argument.

substantial performance: The fulfillment of the material obligations that a person has under a contract so as to constitute complete performance of one's legal obligations under the contract.

substantive law: Statute or common law that creates, defines and regulates a person's rights in a particular area.

substituted service: Service of process upon a person by any authorized means other than personal delivery of the legal order to the person.

subtenant: A person who rents all or part of leased premises from the original lessee of the property for a period less than the term of the original lease; sublessee.

succession: Procedure by which property of a deceased person is transferred to another person, either by operation of statute or will. The act of following in sequence, *e.g.*, the replacement of a retired judge by his successor to the bench.

sudden passion: Anger or fury that is the immediate and direct result of an incident. Most commonly referred to with respect to the definition of manslaughter ("*i.e.*, heat of passion").

sue: To institute legal proceedings; to bring a civil action against another person; to file a cause of action against another.
suffrage: The right or privilege to vote.
suicide: The intentional taking or destruction of one's own life.
sui generis: Lat. Of its own kind. To be unique and different from all others.
sui juris: Lat. Of his own right. The capacity or ability to control one's life and make decisions with respect to how one's life will be ordered.
suit: Any legal proceeding initiated by a person; a civil action brought in a court of law to redress a wrong.
summary: (Noun) A concise description of a legal argument; digest of a judicial decision. (Adj.) Concise; condensed; brief.
summary judgment: Judgment rendered in favor of a party to a legal proceeding on an issue in dispute upon a motion by that party for judgment because there is no factual basis for holding against him and he is therefore entitled to prevail on the issue as a matter of law.
summary proceeding: Legal dispute which is settled promptly through the use of abbreviated judicial procedures, such as limited discovery and the use of a bench trial rather than a trial by jury, *e.g.*, a small claims court proceeding.
summing up: The restatement and summarization of evidence and arguments presented by counsel at the end of a trial by jury.
summons: Judicial writ issued by a court that orders a person to appear before the court so a civil action brought against the person by another party may be adjudicated.
supersede: To replace; to set aside; to displace, *e.g.*, to set aside a prior court ruling.
supersedeas: Judicial writ issued by an appellate court that stays or suspends lower court proceedings or decisions.
superseding cause: Conduct of a person that is so substantially responsible for an injury suffered by another person that the prior negligent conduct of other persons that also caused the injury is waived in determining liability.
supervening cause: The source or origin of an injury which is independent of all other causes and is the direct and proximate cause of the injury.
supplementary proceedings: Judicial hearing that follows a judgment issued by a court on behalf of a creditor against a debtor which has as its purpose the ascertainment of the assets and property of the debtor which are available to satisfy the judgment.
support: (Verb) To sustain; to bolster; to validate by the offering of additional proof, *e.g.*, to bolster a legal argument advanced by another person. (Noun)-Sustenance; maintenance provided for the upkeep of a person or a family; to furnish the necessary means so a person may go on living.
suppressio veri, expresso falsi: Lat. Suppression of the truth is the same as the expression of what is false.
supra: Lat. Above. The word is used to refer to a prior passage in a legal text.
Supreme Court: The highest judicial body in the United States. The highest judicial body in most states.
surcharge: To impose an additional tax; to inflict a supplementary cost on an individual or a corporation. To hold a fiduciary liable for his improper and negligent conduct in the carrying out of his fiduciary duties.
surety: A person who agrees to fulfill a financial obligation of another person upon that person's default of his obligation.
surname: A person's last name; a person's family name; *e.g.*, John Smith's surname is Smith.
surplusage: Extraneous material; nonessential matter.
surprise: (Noun) An unexpected event or happening, *e.g.*, an unexpected occurrence during a trial. (Verb) To stun or catch unaware.
surrebutter: Under common law pleading, the plaintiff's answer of fact to the defendant's rebutter.
surrejoinder: Under common law pleading, the plaintiff's answer of fact to the defendant's rejoinder.
surrender: To give up; yield; relinquish; *e.g.*, to relinquish a claim against property.
surrogate: Person who takes the place of another; a substitute. Title given to a judicial officer entrusted with the responsibility of supervising probate matters.
surtax: An additional tax imposed on top of another tax.
survivorship: Right to property or some other interest that a person possesses because he has outlived another.
suspended sentence: Criminal penalty of imprisonment that is imposed on the convicted person but which he is not required to serve.
suspension: An interruption; a postponement; *e.g.*, the interruption of a lawyer's right to practice law because of his improper conduct.
sustain: To uphold; maintain; to approve; *e.g.*, to uphold a lower court judgment.
syllabus: A summary outline of a decision or an argument.

symbolic delivery: The transferring of possession of real or personal property from one person to another by the transfer of some token object.

syndicate: A group of persons who join together for the express purpose of conducting a commercial transaction, *e.g.*, a group of brokers.

T

tacit: Implied understanding; silent agreement without any opposition.
Taft-Hartley Act: Federal labor legislation enacted in 1947, amending the Wagner Act of 1935, by limiting the power of labor unions. The Act imposed certain duties on unions, established unfair labor practices for unions, abolished the closed shop, established the rights of employees to revoke the union as their bargaining agent, and provided for the equal treatment of independent and affiliated unions.
tail: In property law, an "estate in tail" or "fee tail" is an estate which, at the death of the owner, goes to the lineal descendants or the "heirs of the body" of the owner, as long as there are lineal descendants. Today, the fee tail is rarely used in the United States.
talesman: A person added to the jury from among the bystanders at the courthouse, rather than being summoned in the normal manner.
tangible: Having a definite, physical existence. In property law, "tangible property" includes things like objects, buildings, and money. In evidence, "tangible evidence" refers to physical evidence which can be seen at trial, *e.g.*, the gun, the contract, the photographs.
tangible property: In property law, referring to things with a definite physical existence, *e.g.*, an object, a building, a bank account. "Intangible property" is not physical, *e.g.*, a copyright, an easement, goodwill, or rights under a contract.
tariff: The payment of customs or duties on goods imported into the United States. The "tariff schedule" lists rates for the various imports which are subject to the tariff. Tariffs may be "protective" (to help United States businesses against foreign competition), "retaliatory" (to force another nation to reduce its tariffs on United States goods) or "fiscal" (to raise revenue).
tax: The money or rate of money paid to government by its citizens for governmental services. A tax may be assessed on income, property, business, sales, inheritances, roads, mining, gifts, excess profits, capital gains, etc.
taxable income: The amount of income taxed, at varying rates depending on the amount. For individuals, taxable income is adjusted gross income minus deductions and exceptions. For businesses, taxable income is gross income.
tax evasion: Illegally paying less taxes than the law requires, a crime under *Internal Revenue Code §7201*. In contrast, "tax avoidance" is paying only the minimum amount of taxes required.
teller: An official counter. In banks, tellers take deposits and disburse withdrawals of money. In legislatures, tellers count the votes.
temporary injunction: A remedy granted temporarily by the court at the start of the litigation to prevent future injury to the person seeking the injunction, until the court has had an opportunity to make a final decision in the case. Also called "interlocutory injunction."
temporary restraining order (T.R.O.): A remedy granted temporarily by the court only in exceptional circumstances when the court cannot hold an immediate hearing. T.R.O. is granted to prevent further immediate and irreparable injury to the person seeking the order. The order may be granted without advance notice to the adverse party and lasts only until the court holds a hearing. *See Federal Rule of Civil Procedure 65(b).*
tenancy: The right to possess real property under a lease, subject to another's valid title. The landlord, who holds title, leases the exclusive right of possession to the tenant, withholding the landlord's right to enter to demand rent or to make repairs.
tenancy by the entirety: Ownership of property by a husband and wife together so that upon the death of either spouse the other will take full and complete ownership of the entire property. Neither spouse can sell the property without the consent of the other. A divorce terminates the tenancy by the entirety and creates a "tenancy in common."
tenancy in common: Undivided ownership in property by two or more persons, each having the same right to the use and possession of the property. Thus

each owner may separately partition, convey, sell, or dispose by will his share of the property.
tenant: Generally, one who possesses real property. Specifically, one who possesses real property under a lease given by the owner or "landlord," subject to the landlord's title.
tenant at sufferance: One who continues to possess real estate after his right to possession has terminated; also called a "holdover tenant." A tenant at sufferance has no estate and no privity with the landlord; he is not entitled to stay unless the landlord agrees to extend the lease. However, he may not be sued for trespass unless the landlord enters and demands possession.
tenant at will: One who possesses real estate under a lease which does not set a fixed term of tenancy. The tenancy may be terminated, upon proper notice, by either the landlord or the tenant at any time.
tenant for life: One who possesses real property for the term of his life, or the life of another person.
tender: Unconditional offer to pay or perform one's duties under a contract, along with the present ability to carry out the offer. If the other party refuses the offer, that party is in default, and the tendering party then has a right to sue for breach of contract. To make payment of money; to deliver a deed; to deliver stock certificates.
tender offer: In securities law, a corporation's direct offer to the shareholders of another corporation to purchase a certain number of shares at a given price or at a maximum price, in order to achieve control of the corporation. Tender offers are public and are regulated by federal and state securities laws.
tenement: Any structure permanently attached to land, *e.g.,* buildings, houses, apartments. Today, "tenements" usually refers to slum housing for the poor. Traditionally, it referred to any real property which might be possessed permanently.
Tennessee Valley Authority (T.V.A.): Established in 1933 to conduct a unified resource development program to promote economic growth in the Tennessee Valley area.
tenor: In pleadings, used to mean that the exact language of the deed or contract is included, rather than a paraphrasing of the language; *e.g.,* "the tenor of the contract that . . ."
tenure: Generally, the right to possess property. The duration of the right to hold public office; *e.g.,* federal judges hold tenure for life and good behavior. The right of some public employees (*e.g.,* teachers) to hold their positions permanently, subject only to removal for cause or for economic necessity (*e.g.,* declining enrollment). Tenure is also granted to teachers in some private schools and colleges.
term: A fixed period of time in contracts or deeds, *e.g.,* time to make payments, time of employment, time of lease. Any segment of a contract concerning a particular item, *e.g.,* price term, delivery term, payment term, etc. The period of time a court is mandated by law to hear cases. A "session" is the period of time a court actually hears cases.
territorial waters: Designated waters which are within the legal and political control of a nation, including inland rivers, waters within the tides, and seawaters extending three miles beyond the shore.
territory: Geographical area under control of an outside power. In the United States, territories are lands which are not part of any state, have not been admitted as a state, but are organized with legislatures and executive officers appointed by the president. *See U.S. Constitution, article IV, section 3.*
testacy: The condition of having left a will at one's death, opposed to "intestacy," having died without leaving a will.
testament: Formerly, one's statement regarding disposition of his personal property at his death, distinguished from a "will" which controlled disposition of real property, *e.g.,* "last will and testament." Today, the word "testament" is unnecessary, since a will may dispose of both real and personal property.
testamentary: Concerning a will or testament; describing a deed, contract, instrument, gift, etc., which takes effect only upon the death of the maker.
testamentary disposition: Disposition of property by gift, will, deed, or contract, which takes effect only upon the death of the grantor.
testamentum omne morte consummatur: Lat. Every will is perfected at death. Principle that a will must take effect only upon the death of the testator.
testate: Having left a will at one's death, opposed to "intestate," having died without leaving a will.
testator: A man who dies having left a will or testament.
testatrix: A woman who dies having left a will or testament.
testes ponderantur, non numerantur: Lat. Witnesses are weighed, not numbered. Principle that the credibility and strength of testimony should determine conflicts in the evidence, not the number of witnesses each side presents.
testimony: Statements by a witness under oath or affirmation, usually in court, connected with a legal proceeding. Testimony is one form of evidence.
theft: The illegal taking of another's property without the owner's consent, with the intent to permanently deprive the owner of its use. *See* larceny and robbery.
third degree: Using extended periods of interrogation, threatening violence, or employing actual vio-

lence when trying to extract a statement or confession from a criminal suspect. *See Miranda* warning.

third party: A person not involved in the specific litigation, contract, or transaction under consideration, but who may have incidental rights or interests to assert.

third party beneficiary: One who may receive a benefit under a contract without being a party to the contract, *e.g.*, the beneficiary under a life insurance policy stands to receive the proceeds of the policy, but never signs or agrees to the policy. Two parties may validly contract to confer benefits on a third party, even though the third party provides no consideration.

threat: Statement of intention to injure person or property through an unlawful act, along with the ability to injure, in order to coerce another.

three-mile limit: The distance offshore of three miles (or one marine league) represents the waters which are within the legal and political control of the nation inhabiting the shoreline.

ticket: In contracts, a receipt indicating that the holder has a specific and described right, *e.g.*, pawn tickets, baseball tickets, discount tickets, etc. Form for recording violations of the motor vehicle laws.

tipstaff: Traditionally, a court officer similar to the bailiff, appointed to guard prisoners, preserve good order, assist the judges and jury, etc.

title: In property law, the right to own and possess real and personal property. Usually applied to real property, "title" identifies the legal owner of the land. Designated at the beginning of each pleading, the identification of the court and the name of the parties. Generally, any mark or designation, *e.g.*, a book title, a patent title, or the title of an official.

to have and to hold: The traditional phrase used in a conveyance which signifies the estate granted; *e.g.*, "To *A* and his heirs, to have and to hold Blackacre, unto and for the use of *A* and his heirs forever."

toll: A charge for the use of public highways, *e.g.*, roads, bridges, or telephone lines. To end; to defeat; *e.g.*, the statute of limitations "tolls" the right to sue after a specified period of time.

tontine: A special kind of financial agreement, sometimes used in insurance policies, by which a group of investors share all the benefits exclusively. When any of them dies or defaults, the benefits are equally divided among those remaining.

tort: A wrongful injury; a private or civil wrong which is not a breach of contract. A tort is some action or conduct by the defendant which results from a breach of a legal duty owed by the defendant to the plaintiff, which proximately causes injury or damage to the plaintiff. Torts may be "intentional" (when the defendant intends to violate a legal duty) or "negligent" (when the defendant fails to exercise the proper degree of care established by law).

tortfeasor: The person who commits a tort.

tortious: Describing action or conduct which results from a breach of a legal duty which may subject the actor to liability.

total disability: The disability which prevents the employee from performing the substantial, gainful work required in his usual occupation, resulting in a loss of earning power, whether or not the disability is permanent, crippling, or physical.

total loss: In fire insurance policies, the complete destruction of the building or property, so that there are no substantial remains to reconstruct or restore to the original condition.

Totten trust: A trust arrangement by which the creator of the trust becomes the trustee for the beneficiary of the trust. The Totten trust may be revoked by the creator until the death of the creator or until the creator transfers control to the beneficiary.

to wit: Namely; that is to say. Phrase used to introduce an explanation, *e.g.*, "Defendant breached the contract, to wit, he did not deliver the goods."

town: A civil and political division of a state. In many states, the town is the unit of local government; in others, the county is the unit of local government and a town is part of the county.

township: In the United States government public lands survey, a township is a six-mile square tract of land. In many states, a township is simply a political unit for local government.

trademark: Any mark, picture, symbol, or stamp used to designate a certain product of a certain manufacturer and to distinguish it from other manufacturer's similar products. The trademark must be adopted by the manufacturer or merchant and affixed to the product. Generic names, personal names, place names, and common adjectives are not valid trademarks. The federal government gives trademark holders exclusive rights to use the trademark for 28 years; actions for infringement of trademark, may be brought in federal court.

trade-name: A description, including words or symbols, of the dealer or manufacturer of particular goods, distinguished from a trademark which is a description of the goods.

trade secret: A secret formula or other kind of information used in one's business for commercial advantage, *e.g.*, the recipe for Coca-Cola.

trade union: An organization of workers in the same trade or related trades with the purpose of achieving better wages, hours, or conditions of employment, *e.g.*, United Steelworkers, Ladies Garment Workers.

trade usage: The practice and customs of the participants in a particular trade relating to the forming and performing of contracts.

transaction: The activities around which a contract, crime, or some other legal matter develops, including negotiations, business management, other conversations, or events.

transcript: Anything transcribed or copied from an original (especially original legal documents). A "trial transcript" is a copy of the questions, answers, and statements made at a trial and recorded by the court reporter.

transfer: To convey, sell, or in any other way give possession or control of land to another. The act of conveying, selling, or giving away property.

transferred intent: Legal principal used in tort law which states that if a person intends to harm *A* and instead harms *B*, he is liable to *B* in tort even though the intent was not directed to *B*. The principle is also used in criminal law: when a person intends to murder *A* but instead murders *B*, the requisite intent for murder of *B* may be established.

transfer tax: Tax on the transfer of property, whether by sale or gift. The tax may be placed on the deed, on the gift, on the inheritance, or on securities.

transitory action: A cause of action which may be pursued in several places, as opposed to a "local" action which may be brought only in one place. Property and criminal actions are "local"; contract and tort actions are generally transitory.

trauma: A physical injury to the body, including any wound, shock, or psychological damage resulting from a particular emotional disturbance.

traverse: In common law pleading, a denial of the preceding pleading. The traverse may be "common" (a denial with no argument) or "special" (including an affirmative argument or explanation). A "general traverse" denies all allegations.

treason: Rebellion against one's own civil government. Treason against the United States is defined as "levying war against them, or, in adhering to their Enemies, giving them Aid and Comfort." *U.S. Constitution, article III, section 3.*

treasury notes: Promissory note with interest-bearing coupons issued by the United States for one to five years.

treaty: In international law, an agreement between two or more nations relating to international or external affairs. In the United States, the President may make a treaty which must be approved by the Senate before it takes effect.

treble damages: Damages awarded to the plaintiff three times the amount of his actual injury as found by the jury. Treble damages may be given only by statute, *e.g.,* they are awarded in antitrust cases under section 4 of the Clayton Act. *15 U.S.C. § 15.*

trespass: Wrongful interference with or damage to another's property (real and personal), including entering onto land, physical assault, or destruction of legal rights. In the old common law, any type of broad civil wrong or tort.

trial: Courtroom proceedings before a judge and jury to examine evidence, hear arguments, and decide the factual and legal questions presented in making a final decision.

tribunal: A court, composed of several judges, each with legal authority to decide cases.

tripartite: Having three parts.

trover: An old common law pleading to recover damages for a wrongful taking of property or to recover actual possession of the property. Trover originally developed for the recovery of lost property and later expanded to include taken property.

true bill: An indictment approved by the grand jury which indicates it is satisfied that the evidence presents a prima facie case against the accused.

trust: Property held by one person as trustee for the benefit of another. The trustee holds the legal title of the trust property and the beneficiary or "cestui que trust" holds the "equitable title" of the property. *See* constructive trust, precatory trust, and resulting trust.

trust deed: Document by which one person gives legal title to real property to another person as trustee where the property is given as security for the payment of a debt or performance of an obligation.

trustee: The person appointed to hold and manage property in trust for the benefit of another.

trustee in bankruptcy: Person who will take control of the property of the debtor, by running his business, liquidating his assets, defending his suits, contesting the claims, and eventually distributing his assets.

trust fund: The property or money held by the trustee in a trust for the benefit of another. Also called the "corpus" or the "res" of the trust.

trust receipt: A receipt stating the security arrangements surrounding bank-funded commercial sales of goods. The bank holds title (under the trust receipts) to the goods until the debt is paid by the buyer.

try: To examine or present evidence in courtroom proceedings in order to decide the issues raised.

turpis causa: Lat. Base cause. Immoral or base consideration is invalid to support a contract, *e.g.,* prostitution, embezzlement, or kidnapping.

turpitude: Conduct which is inherently immoral or dishonest. Some statutes provide that a witness may be impeached with evidence of a crime involving moral turpitude because it tends to contradict his credibility.

T.V.A.: *See* Tennessee Valley Authority.
tying in: Unfair contracting by a seller with substantial market power who refuses to sell a certain product unless the buyer also buys another product from the seller. Tie-in sales are illegal under the Clayton Act.

U

ultimate facts: Final and resulting facts inferred from evidentiary facts presented to a court and which are necessary for a court to reach a decision.
ultimatum: Lat. The last. The last and conclusive offer asserted by a person; the final proposal advanced by a party involved in negotiations or a dispute, *e.g.*, the last offer made by a person who is negotiating an employment contract.
ultra: Lat. Beyond. Extreme; *e.g.*, a person who is an ultraconservative is extremely conservative in his beliefs.
ultra vires: Lat. Beyond granted powers. Conduct that exceeds the powers granted to an entity, most commonly used in reference to corporate actions that exceed the powers granted to the corporation through its articles of incorporation or by state law.
unclean hands: Doctrine that asserts that a person who has defrauded his opponent in a transaction may not seek to avail himself of the equitable powers of a court with respect to that transaction.
unconscionability: Contract doctrine that holds where a commercial transaction or contract is so one-sided and beneficial to one party in the transaction that the contract will be voided because its terms when applied are onerous, burdensome and oppressive to the other party. The court may void the entire contract or that portion which it finds offensive.
unconstitutional: That which violates or contravenes the provisions of a constitution, *e.g.*, a state statute which violates the first amendment of the United States Constitution.
under-lease: A sublease; the leasing of property by a lessee to another person for a period of time less than the full term of the lease. The subleasing of a portion of the property leased by the lessee to another person for the duration of the lease.
understand: To perceive; discern; realize; know.
understanding: A contract; an agreement; an informal agreement, either written or oral, based upon the express provisions of a contract.
undertake: To engage in; to enter into, *e.g.*, to enter into a compact with another person.
undertaking: Compact; promise; agreement. Enterprise; venture; business endeavor.
underwrite: To insure against losses; to guarantee against loss or destruction, *e.g.*, to insure property. To assume financial responsibility; to insure the sale of stock or other securities.
underwriter: A financial institution or business, and any person associated with such entity, that insures the sale of stock or other securities issued by a business, government or a public agency. In insurance, the one who assumes the risk in exchange for the payment of a premium.
undisclosed principal: A person who engages an agent to act on his behalf in regard to a transaction while the other party to the transaction is not aware that the agent is acting on behalf of someone else.
undue influence: Inappropriate persuasion of another person which destroys that person's opportunity to make a rational choice, *e.g.*, the improper inducement of a person so that his last will and testament does not reflect his own wishes.
unethical conduct: Behavior that does not comport with the rules of conduct or standard of morality in a given situation, *e.g.*, conduct engaged in by a lawyer that does not meet the accepted and recognized standards of the profession.
unfair competition: Improper business conduct; dishonest commercial practices; fraudulent or deceptive business activities.
unfair labor practice: Action taken by an employer that violates an employee's rights as set forth in the National Labor Relations Act, *e.g.*, the interference by an employer in the internal affairs of a labor union.
uniform: Unchanging; invariable; consistent. The distinctive wardrobe of a group or organization, *e.g.*, the wardrobe worn by members of a police department.
uniform acts or laws: Statutes in particular subject areas that are drafted, formulated, and approved by the Commissioners on Uniform State Laws and

which are enacted, in whole or in part, by state governments.
Uniform Commercial Code (U.C.C.): Statute drafted, formulated, and approved by the Commissioners on Uniform State Laws that sets forth the rules which control commercial transactions and contracts. The statute has been enacted by all states except Louisiana.
unilateral: Pertaining to or involving one person, object or thing; one-sided, *e.g.*, action taken by one country without the assent, knowledge, or approval of another country.
unilateral contract: Agreement whereby one person makes an express promise to perform upon actual performance by the other party. The agreement is the exchange of a promise for an act.
unilateral mistake: Misunderstanding or erroneous judgment made by only one party to a contract with respect to the contract's terms or provisions.
union shop: Place of employment where all employees belong to a union.
United Nations: International political organization whose major purposes are the promotion of peace and justice and the protection of human rights.
United States Code Annotated (U.S.C.A.): Legal publication, in multi-volume form, that is comprised of the complete text of all federal statutes, brief summaries of federal and state court decisions that refer to the statutes, and historical and research references that relate to the statutes.
United States Code of Military Justice: Body of law that provides both the substantive and procedural law that governs the United States military and its members.
United States Commissioners: Officers of a federal district court, appointed by a judge of that court, who handle preliminary trial matters. This position has been replaced by that of United States Magistrate.
United States Courts of Appeals: Federal appellate courts. There is a court of appeals for each of the eleven federal circuits. The judges who sit on these courts of appeals are appointed by the President subject to approval by the United States Senate.
United States International Trade Commission (U.S.I.T.C.): Established in 1916; among other things, it has been called upon to carry out provisions of the Tariff Act of 1930, the Agricultural Adjustment Act of 1934, the Trade Expansion Act of 1962, the Trade Act of 1974, and the Trade Agreements Act of of 1979.
United States of America: Sovereign nation located in the Western Hemisphere which is composed of fifty states and other territories.
unity: Oneness; concurrent interests; the condition of being one in interest or possession of real or personal property.
unity of interest: The condition that cotenants' shares in a joint tenancy be equal and that they be acquired in the same transaction.
unity of possession: One of the essential properties of a joint estate, which requires that each joint tenant hold the same undivided possession of the whole.
unity of title: Phrase that recognizes that cotenants in a joint tenancy own their property under the same legal title.
universal agent: Person who has the power to act on behalf of another in all areas and who also has the authority to entrust this power of agency to another person as well.
universal partnership: Partnership where the partners agree to pool all of their assets or the benefit of the partnership for the length of their association.
unjust enrichment: Improper acquisition of property or money by a person at the expense of another which neither equity nor justice would condone, and is, therefore, a legally sufficient cause for failure to enforce a contract.
unlawful: Illegal; criminal conduct; extralegal activity.
unlawful assembly: The illegal meeting of a group of persons for the purpose of causing a civil disturbance or similar strife.
unlawful detainer: The illegal possession of real property by a person whose once valid right to possess the property is now extinguished.
unsound mind: Unhealthy intellect; infirm or sick mind.
unwritten law: Case law; any rule of law not set forth by statute or regulation enacted by a legislative body.
upset price: The minimum price for which real or personal property that is to be sold at an auction may be purchased.
usage: Customary practice; habitual act, *e.g.*, a well-known local custom.
use: (Noun) Practice; employ; usage. (Verb) To utilize; employ; operate.
usufruct: The privilege possessed by a person to the benefits of property owned by another.
usury: The lending of funds at an exorbitant rate or at a rate above that permitted by law.
utter: To speak; to make a sound. To issue; publish; emit, *e.g.*, to issue a forged security under the pretense that it is legitimate.
uxor: Lat. A wife.
uxoricide: The killing of a woman by her spouse.

V

v.: Abbreviation for "versus" in the name of a case; also used as an abbreviation for "vide" (see); "voce" (voice); "verb"; or "volume."
V.A.: *See* Veteran's Administration.
vacant: Empty, unoccupied.
vacate: To cancel; annul; set aside; rescind. To make an act void as "to vacate a judgment." To move out as in "vacating premises."
vagrant: An idle wanderer; a person who is capable of maintaining himself by lawful labor, but who refuses to work and lives without labor or on the charity of others.
vague: Indefinite; uncertain; imprecise; not capable of being understood.
valid: Legally binding; authentic; executed with proper formalities; authorized by law; incapable of being rightfully overthrown or set aside.
valuable consideration: A type of consideration upon which a promise may be founded. Some right, interest, profit, or benefit accruing to one party, or some forebearance, detriment, loss, or responsibility given, suffered, or undertaken by the other. Consideration in money or something which has monetary value.
value: The utility or worth of an object. "Value" is often used as an abbreviation for "valuable consideration," such as in the phrases "purchaser for value" and "holder for value."
value received: Phrase denoting that consideration has been given; usually used in a bill of exchange or promissory note to denote that lawful consideration has been given for it.
variance: In pleading, a discrepancy between two instruments or two allegations in the same cause, which should by law be consonant; such as a disagreement between the statements in the pleadings and the evidence adduced in proof thereof. In zoning, permission to use property in such a way as is otherwise prohibited by the zoning law.
vendee: A purchaser or buyer; one to whom anything is sold. Term generally refers to one who buys land. One who buys goods is usually called a "buyer."
vendor: A seller; one who sells anything. Generally refers to one selling real estate. One who sells goods is usually called a "seller."
vendor's lien: In equity a lien belonging to a vendor for the unpaid purchase price of land where the vendor has not taken any other lien or security. Also applies to the sale of chattels.
venire facias: Lat. Make to come. A writ to a sheriff to summon a jury.
venire facias de novo: Lat. A writ to summon a jury for a new trial; a writ to compel a new trial of an action.
venue: (Formerly spelled "visne.") The neighborhood; the particular county or geographical area in which a court with jurisdiction may hear and determine a case. In common law pleading and practice venue referred to the place, neighborhood, or county in which an injury took place.
verdict: The formal decision of a jury concerning the matters submitted to it in the trial of a lawsuit. A verdict may be general or special. In a general verdict the jury decides which side wins, and how much, if applicable. A verdict is special when the jury is given specific questions of fact to answer and based on those answers the court determines which party is to have judgment.
verification: Confirmation of the correctness, truth, or authenticity of something (such as a pleading) by means of an affidavit, oath, or deposition.
versus: Lat. Against. In the title of a case the plaintiff's name is put first followed by "versus" and the defendant's name. Commonly abbreviated as "v." or "vs.," *e.g., Smith v. Jones.*
vest: To give an immediate, fixed right of present or future enjoyment.
vested: Fixed, accrued, absolute, fixed in interest, indefeasible, not contingent. Generally used to describe any right or title to something which is not dependent upon the occurrence or nonoccurrence of some condition precedent. The right must be more than a mere expectation; it must become a title, legal or equitable, to the present or future enforcement of

some demand. *E.g.*, pension plan benefits are vested if they are not contingent on the employee continuing to work for the employer.

Veteran's Administration (V.A.): Federal government agency that administers the system of benefits for veterans of the armed services and their dependents. Benefits include: medical care; monetary benefits for illness, injury, or death related to military service; benefits to widows and minors of deceased veterans; education and rehabilitation; home loan guaranty; and burial.

veto: Lat. I forbid. To refuse to sign a law enacted by the legislative branch of the government.

vexatious litigation: Proceeding instituted which is not bona fide, but which is instituted without probable cause, maliciously, or intended to harass the opponent.

viability: Capability of living. Generally term is applied to a newborn child to denote the power it possesses to continue its independent existence.

vicarious liability: The liability of one person for the acts of another; indirect legal responsibility, *e.g.*, the liability of the employer for the acts of an employee.

vice: (Noun) A fault, defect, or imperfection. Immoral conduct, practice, or habit. (Adj.) Lat. Instead of; in the place of; *e.g.*, vice president.

vi et armis: Lat. With force and arms.

violation: Breach of right, duty, or law; injury; rape.

vis: Lat. Force or violence.

visa: The endorsement on a passport or other official document by foreign authorities allowing a person to enter another country.

vis major: Lat. A higher force, an irresistible force, *e.g.*, a storm or earthquake.

vitiate: To destroy the legal or binding effect of something, such as an act or instrument; to invalidate; to impair. *E.g.*, fraud vitiates a contract.

viva voce: Lat. The living voice; by word of mouth. In evidence, term means oral testimony as opposed to written evidence such as affidavits or depositions. In relation to voting, term means voting by outcry rather than by written ballots.

viz: Lat. Abbreviation of "videlicet." Namely; that is to say; to wit.

void: Of no legal force or binding effect, null, nugatory, incapable of being ratified. *Contrast* with voidable.

voidable: Defective, but capable of confirmation or ratification. *E.g.*, a minor does not have the capacity to enter into a contract; therefore, any contract he makes is voidable. However, the contract is not void, and, therefore, it is binding on the competent party unless the minor repudiates it. A voidable transaction is one which can be affirmed by a party entitled to void it.

voir dire: Lat. To speak the truth. An examination of a person as a prospective juror to test his competency and prejudice. Preliminary examination of a witness in order to determine his or her competency to speak the truth.

volenti non fit injuria: Lat. To a willing person no injury is done. Torts maxim meaning that one cannot usually claim damages when he, knowing and comprehending the danger, consented to the action which caused the damage.

Volstead Act: Federal law passed under the eighteenth amendment to the U.S. Constitution which prohibited the manufacture, sale, or transportation of liquor. Repealed by the twenty-first amendment.

voluntary: Acting without compulsion, intended; acting on one's own initiative without being paid to do so; unimpelled by another's influence. In regards to statutes, often implies knowledge of essential facts.

volunteer: A person who acts without an express or implied promise or remuneration. A person who enlists in the armed services without being compelled by a military draft. An intruder who intermeddles.

voting trust: An arrangement by which shares of stock in a corporation are pooled and held in trust for the purpose of voting them at stockholder's meetings. Voting trusts are generally created for the purpose of electing officers or controlling the activities of the corporation.

voucher: A receipt or other evidence of payment; written proof of a transaction; a book of accounts containing the company's receipts; a document giving evidence of an expenditure.

W

wager: A gamble or bet; an agreement between two persons that one will pay the other a sum of money or other stake if a certain thing happens or does not happen. The parties have no interest in the event except that arising from the possibility of such gain or loss.
wager of law: Obsolete common law procedure by which a defendant would give security in an action on a debt that he would "wage" his law, meaning that he would appear at the set time and would give an oath as to his innocence, and bring with him eleven neighbors (called compurgators) to swear that they believed his truthfulness.
Wagner Act: The National Labor Relations Act, federal law giving employees the right to organize, to form unions, and to bargain collectively with employers. The Act also set up the National Labor Relations Board to help enforce the new labor laws. *See U.S.C. §§ 151 et seq; 49 Stat. 449 (1935).*
waive: To voluntarily give up, relinquish, renounce, or disclaim a privilege, right, or benefit. It is assumed that one who waives a right does so intentionally and with full knowledge of the facts.
waiver: The voluntary and intentional giving up or renouncing of a known right, benefit, or privilege. A waiver may be either "express," such as an oral or written statement, or "implied" from circumstances.
wanton: Reckless, heedless, malicious; extreme recklessness or foolhardiness; disregardful of the rights or safety of others or of consequences.
ward: A person, usually a minor or incompetent, who is under guardianship. Subdivision of a city, borough, county, or parish for election and other purposes.
warden: Guardian; keeper; guard; the superintendent of a prison.
ward of the court: Person whose rights and safety are guarded by the court, *e.g.,* minors and mentally incompetent people.
warehouseman: A person who is engaged in the business of accepting and storing goods for compensation or profit. *See U.C.C. §7-102.*
warehouse receipt: A receipt issued by a person engaged in the business of storing goods for hire. *See U.C.C. §1-201(45).*
warrant: Written authority. An order from a court or other authorized body to an officer, directing the officer to arrest a person, search a house, etc. In commercial and property law, to state that something is true; act of guaranteeing, assuring. An order authorizing a payment of money by one person to a third person.
warranty: Promise that certain facts are true. Guarantee concerning goods or land, which is expressly or impliedly made to a purchaser by the vendor. Statement or promise made as part of a transaction upon which the transaction depends; *e.g.,* in an insurance contract, the insurance company could refuse to pay a claim if a statement made in the application is false. An agreement to be responsible for all damages that arise from the falsity of a statement or assurance of a fact.
warranty of fitness: Where the seller has reason to know any particular purpose for which the goods are required, and that the buyer is relying on the seller's skill or judgment to select or furnish suitable goods, there is, unless excluded or modified, an implied warranty that the goods shall be fit for such purpose. *See U.C.C. §2-315.*
warranty of merchantability: Warranty made by the seller that the goods are reasonably fit for general purposes for which they are sold. *See U.C.C. §2-314.*
waste: Abuse, destruction, misuse, alteration, or neglect of property in one's rightful possession, but belonging to somebody else. Waste may be permissive (mere neglect or omission to do what is necessary to prevent injury), voluntary (doing some act which causes the damage), or ameliorative (making unauthorized, unnecessary improvements).
watercourse: A stream of water flowing in a definite direction or channel with banks.
watered stock: Stock that is issued by a company as though it were paid in full when it has not been, *e.g.,* shares issued for no consideration or at a discount.

weapon: An instrument used for offensive or defensive combat, *e.g.,* gun, knife, club, or any device for inflicting harm or for protecting oneself against an attacker. Often defined by state statute.

weight of the evidence: The balance or preponderance of evidence; the weight of the evidence is that which is more believable and is superior to the evidence submitted by the other side in a case. "Weight" does not refer to quantity, but rather to how convincing is each side's evidence.

wergild, wergeld: In Saxon law, the fine or price imposed for homicide or other atrocious personal offense. Part of the fine went to the king for the loss of a subject and part went to the relatives of the deceased.

wharfage: Compensation for the use of a wharf; money paid for landing goods upon or loading them from a wharf.

wharfinger: A person who owns or keeps a wharf for the purpose of receiving and shipping goods thereon for hire.

whereas: When in fact; that being the case; considering that; because; in view of the following facts; a word introducing the recital of a fact.

whiplash injury: A personal injury involving the neck where the head is thrown violently forward and back or from side to side. Commonly caused by an automobile accident.

white slaver: The interstate transportation of females for immoral purposes; holding females for prostitution. *See* Mann Act.

wildcat strike: A strike by union workers that is not authorized by union officials.

Wild's Case, Rule in: In property law, a rule of construction that a devise to *B* and his children or issue, *B* having no issue at the time of the devise, gives him an estate tail; but if he has issue at the time, *B* and his children take as joint tenants, or as tenants in common according to the other words of the will. *77 E.R. 277 (1599).*

will: A person's declaration of how he wishes his property to be disposed of after his death. A will is revocable during the testator's or testatrix's lifetime. Most states require that it be in writing and be witnessed. Minors and persons of unsound mind have no legal capacity to make a will.

willful, wilful: An act which is intentional, deliberate, knowing, or voluntary, as distinguished from accidental. With evil motive or unlawful intent; malicious.

winding up: The liquidation of a partnership or corporation by finishing current business, settling accounts, turning property into cash, and splitting up the assets. Winding up may be either voluntary or involuntary, such as when it is court ordered. Liquidation procedures are usually prescribed by state statutes.

withdrawal: Removal of money or security from the place where it is deposited, such as a bank. The abandonment of a crime by a coconspirator. Withdrawal requires that the coconspirator must evidence dissapproval of or opposition to the criminal activities and communicate it to the coconspirators or give complete disclosure to authorities.

without prejudice: Phrase declaring that no rights or privileges of the contesting parties have been affected by the disposition of the matter before the court. A dismissal "without prejudice" allows a new suit to be brought on the same cause of action without being affected by res judicata.

without recourse: Phrase used in a qualified endorsement of a negotiable instrument, stating that the indorser will not be responsible for payment if the party primarily liable does not pay. *See U.C.C. §3-414(1).*

witness: One who sees or perceives an act or event being done. One who testifies under oath at a trial or hearing as to what he has seen, heard, or otherwise observed. To be present at the signing of, and often to sign, a legal document such as a deed or a will. One who is a witness to a signature on a will or deed attests to its authenticity.

words of art: Terms that are used in a special way by members of a profession, line of work or study, *e.g.*, legal words of art have either no meanings or different meanings outside of a legal context.

words of limitation: A clause in a conveyance which declares how long the estate transferred thereby shall continue. Words of limitation actually indicate the type of estate transferred. Phrases such as "heirs" or "heirs of the body" are words of limitation.

worker's compensation laws: Statutes that provide funds to pay workers for injuries or illnesses arising out of or in the course of employment, regardless of whether the injury was due to the fault or negligence of the employee. The statutes generally establish the liability of the employer and, if the injury is covered by the statute, the employee's only remedy against the employer is that which the statute provides.

work-product: In civil practice, a class of materials which are given protection from discovery, such as work done by an attorney in the process of representing his client. The adverse party may obtain discovery only upon a showing of substantial need of the materials in preparation of his case and that he is unable without undue hardship to obtain the substantial equivalent by other means. *See 34 F.R.D. 212, 213.*

wound: (Noun) An injury to the body usually involving the breaking of the skin or mucous membranes as the result of violence. (Verb) To inflict a cut, laceration, or bruise.

writ: A formal written command or authorization of the court issued to an officer, directing him to act in some way.

writing, written: Printing, typewriting, or any other intentional reduction to tangible form. A document as opposed to mere spoken words. *See U.C.C. §1-201(46).*

writ of coram nobis: In our presence; before us, *i.e.*, before our court. Writ used to obtain review of a judgment for the purpose of correcting errors of fact in a criminal or civil proceeding. Also referred to simply as "coram nobis."

writ of execution: Court's order to the sheriff to enforce a judgment of the court issuing the writ.

wrong: A violation or invasion of the legal rights of another or of a legal duty. A wrong may be private which would allow for compensation to an individual or public such as a crime.

wrongful death statute: Statute which allows a survivor or executor of a decedent's estate the right to sue for any wrongful act or negligence that caused the decedent's death. Wrongful death statutes exist in every state. At common law the death of an individual could not be a cause of action in a civil suit.

Y

year books: Annual reports of old English cases from the time of King Edward II to Henry VIII.
yellow dog contract: Employment contract which states that an employee will not join a labor union under penalty of dismissal. Such contracts are now illegal under NLRA.
yield: To give up, relinquish, surrender, succumb, submit, cease opposition. Return from an investment or expenditure of money or labor. Real property law: To perform a service due by a tenant to his lord.

Z

zoning: Legislative action dividing a city or county into areas for the purpose of limiting the use to which land may be put, minimum size of lots, building types, etc.

Appendix A

The Declaration of Independence

In Congress, July 4, 1776

The Unanimous Declaration of the thirteen united States of America

When in the Course of human events, it becomes necessary for one people to dissolve the political bands which have connected them with another, and to assume among the powers of the earth, the separate and equal station to which the Laws of Nature and of Nature's God entitle them, a decent respect to the opinions of mankind requires that they should declare the causes which impel them to the separation.—We hold these truths to be self-evident, that all men are created equal, that they are endowed by their Creator with certain unalienable Rights, that among these are Life, Liberty and the pursuit of Happiness.—That to secure these rights, Governments are instituted among Men, deriving their just powers from the consent of the governed,—That whenever any Form of Government becomes destructive of these ends, it is the Right of the People to alter or to abolish it, and to institute new Government, laying its foundation on such principles and organizing its powers in such form, as to them shall seem most likely to effect their Safety and Happiness. Prudence, indeed, will dictate that Governments long established should not be changed for light and transient causes; and accordingly all experience hath shown, that mankind are more disposed to suffer, while evils are sufferable, than to right themselves by abolishing the forms to which they are accustomed. But when a long train of abuses and usurpations, pursuing invariably the same Object evinces a design to reduce them under absolute Despotism, it is their right, it is their duty, to throw off such Government, and to provide new Guards for their future security.—Such has been the patient sufferance of these Colonies; and such is now the necessity which constrains them to alter their former Systems of Government. The history of the present King of Great Britain is a history of repeated injuries and usurpations, all having in direct object the establishment of an absolute Tyranny over these States. To prove this, let Facts be submitted to a candid world.—He has refused his Assent to Laws, the most wholesome and necessary for the public good.—He has forbidden his Governors to pass Laws of immediate and pressing importance, unless suspended in their operation till his Assent should be obtained; and when so suspended, he has utterly neglected to attend to them.—He has refused to pass other Laws for the accommodation of large districts of people, unless those people would relinquish the right of Representation in the Legislature, a right inestimable to them and formidable to tyrants only.—He has called together legislative bodies at places unusual, uncomfortable, and distant from the depository of their public Records, for the sole purpose of fatiguing them into compliance with his measures.—He has dissolved Representative Houses repeatedly, for opposing with manly firmness his invasions on the rights of the people.—He has refused for a long time, after such dissolutions, to cause others to be elected; whereby the Legislative powers, incapable of Annihilation, have returned to the People at large for their exercise; the State remaining in the mean time exposed to all the dangers of invasion from without, and convulsions within.—He has endeavored to prevent the population of these States; for that purpose obstructing the Laws for Naturalization of Foreigners; refusing to pass others to encourage their migration hither, and raising the conditions of new Appropriations of Lands.—He has obstructed the Administration of Justice, by refusing his Assent to Laws for establishing Judiciary powers.—He has made Judges dependent on his Will alone, for the tenure of their offices, and the amount and payment of their salaries.—He has erected a multitude of New Offices, and sent hither swarms of Officers to harrass our people, and eat out their substance.—He has kept among us, in times of peace, Standing Armies, without the Consent of our legislatures.—He has affected to render the Military independent of and superior to the Civil power.—He has combined with others to subject us to a jurisdiction foreign to our constitution, and unacknowledged by our laws; giving his Assent to their Acts of pretended Legislation:—For quartering large bodies of armed troops among us:—For protecting them, by a mock Trial, from punishment for any Murders which they should commit on the Inhabitants of these States:—For cutting off our Trade with all parts of the world:—For imposing Taxes on us without our Consent:—For depriving us in many cases, of the benefits of Trial by Jury:—For transporting us beyond Seas to be tried for pretended offences:—For abolishing the free System of English Laws in a neighbouring Province, establishing therein an Arbitrary government, and enlarging its Boundaries so as to render it at once an example and fit instrument for introducing the same absolute rule into these Colonies:—For taking away our Charters, abolishing our most valuable Laws, and altering fundamentally the Forms of our Governments:—For suspending our own Legislatures, and declaring themselves invested with power to legislate for us in all cases whatsoever.—He has abdicated Government here, by declaring us out of his Protection and waging War against us.—He has plundered our seas, ravaged our Coasts, burnt our towns, and destroyed the lives of our people.—He is at this time transporting large Armies of foreign Mercenaries to compleat the works of death, desolation and tyranny, already begun with circumstances of Cruelty & perfidy scarcely paralleled in the most barbarous ages, and totally unworthy the Head of a civilized nation.—He has constrained our fellow Citizens taken Captive on the high Seas to bear Arms against their Country, to become the executioners of their friends and Brethren, or to fall themselves by their Hands.—He has excited domestic insurrections amongst us, and has endeavoured to bring on the inhabitants of our frontiers, the merciless Indian Savages, whose known rule of warfare, is an undistinguished destruction of all ages, sexes and conditions. In every stage of these Oppressions We have Petitioned for Redress in the most humble terms: Our repeated Petitions have been answered only by repeated injury. A Prince, whose character is thus marked by every act which may define a Tyrant, is unfit to be the ruler of a free people. Nor have We been wanting in attentions to our British brethren. We have warned them from time to time of attempts by their legislature to extend an unwarrantable jurisdiction over us. We have reminded them of the circumstances of our emigration and settlement here. We have appealed to their native justice and magnanimity, and we have conjured them by the ties of our common kindred to disavow these usurpations, which, would inevitably interrupt our connections and correspondence. They too have been deaf to the voice of justice and of consanguinity. We must, therefore, acquiesce in the necessity, which denounces our Separation, and hold them, as we hold the rest of mankind, Enemies in War, in Peace Friends.—

We Therefore, the Representatives of the United States of America, in General Congress, Assembled, appealing to the Supreme Judge of the world for the rectitude of our intentions, do, in the Name, and by Authority of the good People of these Colonies, solemnly publish and declare, That these United Colonies are, and of Right ought to be Free and Independent States; that they are Absolved from all Allegiance to the British Crown, and that all political connection between them and the State of Great Britain, is and ought to be totally disolved; and that as Free and Independent States, they have full Power to levy War, conclude Peace, contract Alliances, establish Commerce, and to do all other Acts and Things which Independent States may of right do.—And for the support of this Declaration, with a firm reliance on protection of Divine Providence, we mutually pledge to each other our Lives, our Fortunes and our sacred Honor.

John Hancock
Button Gwinnett
Lyman Hall
Geo. Walton
Wm. Hooper
Joseph Hewes
John Penn
Edward Rutledge
Thos. Heyward, Jr.
Thomas Lynch, Jr.
Arthur Middleton
Samuel Chase
Wm. Paca
Thos. Stone
Charles Carroll of Carrollton
George Wythe
Richard Henry Lee
Th. Jefferson

Benj. Harrison
Thos. Nelson, Jr.
Francis Lightfoot Lee
Carter Braxton
Robt. Morris
Benjamin Rush
Benj. Franklin
John Morton
Geo. Clymer
Jas. Smith
Geo. Taylor
James Wilson
Geo. Ross
Caesar Rodney
Geo. Read
Tho. McKean
Wm. Floyd
Phil. Livingston
Frans. Lewis

Lewis Morris
Richd. Stockton
Jon. Witherspoon
Fras. Hopkinson
John Hart
Abra. Clark
Josiah Bartlett
Wm. Whipple
Saml. Adams
John Adams
Robt. Treat Paine
Elbridge Gerry
Step. Hopkins
William Ellery
Roger Sherman
Sam. Huntington
Wm. Williams
Oliver Wolcott
Matthew Thornton

Appendix B

CONSTITUTION OF THE UNITED STATES OF AMERICA

WE THE PEOPLE of the United States, in Order to form a more perfect Union, establish Justice, insure domestic Tranquility, provide for the common defence, promote the general Welfare, and secure the Blessings of Liberty to ourselves and our posterity, do ordain and establish this Constitution for the United States of America.

ARTICLE I.

Section 1. All legislative Powers herein granted shall be vested in a Congress of the United States, which shall consist of a Senate and House of Representatives.

Section 2. The House of Representatives shall be composed of Members chosen every second Year by the People of the several States, and the Electors in each State shall have the Qualifications requisite for Electors of the most numerous Branch of the State Legislature.

No person shall be a Representative who shall not have attained to the Age of twenty five Years, and been seven Years a Citizen of the United States, and who shall not, when elected, be an Inhabitant of that State in which he shall be chosen.

Representatives and direct Taxes shall be apportioned among the several States which may be included within this Union, according to their respective Numbers, which shall be determined by adding to the whole Number of free Persons, including those bound to Service for a Term of Years, and excluding Indians not taxed, three fifths of all other Persons. The actual Enumeration shall be made within three Years after the first Meeting of the Congress of the United States, and within every subsequent Term of ten Years, in such Manner as they shall by Law direct. The Number of Representatives shall not exceed one for every thirty Thousand, but each State shall have at Least one Representative; and until such enumeration shall be made, the State of New Hampshire shall be entited to chuse three, Massachusetts eight, Rhode Island and Providence Plantations one, Connecticut five, New York six, New Jersey four, Pennsylvania eight, Delaware one, Maryland six, Virginia ten, North Carolina five, South Carolina five, and Georgia three.

When vacancies happen in the Representation from any State, the Executive Authority thereof shall issue Writs of Election to fill such vacancies.

The House of Representatives shall chuse their Speaker and other Officers; and shall have the sole Power of Impeachment.

Section 3. The Senate of the United States shall be composed of two Senators from each State, chosen by the Legislature thereof, for six Years; and each Senator shall have one Vote.

Immediately after they shall be assembled in Consequence of the first Election, they shall be divided as equally as may be into three Classes. The Seats of the Senators of the first Class shall be vacated at the Expiration of the second Year, of the second Class at the Expiration of the fourth Year, and of the third Class at the Expiration of the sixth Year, so that one third may be chosen every second Year; and if Vacancies happen by Resignation, or otherwise, during the Recess of the Legislature of any State, the Executive thereof may make temporary Appointments until the next Meeting of the Legislature, which shall then fill such Vacancies.

No person shall be a Senator who shall not have attained to the Age of thirty Years, and been nine Years a Citizen of the United States, and who shall not, when elected, be an Inhabitant of that State for which he shall be chosen.

The Vice President of the United States shall be President of the Senate, but shall have no Vote, unless they be equally divided.

The Senate shall chuse their other Officers, and also a President pro tempore, in the Absence of the Vice President, or when he shall exercise the Office of President of the United States.

The Senate shall have the sole Power to try all Impeachments. When sitting for that Purpose, they shall be on Oath or Affirmation. When the President of the United States is tried the Chief Justice shall preside: And no Person shall be convicted without the Concurrence of two thirds of the Members present.

Judgment in Cases of Impeachment shall not extend further than to removal from Office, and disqualification to hold and enjoy any Office of honor, Trust or Profit under the United States: but the Party convicted shall nevertheless be liable and subject to Indictment, Trial, Judgment and Punishment, according to Law.

Section 4. The Times, Places and Manner of holding Elections for Senators and Representatives, shall be prescribed in each State by the Legislature thereof; but the Congress may at any time by Law make or alter such Regulations, except as to the Places of chusing Senators.

The Congress shall assemble at least once in every Year, and such Meeting shall be on the first Monday in December, unless they shall by Law appoint a different Day.

Section 5. Each House shall be the Judge of the Elections, Returns and Qualifications of its own Members, and a Majority of each shall constitute a Quorum to do Business; but a smaller Number may adjourn from day to day, and may be authorized to compel the Attendance of absent Members, in such manner, and under such Penalties as each House may provide.

Each House may determine the Rules of its Proceedings, punish its Members for disorderly Behavior, and, with the Concurrence of two thirds, expel a Member.

Each House shall keep a Journal of its Proceedings, and from time to time publish the same, excepting such Parts as may in their Judgment require Secrecy; and the Yeas and Nays of the Members of either House on any question shall, at the Desire of one fifth of those present, be entered on the Journal.

Neither House, during the Session of Congress, shall, without the Consent of the other, adjourn for more than three days, nor to any other Place than that in which the two Houses shall be sitting.

Section 6. The Senators and Representatives shall receive a Compensation for their Services, to be ascertained by Law, and paid out of the Treasury of the United States. They shall in all Cases, except Treason, Felony and Breach of the Peace, be privileged from Arrest during their Attendance at the Session of their respective Houses, and in going to and returning from the same; and for any Speech or Debate in either House, they shall not be questioned in any other Place.

No Senator or Representative shall, during the Time for which he was elected, be appointed to any civil Office under the Authority of the United States, which shall have been created, or the Emoluments whereof shall have been encreased during such time; and no Person holding any Office under the United States, shall be a Member of either House during his Continuance in Office.

Section 7. All Bills for raising Revenue shall originate in the House of Representatives; but the Senate may propose or concur with Amendments as on other Bills.

Every Bill which shall have passed the House of Representatives and the Senate, shall, before it become a Law, be presented to the President of the United States; If he approves he shall sign it, but if not he shall return it, with his Objections to that House in which it shall have originated, who shall enter the Objections at large on their Journal, and proceed to reconsider it. If after such Reconsideration two thirds of that House shall agree to pass the Bill, it shall be sent together with the Objections, to the other House, by which it shall likewise be reconsidered, and if approved by two thirds of that House, it shall become a Law. But in all such Cases the Votes of both Houses shall be determined by Yeas and Nays, and the Names of the Persons voting for and against the Bill shall be entered on the Journal of each House respectively. If any Bill shall not be returned by the President within ten Days (Sundays excepted) after it shall have been presented to him, the

Same shall be a Law, in like Manner as if he had signed it, unless the Congress by their Adjournment prevent its Return, in which Case it shall not be a Law.

Every Order, Resolution, or Vote to which the Concurrence of the Senate and House of Representatives may be necessary (except on a question of Adjournment) shall be presented to the President of the United States; and before the Same shall take Effect, shall be approved by him, or being disapproved by him, shall be repassed by two thirds of the Senate and House of Representatives, according to the Rules and Limitations prescribed in the Case of a Bill.

Section 8. The Congress shall have Power To lay and collect Taxes, Duties, Imposts and Excises, to pay the Debts and provide for the common Defence and general Welfare of the United States; but all Duties, Imposts and Excises shall be uniform throughout the United States;

To borrow Money on the credit of the United States;

To regulate Commerce with foreign Nations; and among the several States, and with the Indian Tribes;

To establish a uniform Rule of Naturalization, and uniform Laws on the subject of Bankruptcies throughout the United States;

To coin Money, regulate the Value thereof, and of foreign Coin, and fix the Standard of Weights and Measures;

To provide for the Punishment of counterfeiting the Securities and current Coin of the United States;

To establish Post Offices and post Roads;

To promote the Progress of Science and Useful Arts, by securing for limited Times to Authors and Inventors the exclusive Right to their respective Writings and Discoveries;

To constitute Tribunals inferior to the supreme Court;

To define and punish Piracies and Felonies committed on the high Seas, and Offences against the Law of Nations;

To declare War, grant Letters of Marque and Reprisal, and make Rules concerning Captures on Land and Water;

To raise and support Armies, but no Appropriation of Money to that Use shall be for a longer Term than two Years;

To provide and maintain a Navy;

To make Rules for the Government and Regulation of the land and naval Forces;

To provide for calling forth the Militia to execute the Laws of the Union, suppress Insurrections and repel Invasions;

To provide for organizing, arming, and disciplining, the Militia, and for governing such Part of them as may be employed in the Service of the United States, reserving to the States respectively, the Appointment of the Officers, and the Authority of training the Militia according to the discipline prescribed by Congress;

To exercise exclusive Legislation in all Cases whatsoever, over such District (not exceeding ten Miles square) as may, by Cession of particular States, and the Acceptance of Congress, become the Seat of the Government of the United States, and to exercise like Authority over all Places purchased by the Consent of the Legislature of the State in which the Same shall be, for the Erection of Forts, Magazines, Arsenals, dock-Yards, and other needful Buildings;—And

To make all Laws which shall be necessary and proper for carrying into Execution the foregoing Powers, and all other Powers vested by this Constitution in the Government of the United States, or in any Department or Officer thereof.

Section 9. The Migration or Importation of such Persons as any of the States now existing shall think proper to admit, shall not be prohibited by the Congress prior to the Year one thousand eight hundred and eight, but a Tax or duty may be imposed on such Importation, not exceeding ten dollars for each Person.

The Privilege of the Writ of Habeas Corpus shall not be suspended, unless when in Cases of Rebellion or Invasion the public Safety may require it.

No Bill of Attainder or ex post facto Law shall be passed.

No Capitation, or other direct, Tax shall be laid, unless in Proportion to the Census or Enumeration herein before directed to be taken.

No Tax or Duty shall be laid on Articles exported from any State.

No Preference shall be given by any Regulation of Commerce or Revenue to the Ports of one State over those of another; nor shall Vessels bound to, or from, one State, be obliged to enter, clear, or pay Duties in another.

No Money shall be drawn from the Treasury, but in Consequence of Appropriations made by Law; and a regular Statement and Account of the Receipts and Expenditures of all public Money shall be published from time to time.

No Title of Nobility shall be granted by the United States; And no Person holding any Office of Profit or Trust under them, shall, without the Consent of the Congress, accept of any present, Emolument, Office, or Title, of any kind whatever, from any King, Prince, or foreign State.

Section 10. No State shall enter into any Treaty, Alliance, or Confederation; grant Letters of Marque and Reprisal; coin Money; emit Bills of Credit; make any Thing but gold and silver Coin a Tender in Payment of Debts; pass any Bill of Attainder, ex post facto Law, or Law impairing the Obligation of Contracts, or grant any Title of Nobility.

No State, shall, without the Consent of the Congress, lay any Imposts or Duties on Imports or Exports, except what may be absolutely necessary for executing its inspection Laws: and the net Produce of all Duties and Imposts, laid by any State on Imports or Exports, shall be for the Use of the Treasury of the United States; and all such Laws shall be subject to the Revision and Controul of the Congress.

No State shall, without the Consent of Congress, Lay any Duty of Tonnage, keep Troops, or Ships of War in time of Peace, enter into any Agreement or Compact with another State, or with a foreign Power, or engage in War, unless actually invaded, or in such imminent Danger as will not admit of delay.

ARTICLE II.

Section 1. The executive Power shall be vested in a President of the United States of America. He shall hold his Office during the Term of four Years, and, together with the Vice President, chosen for the Same Term, be elected, as follows.

Each State shall appoint, in such Manner as the Legislature thereof may direct, a Number of Electors, equal to the whole Number of Senators and Representatives to which the State may be entitled in the Congress:

but no Senator or Representative, or Person holding an Office of Trust or Profit under the United States, shall be appointed an Elector.

The Electors shall meet in their respective States, and vote by Ballot for two Persons of whom one at least shall not be an Inhabitant of the same State with themselves. And they shall make a List of all the Persons voted for, and of the Number of Votes for each; which List they shall sign and certify, and transmit sealed to the Seat of the Government of the United States, directed to the President of the Senate. The President of the Senate shall, in the Presence of the Senate and House of Representatives, open all the Certificates, and the Votes shall then be counted. The Person having the greater Number of Votes shall be the President, if such Number be a Majority of the whole Number of Electors appointed; and if there be more than one who have such Majority, and have an equal Number of Votes, then the House of Representatives shall immediately chuse by Ballot one of them for President; and if no Person have a Majority, then from the five highest on the List the said House shall in like Manner chuse the President. But in chusing the President, the Votes shall be taken by States, the Representation from each State having one Vote; A quorum for this Purpose shall consist of a Member or Members from two thirds of the States, and a Majority of all the States shall be necessary to a Choice. In every Case, after the Choice of the President, the Person having the greatest Number of Votes of the Electors shall be the Vice President. But if there should remain two or more who have equal Votes, the Senate shall chuse from them by Ballot the Vice President.

The Congress may determine the Time of chusing the Electors, and the Day on which they shall give their Votes; which Day shall be the same throughout the United States.

No Person except a natural born Citizen, or a Citizen of the United States, at the time of the Adoption of this Constitution, shall be eligible to the Office of President; neither shall any Person be eligible to that Office who shall not have attained to the Age of thirty five Years, and been fourteen Years a Resident within the United States.

In Case of the Removal of the President from Office, or of his Death, Resignation, or Inability to discharge the Powers and Duties of the said Office, the same shall devolve on the Vice President, and the Congress may by Law provide for the Case of Removal, Death, Resignation or Inability, both of the President and Vice President, declaring what Officer shall then act as President, and such Officer shall act accordingly, until the Disability be removed, or a President shall be elected.

The President shall, at stated Times, receive for his Services, a Compensation, which shall neither be encreased nor diminished during the Period for which he shall have been elected, and he shall not receive within that Period any other Emolument from the United States, or any of them.

Before he enter on the Execution of his Office, he shall take the following Oath or Affirmation:—"I do solemnly swear (or affirm) that I will faithfully execute the Office of President of the United States, and will to the best of my Ability, preserve, protect and defend the Constitution of the United States."

Section 2. The President shall be Commander in Chief of the Army and Navy of the United States, and of the Militia of the several States, when called into the actual Service of the United States; he may require the Opinion, in writing, of the principal Officer in each of the executive Departments, upon any Subject relating to the Duties of their respective Offices, and he shall have Power to grant Reprieves and Pardons for Offences against the United States, except in Cases of Impeachment.

He shall have Power, by and with the Advice and Consent of the Senate, to make Treaties, provided two thirds of the Senators present concur; and he shall nominate, and by and with the Advice and Consent of the Senate, shall appoint Ambassadors, other public Ministers and Consuls, Judges of the supreme Court, and all other Officers of the United States, whose Appointments are not herein otherwise provided for, and which shall be established by Law: but the Congress may by Law vest the Appointment of such inferior Officers, as they think proper, in the President alone, in the Courts of Law, or in the Heads of Departments.

The President shall have Power to fill up all Vacancies that may happen during the Recess of the Senate, by granting Commissions which shall expire at the End of their next Session.

Section 3. He shall from time to time give to the Congress Information of the State of the Union, and recommend to their Consideration such Measures as he shall judge necessary and expedient; he may, on extraordinary Occasions, convene both Houses, or either of them, and in Case of Disagreement between them, with Respect to the Time of Adjournment, he may adjourn them to such Time as he shall think proper; he shall receive Ambassadors and other public Ministers; he shall take Care that the Laws be faithfully executed, and shall Commission all the Officers of the United States.

Section 4. The President, Vice President and all civil Officers of the United States, shall be removed from Office on Impeachment for, and Conviction of, Treason, Bribery, or other high Crimes and Misdemeanors.

ARTICLE III.

Section 1. The judicial Power of the United States, shall be vested in one supreme Court, and in such inferior Courts as the Congress may from time to time ordain and establish. The Judges, both of the supreme and inferior Courts, shall hold their Offices during good Behaviour, and shall, at stated Times, receive for their Services, a Compensation, which shall not be diminished during their Continuance in Office.

Section 2. The judicial Power shall extend to all Cases, in Law and Equity, arising under this Constitution, the Laws of the United States, and Treaties made, or which shall be made, under their Authority;—to all Cases affecting Ambassadors, other public Ministers and Consuls;—to all Cases of admiralty and maritime Jurisdiction;—to Controversies to which the United States shall be a Party;—to Controversies between two or more States;—between a State and Citizens of another State;—between Citizens of different States,—between Citizens of the same State claiming Lands under Grants of different States, and between a State, or the Citizens thereof, and foreign States, Citizens or Subjects.

In all Cases affecting Ambassadors, other public Ministers and Consuls, and those in which a State shall be Party, the supreme Court shall have original Jurisdiction. In all the other Cases before mentioned, the supreme Court shall have appellate jurisdiction, both as to Law and Fact, with such Exceptions, and under such Regulations as the Congress shall make.

The Trial of all Crimes, except in Cases of Impeachment, shall be by Jury; and such Trial shall be held in the State where the said Crimes shall have been committed; but when not committed within any State, the Trial shall be at such Place or Places as the Congress may by Law have directed.

Section 3. Treason against the United States, shall consist only in levying War against them, or in adhering to their Enemies, giving them Aid and Comfort. No Person shall be convicted of Treason unless on the Testimony of two Witnesses to the same overt Act, or on Confession in open Court.

The Congress shall have Power to declare the Punishment of Treason, but no Attainder of Treason shall work Corruption of Blood, or Forfeiture except during the Life of the Person attainted.

ARTICLE IV.

Section 1. Full Faith and Credit shall be given in each State to the public Acts, Records, and judicial Proceedings of every other State. And the Congress may by general Laws prescribe the Manner in which such Acts, Records and Proceedings shall be proved, and the Effect thereof.

Section 2. The Citizens of each State shall be entitled to all Privileges and Immunities of Citizens in the several states.

A Person charged in any State with Treason, Felony, or other Crime, who shall flee from Justice, and be found in another State, shall on Demand of the executive Authority of the State from which he fled, be delivered up, to be removed to the state having Jurisdiction of the Crime.

No Person held to Service or Labour in one State, under the Laws thereof, escaping into another, shall, in Consequence of any Law or Regulation therein, be discharged from such Service or Labour, but shall be delivered up on Claim of the Party to whom such Service or Labour may be due.

Section 3. New States may be admitted by the Congress into this Union; but no new State shall be formed or erected within the Jurisdiction of any other State; nor any State be formed by the Junction of two or more States, or Parts of States, without the Consent of the Legislature of the States concerned as well as of the Congress.

The Congress shall have Power to dispose of and make all needful Rules and Regulations respecting the Territory or other Property belonging to the United States; and nothing in this Constitution shall be so construed as to Prejudice any Claims of the United States, or of any particular State.

Section 4. The United States shall guarantee to every State in this Union a Republican Form of Government, and shall protect each of them against Invasion; and on Application of the Legislature, or of the Executive (when the Legislature cannot be convened) against domestic Violence.

ARTICLE V.

The Congress, whenever two thirds of both Houses shall deem it necessary, shall propose Amendments to this Constitution, or, on the Application of the Legislatures of two thirds of the several States, shall call a Convention for proposing Amendments, which, in either Case, shall be valid to all Intents and Purposes, as Part of this Constitution, when ratified by the Legislatures of three fourths of the several States, or by Conventions in three fourths thereof, as the one or the other Mode of Ratification may be proposed by the Congress; Provided that no Amendment which may be made prior to the Year One thousand eight hundred and eight shall in any Manner affect the first and fourth Clauses in the Ninth Section of the first Article; and that no State, without its Consent, shall be deprived of its equal Suffrage in the Senate.

ARTICLE VI.

All Debts contracted and Engagements entered into, before the Adoption of this Constitution, shall be as valid against the United States under this Constitution, as under the Confederation.

This Constitution, and the laws of the United States which shall be made in Pursuance thereof; and all Treaties made, or which shall be made, under the Authority of the United States, shall be the supreme Law of the Land; and the Judges in every State shall be bound thereby, any Thing in the Constitution or Laws of any State to the Contrary notwithstanding.

The Senators and Representatives before mentioned, and the Members of the several State Legislatures, and all executive and judicial Officers, both of the United States and of the several States, shall be bound by Oath or Affirmation, to support this Constitution; but no religious Test shall ever be required as a Qualification to any Office or public Trust under the United States.

ARTICLE VII.

The Ratification of the Conventions of nine States, shall be sufficient for the Establishment of this Constitution between the States so ratifying the Same.

ARTICLES IN ADDITION TO, AND AMENDMENT OF THE CONSTITUTION OF THE UNITED STATES OF AMERICA, PROPOSED BY CONGRESS, AND RATIFIED BY THE LEGISLATURES OF THE SEVERAL STATES, PURSUANT TO THE FIFTH ARTICLE OF THE ORIGINAL CONSTITUTION.

Amendment I.

Congress shall make no law respecting an establishment of religion, or prohibiting the free exercise thereof; or abridging the freedom of speech, or of the press; or the right of the people peaceably to assemble, and to petition the Government for a redress of grievances.

Amendment II.

A well regulated militia, being necessary to the security of a free State, the right of the people to keep and bear arms, shall not be infringed.

Amendment III.

No Soldier shall, in time of peace be quartered in any house, without the consent of the owner, nor in time of war, but in a manner to be prescribed by law.

Amendment IV.

The right of the people to be secure in their persons, houses, papers, and effects, against unreasonable searches and seizures, shall not be violated, and no warrants shall issue, but upon probable cause, supported by oath or affirmation, and particularly describing the place to be searched, and the persons or things to be seized.

Amendment V.

No person shall be held to answer for a capital, or otherwise infamous crime, unless on a presentment or indictment of a Grand Jury, except in cases arising in the land or naval forces, or in the militia, when in actual service in time of war or public danger; nor shall any person be subject for the same offence to be twice put in jeopardy of life or limb; nor shall be compelled in any criminal case to be a witness against himself, nor be deprived of life, liberty, or property, without due process of law; nor shall private property be taken for public use, without just compensation.

Amendment VI.

In all criminal prosecutions, the accused shall enjoy the right to a speedy and public trial, by an impartial jury of the State and district wherein the crime shall have been committed, which district shall have been previously ascertained by law, and to be informed of the nature and cause of the accusation; to be confronted with the witnesses against him; to have compulsory process for obtaining witnesses in his favor, and to have the assistance of counsel for his defence.

Amendment VII.

In Suits at common law, where the value in controversy shall exceed twenty dollars, the right of trial by jury shall be preserved, and no fact tried by a jury, shall be otherwise reexamined in any Court of the United States, than according to the rules of the common law.

Amendment VIII.

Excessive bail shall not be required, nor excessive fines imposed, nor cruel and unusual punishments inflicted.

Amendment IX.

The enumeration in the Constitution, of certain rights, shall not be construed to deny or disparage others retained by the people.

Amendment X.

The powers not delegated to the United States by the Constitution, nor prohibited by it to the States, are reserved to the States respectively, or to the people.

Amendment XI.

The Judicial power of the United States shall not be construed to extend to any suit in law or equity, commenced or prosecuted against one of the United States by Citizens of another State, or by Citizens or Subjects of any Foreign State.

Amendment XII.

The Electors shall meet in their respective states and vote by ballot for President and Vice-President, one of whom, at least, shall not be an inhabitant of the same state with themselves; they shall name in their ballots the person voted for as President, and in distinct ballots the person voted for as Vice-President, and they shall make distinct lists of all persons voted for as President, and of all persons voted for as Vice-President, and of the number of votes for each, which lists they shall sign and certify, and transmit sealed to the seat of the government of the United States, directed to the President of the Senate;—The President of the Senate shall, in the presence of the Senate and House of Representatives, open all the certificates and the votes shall then be counted;—The person having the greatest number of votes for President, shall be the President, if such number be a majority of the whole number of Electors appointed; and if no person have such majority, then from the persons having the highest numbers not exceeding three on the list of those voted for as President, the House of Representatives shall choose immediately, by ballot, the President. But in choosing the President, the votes shall be taken by states, the representation from each state having one vote; a quorum for this purpose shall consist of a member or members from two-thirds of the states, and a majority of all the states shall be necessary to a choice. And if the House of Representatives shall not choose a President whenever the right of choice shall devolve upon them, before the fourth day of March next following, then the Vice-President shall act as President, as in the case of the death or other constitutional disability of the President—The person having the greatest number of votes as Vice-President, shall be the Vice-President, if such number be a majority of the whole number of Electors appointed, and if no person have a majority, then from the two highest numbers on the list, the Senate shall choose the Vice-President; a quorum for the purpose shall consist of two-thirds of the whole number of Senators, and a majority of the whole number shall be necessary to a choice. But no person constitutionally ineligible to the office of President shall be eligible to that of Vice-President of the United States.

Amendment XIII.

Section 1. Neither slavery nor involuntary servitude, except as a punishment for crime whereof the party shall have been duly convicted, shall exist within the United States, or any place subject to their jurisdiction.

Section 2. Congress shall have power to enforce this article by appropriate legislation.

Amendment XIV.

Section 1. All persons born or naturalized in the United States, and subject to the jurisdiction thereof, are citizens of the United States and of the State wherein they reside. No State shall make or enforce any law which shall abridge the privileges or immunities of citizens of the United States; nor shall any State deprive any person of life, liberty, or property, without due process of law; nor deny to any person within its jurisdiction the equal protection of the laws.

Section 2. Representatives shall be apportioned among the several states according to their respective numbers, counting the whole number of persons in each State, excluding Indians not taxed. But when the right to vote at any election for the choice of electors for President and Vice-President of the United States, Representatives in Congress, the Executive and Judicial officers of a State, or the members of the Legislature thereof, is denied to any of the male inhabitants of such State, being twenty-one years of age, and citizens of the United States, or in any way abridged, except for participation in rebellion, or other crime, the basis of representation therein shall be reduced in the proportion which the number of such male citizens shall bear to the whole number of male ctizens twenty-one years of age in such State.

Section 3. No person shall be a Senator or Representative in Congress, or elector of President and Vice-President, or hold any office, civil or military, under the United States, or under any State, who, having previously taken an oath, as a member of Congress, or as an officer of the United States, or as a member of any State legislature, or as an executive or judicial officer of any State, to support the Constitution of the United States, shall have engaged in insurrection or rebellion against the same, or given aid or comfort to the enemies thereof. But Congress may by a vote of two-thirds of each House remove such disability.

Section 4. The validity of the public debt of the United States, authorized by law, including debts incurred for payment of pensions and bounties for services in suppressing insurrection or rebellion, shall not be questioned. But neither the United States nor any State shall assume or pay any debt or obligation incurred in aid of insurrection or rebellion against the United States, or any claim for the loss or emancipation of any slave; but all such debts, obligations and claims shall be held illegal and void.

Section 5. The Congress shall have power to enforce, by appropriate legislation, the provisions of this article.

Amendment XV.

Section 1. The right of citizens of the United States to vote shall not be denied or abridged by the United States or by any State on account of race, color, or previous condition of servitude.

Section 2. The Congress shall have power to enforce this article by appropriate legislation.

Amendment XVI.

The Congress shall have power to lay and collect taxes on incomes, from whatever source derived, without apportionment among the several States, and without regard to any census or enumeration.

Amendment XVII.

The Senate of the United States shall be composed of two Senators from each State, elected by the people thereof, for six years; and each Senator shall have one vote. The electors in each State shall have the qualifications requisite for electors of the most numerous branch of the State legislatures.

When vacancies happen in the representation of any State in the Senate, the executive authority of such State shall issue writs of election to fill such vacancies: *Provided,* That the legislature of any State may empower the executive thereof to make temporary appointments until the people fill the vacancies by election as the legislature may direct.

This amendment shall not be so construed as to affect the election or term of any Senator chosen before it becomes valid as part of the Constitution.

Amendment XVIII.

Section 1. After one year from the ratification of this article the manufacture, sale, or transportation of intoxicating liquors within, the importation thereof into, or the exportation thereof from the United States and all territory subject to the jurisdiction thereof for beverage purposes is hereby prohibited.

Section 2. The Congress and the several States shall have concurrent power to enforce this article by appropriate legislation.

Section 3. This article shall be inoperative unless it shall have been ratified as an amendment to the Constitution by the legislatures of the several States, as provided in the Constitution, within seven years from the date of the submission hereof to the States by the Congress.

Amendment XIX.

The right of citizens of the United States to vote shall not be denied or abridged by the United States or by any State on account of sex.

Congress shall have power to enforce this article by appropriate legislation.

Amendment XX.

Section 1. The terms of the President and Vice President shall end at noon on the 20th day of January, and the terms of Senators and Representatives at noon on the 3d day of January, of the years in which such terms would have ended if this article had not been ratified; and the terms of their successors shall then begin.

Section 2. The Congress shall assemble at least once in every year, and such meeting shall begin at noon on the 3d day of January, unless they shall by law appoint a different day.

Section 3. If, at the time fixed for the beginning of the term of the President, the President elect shall have died, the Vice President elect shall become President. If a President shall not have been chosen before the time fixed for the beginning of his term, or if the President elect shall have failed to qualify, then the Vice President elect shall act as President until a President shall have qualified; and the Congress may by law provide for the case wherein neither a President elect nor a Vice President elect shall have qualified, declaring who shall then act as President, or the manner in which one who is to act shall be selected, and such person shall act accordingly until a President or Vice President shall have qualified.

Section 4. The Congress may by law provide for the case of the death of any of the persons from whom the House of Representatives may choose a President whenever the rights of choice shall have devolved upon them, and for the case of the death of any of the persons from whom the Senate may choose a Vice President whenever the right of choice shall have devolved upon them.

Section 5. Sections 1 and 2 shall take effect on the 15th day of October following the ratification of this article.

Section 6. This article shall be inoperative unless it shall have been ratified as an amendment to the Constitution by the legislatures of three-fourths of the several States within seven years from the date of its submission.

Amendment XXI.

Section 1. The eighteenth article of amendment to the Constitution of the United States is hereby repealed.

Section 2. The transportation or importation into any State, Territory, or possession of the United States for delivery or use therein of intoxicating liquors, in violation of the laws thereof, is hereby prohibited.

Section 3. This article shall be inoperative unless it shall have been ratified as an amendment to the Constitution by conventions in the several States, as provided in the Constitution, within seven years from the date of the submission hereof to the States by the Congress.

Amendment XXII.

Section 1. No person shall be elected to the office of the President more than twice, and no person who has held the office of President, or acted as President, for more than two years of a term to which some other person was elected President shall be elected to the office of the President more than once. But this Article shall not apply to any person holding the office of President when this Article was proposed by the Congress, and shall not prevent any person who may be holding the office of President, or acting as President, during the term within which this Article becomes operative from holding the office of President or acting as President during the remainder of such term.

Section 2. This article shall be inoperative unless it shall have been ratified as an amendment to the Constitution by the legislatures of three-fourths of the several States within seven years from the date of its submission to the States by the Congress.

Amendment XXIII.

Section 1. The District constituting the seat of Government of the United States shall appoint in such manner as the Congress may direct:

A number of electors of President and Vice President equal to the whole number of Senators and Representatives in Congress to which the District would be entitled if it were a State, but in no event more than the least populous State; they shall be in addition to those appointed by the States but they shall be considered, for the purposes of the election of President and Vice President, to be electors appointed by a State; and they shall meet in the District and perform such duties as provided by the twelfth article of amendment.

Section 2. The Congress shall have power to enforce this article by appropriate legislation.

Amendment XXIV.

Section 1. The right of citizens of the United States to vote in any primary or other election for President or Vice President, for electors for President or Vice President, or for Senator or Representative in Congress, shall not be denied or abridged by the United States or any State by reason of failure to pay any poll tax or other tax.

Section 2. The Congress shall have power to enforce this article by appropriate legislation.

Amendment XXV.

Section 1. In case of the removal of the President from office or of his death or resignation, the Vice President shall become President.

Section 2. Whenever there is a vacancy in the office of the Vice President, the President shall nominate a Vice President who shall take office upon confirmation by a majority vote of both Houses of Congress.

Section 3. Whenever the President transmits to the President pro tempore of the Senate and the Speaker of the House of Representatives his written declaration that he is unable to discharge the powers and duties of his office, and until he transmits to them a written declaration to the contrary, such powers and duties shall be discharged by the Vice President as Acting President.

Section 4. Whenever the Vice President and a majority of either the principal officers of the executive departments or of such other body as Congress may by law provide, transmit to the President pro tempore of the Senate and the Speaker of the House of Representatives their written declaration that the President is unable to discharge the powers and duties of his office, the Vice President shall immediately assume the powers and duties of the office as Acting President.

Thereafter, when the President transmits to the President pro tempore of the Senate and the Speaker of the House of Representatives his written declaration that no inability exists, he shall resume the powers and duties of his office unless the Vice President and a majority of either the principal officers of the executive department or of such other body as Congress may by law provide, transmit within four days to the President pro tempore of the Senate and the Speaker of the House of Representatives their written declaration that the President is unable to discharge the powers and duties of his office. Thereupon Congress shall decide the issue, assembling within forty-eight hours for that purpose if not in session. If the Congress, within twenty-one days after receipt of the latter written declaration, or, if Congress is not in session, within twenty-one days after Congress is required to assemble, determines by two-thirds vote of both Houses that the President is unable to discharge the powers and duties of his office, the Vice President shall continue to discharge the same as Acting President; otherwise, the President shall resume the powers and duties of his office.

Amendment XXVI.

Section 1. The right of citizens of the United States, who are eighteen years of age or older, to vote shall not be denied or abridged by the United States or by any State on account of age.

Section 2. The Congress shall have power to enforce this article by appropriate legislation.

Appendix C

Periodical Abbreviations

Administrative Law Review	Ad. L. Rev.
Alabama Law Review	Ala. L. Rev.
Albany Law Review	Alb. L. Rev.
American Bankruptcy Law Journal	Am. Bankr. L.J.
American Bar Association Journal	A.B.A. J.
American Federal Tax Reports	AFTR
American Journal of International Law	Am. J. Int. L.
American Journal of Jurisprudence	Am. J. Juris.
American Law Institute	A.L.I.
American Law Reports	A.L.R.
American Trial Lawyers Association Journal	A.T.L.A. J.
American University Law Review	Am. U.L. Rev.
Arizona Law Review	Ariz. L. Rev.
Arizona State Law Journal	Ariz. St. L.J.
Arkansas Law Review	Ark. L. Rev.
Banking Law Journal	Banking L.J.
Baylor Law Review	Baylor L. Rev.
Black Law Journal	Black L.J.
Blackstone's Commentary on the Law of England	Black. Com.
Boston College Law Review	B.C.L. Rev.
Boston University Law Review	B.U.L. Rev.
Brigham Young University Law Review	B.Y.U. L. Rev.
Brooklyn Law Review	Brooklyn L. Rev.
Buffalo Law Review	Buffalo L. Rev.
Business Law Review	Bus. L. Rev.
California Law Review	Calif. L. Rev.
California State Bar Journal	Cal. St. B.J.
Cambridge Law Journal	Cambridge L.J.
Catholic Lawyer	Cath. Law.
Catholic University Law Review	Cath. U.L. Rev.
Chicago-Kent Law Review	Chi.-Kent L. Rev.
Chicago Law Journal	Chicago L.J.
Chicago Law Record	Chicago L. Rec.
Cincinnati Law Review	Cin. L. Rev.
Cleveland State Law Review	Clev. St. L. Rev.
Cleveland-Marshall Law Review	Clev.-Mar. L. Rev.
Columbia Law Review	Colum. L. Rev.
Commercial Law Journal	Com. L. J.
Congressional Digest	Cong. Dig.
Congressional Record	Cong. Rec.
Connecticut Bar Journal	Conn. B.J.
Connecticut Law Review	Conn. L. Rev.
Cornell Law Forum	Cornell L.F.
Cornell Law Review	Cornell L. Rev.
Creighton Law Review	Creighton L. Rev.
Criminal Law Reporter	Crim. L. Rptr.
Cumberland Law Review	Cum. L. Rev.
Cyclopedia of Law and Procedure	Cyc.
Dakota Law Review	Dak. L. Rev.

District of Columbia Bar Journal	D.C.B.J.
De Paul Law Review	De Paul L. Rev.
Denver Law Journal	Den. L.J.
Detroit Law Journal	Det. L.J.
Dickinson Law Review	Dick. L. Rev.
Drake Law Review	Drake L. Rev.
Duke Law Journal	Duke L.J.
Duquesne University Law Review	Duquesne L. Rev.
Ecology Law Quarterly	Ecology L.Q.
Emory Law Journal	Emory L.J.
Environmental Law Review	Env. L. Rev.
European Law Review	Eur. L. Rev.
Faculty Law Review	Faculty L. Rev.
Family Law Quarterly	Family L.Q.
Federal Law Review	Fed. L. Rev.
Federal Register	Fed. Reg.
Florida Bar Journal	Fla. B.J.
Florida Law Journal	Fla. L.J.
Florida State University Law Review	Fla. St. U.L. Rev.
Fordham Law Review	Fordham L. Rev.
George Washington Law Review	Geo. Wash. L. Rev.
Georgetown Law Journal	Geo. L.J.
Georgia Law Review	Ga. L. Rev.
Georgia State Bar Journal	Ga. St. B.J.
Glendale Law Review	Glendale L. Rev.
Golden Gate Law Review	Golden Gate L. Rev.
Harvard Civil Rights-Civil Liberties Law Review	Harv. C.R.-C.L. L. Rev.
Harvard International Law Journal	Harv. Int'l L.J.
Harvard Journal on Legislation	Harv. J. on Legis.
Harvard Law Review	Harv. L. Rev.
Harvard Women's Law Journal	Harv. Women's L.J.
Hastings Law Journal	Hastings L.J.
Hawaii Bar Journal	Hawaii B.J.
Houston Law Review	Hous. L. Rev.
Howard Law Journal	How. L.J.
Idaho Law Review	Idaho L. Rev.
Illinois Bar Journal	Ill. B.J.
Indiana Law Journal	Ind. L.J.
Indiana Law Review	Ind. L. Rev.
Industrial and Labor Relations Review	Indus. & Lab. Rel. Rev.
Industrial Law Journal	Indus. L.J.
Insurance Law Journal	Ins. L.J.
Iowa Law Review	Iowa L. Rev.
John Marshall Law Journal	J. Mar. L.J.
Journal of the American Medical Association	J. A.M.A.
Journal of American Trial Lawyers Association	J.A.T.L.A.
Journal of Business Law	J. Bus. L.
Journal of Criminal Law and Criminology	Jour. Crim. L.
Journal of Family Law	J. Fam. L.
Juridical Review	Jurid. Rev.

Jurist	Jurist
Justice System Journal	Just. Sys. J.
Kansas Bar Journal	K.B.J.
Kansas Law Journal	Kan. L.J.
Kentucky Law Journal	Ky. L.J.
Labor Law Journal	Lab. L.J.
Law Quarterly Review	Law Q. Rev.
Lawyer's Reports Annotated	L.R.A.
Lehigh Law Journal, Pa.	Leh. L.J.
Louisiana Law Journal	La. L.J.
Louisiana Law Review	La. L. Rev.
Loyola Law Review (New Orleans)	Loy. L. Rev.
Loyola of Los Angeles Law Review	Loy. L.A.L. Rev.
Loyola University of Chicago Law Journal	Loy. U. Chi. L.J.
Luzerne Law Journal	Luz. L.J.
McGill Law Journal	McGill L.J.
Maine Law Review	Me. L. Rev.
Marquette Law Review	Marq. L. Rev.
Maryland Law Review	Md. L. Rev.
Massachusetts Law Review	Mass. L. Rev.
Memphis Law Journal, Tenn.	Mem. L.J.
Memphis State University Law Review	Mem. St. U.L. Rev.
Mercer Law Review	Mercer L. Rev.
Michigan Law Review	Mich. L. Rev.
Minnesota Law Review	Minn. L. Rev.
Mississippi Law Journal	Miss. L.J.
Missouri Bar Journal	Mo. B.J.
Missouri Law Review	Mo. L. Rev.
Montana Law Review	Mont. L. Rev.
National Law Review	Nat. L. Rev.
Nebraska Law Review	Neb. L. Rev.
New England Law Review	New Eng. L. Rev.
New Hampshire Bar Journal	N.H.B.J.
New Jersey Law Journal	N.J.L.J.
New Law Journal	New L.J.
New Mexico Law Review	N.M.L. Rev.
New York Law School Law Review	N.Y.L. Sch. L. Rev.
New York Law Review	N.Y.L. Rev.
New York State Bar Journal	N.Y. St. B.J.
New York University Law Review	N.Y.U. L. Rev.
North Carolina Law Review	N.C.L. Rev.
North Dakota Law Review	N.D.L. Rev.
Northwestern University Law Review	Nw. U.L. Rev.
Notre Dame Lawyer	Notre Dame Law.
Ohio Law Journal	Ohio L.J.
Ohio State Law Journal	Ohio St. L.J.
Oklahoma Law Review	Okla. L. Rev.
Oregon Law Review	Or. L. Rev.
Pacific Law Journal	Pac. L.J.
Patent Law Review	Pat. L. Rev.

Pepperdine Law Review	Pepperdine L. Rev.
Pittsburgh Legal Journal	Pitt. L.J.
Rutgers Law Review	Rutgers L. Rev.
Rutgers-Camden Law Review	Rutgers-Camden L. Rev.
St. John's Law Review	St. John's L. Rev.
St. Louis University Law Journal	St. Louis U.L.J.
St. Mary's Law Journal	St. Mary's L.J.
San Diego Law Review	San Diego L. Rev.
San Francisco Law Journal	San Fran. L.J.
Smith's Law Journal	Smith L.J.
South Carolina Law Review	S.C.L. Rev.
South Dakota Law Review	S.D.L. Rev.
South Texas Law Journal	S. Tex. L.J.
Southern California Law Review	S. Cal. L. Rev.
Southern University Law Review	So. U. L. Rev.
Southwestern Law Journal	Sw. L.J.
Southwestern University Law Review	Sw. U. L. Rev.
Stanford Law Review	Stan. L. Rev.
Stetson Law Review	Stetson L. Rev.
Suffolk University Law Review	Suffolk U.L. Rev.
Supreme Court Review	Sup. Ct. Rev.
Syracuse Law Review	Syracuse L. Rev.
Tax Law Review	Tax L. Rev.
Tennessee Law Review	Tenn. L. Rev.
Texas Law Journal	Tex. L.J.
Texas Law Review	Tex. L. Rev.
Texas Tech Law Review	Tex. Tech L. Rev.
Tulane Law Review	Tul. L. Rev.
Tulsa Law Journal	Tulsa L.J.
U.C. Davis Law Review	U.C.D. L. Rev.
U.C.L.A. Law Review	U.C.L.A. L. Rev.
Uniform Commercial Code Law Journal	U.C.C. L.J.
United States Law Journal	U.S.L.J.
University of Baltimore Law Review	U. Balt. L. Rev.
University of Chicago Law Review	U. Chi. L. Rev.
University of Cincinnati Law Review	U. Cin. L. Rev.
University of Colorado Law Review	U. Colo. L. Rev.
University of Detroit Journal of Urban Law	U. Det. J. Urb. L.
University of Florida Law Review	U. Fla. L. Rev.
University of Hawaii Law Review	U. Hawaii L. Rev.
University of Illinois Law Forum	U. Ill. L. F.
University of Kansas Law Review	U. Kan. L. Rev.
University of Miami Law Review	U. Miami L. Rev.
University of Michigan Journal of Law Reform	U. Mich. J.L. Ref.
University of Pennsylvania Law Review	U. Pa. L. Rev.
University of Pittsburgh Law Review	U. Pitt. L. Rev.
University of Richmond Law Review	U. Rich. L. Rev.
University of San Francisco Law Review	U.S.F.L. Rev.
University of Toledo Law Review	U. Tol. L. Rev.
University of West Los Angeles Law Review	U. West L.A. L. Rev.
Utah Law Review	Utah L. Rev.

Valparaiso University Law Review	Val. U.L. Rev.
Vanderbilt Law Review	Vand. L. Rev.
Villanova Law Review	Vill. L. Rev.
Virginia Law Review	Va. L. Rev.
Wake Forest Law Review	Wake Forest L. Rev.
Washburn Law Journal	Washburn L.J.
Washington Law Review	Wash. L. Rev.
Washington & Lee Law Review	Wash. & Lee L. Rev.
Wayne Law Review	Wayne L. Rev.
West Virginia Law Review	W. Va. L. Rev.
Willamette Law Journal	Willamette L.J.
William and Mary Law Review	Wm. & Mary L. Rev.
Wisconsin Law Review	Wis. L. Rev.
Yale Law Journal	Yale L.J.

Appendix D

Abbreviations of Governmental Agencies and Departments

ACDA	Arms Control and Disarmament Agency
ADAMHA	Alcohol, Drug Abuse, and Mental Health Administration
AFDC	Aid to Families with Dependent Children
AFIS	American Forces Information System
AID	Agency for International Development
Amtrak	National Railroad Passenger Corporation
ANA	Administration for Native Americans
APS	Administration for Public Services
BEA	Bureau of Economic Analysis
BIA	Bureau of Indian Affairs
BJS	Bureau of Justice Statistics
BLM	Bureau of Land Management
BLS	Bureau of Labor Statistics
CAB	Civil Aeronautics Board
CDC	Centers for Disease Control
CEA	Council of Economic Advisers
CENTO	Central Treaty Organization
CEQ	Council on Environmental Quality
CETA	Comprehensive Employment and Training Act
CIA	Central Intelligence Agency
Comcen's	Federal Communications Centers
Conrail	Consolidated Rail Corporation
CRS	Community Relations Service
CSC	Civil Service Commission
DEA	Drug Enforcement Administration
DIA	Defense Intelligence Agency
DNA	Defense Nuclear Agency
DOD	Department of Defense
DOE	Department of Energy
DOT	Department of Transportation
EDA	Economic Development Administration
EEC	European Economic Community
EEOC	Equal Employment Opportunity Commission
EIA	Energy Information Administration
EPA	Environmental Protection Agency
ERISA	Employee Retirement Income Security Act
ESA	Employment Standards Administration
FAA	Federal Aviation Administration
FAO	Food and Agriculture Organization of the United Nations
FBI	Federal Bureau of Investigation
FCA	Farm Credit Administration
FCC	Federal Communications Commission
FCIC	Federal Crop Insurance Corporation
FDA	Food and Drug Administration
FDAA	Federal Disaster Assistance Administration
FDIC	Federal Deposit Insurance Corporation
FEC	Federal Election Commission

FHA	Federal Housing Administration
FHWA	Federal Highway Administration
FIC	Federal Information Centers
FMC	Federal Maritime Commission
FOIA	Freedom of Information Act
FRA	Federal Railroad Administration
FRS	Federal Reserve System
FSLIC	Federal Savings and Loan Insurance Corporation
FTC	Federal Trade Commission
GAO	General Accounting Office
GPO	Government Printing Office
GSA	General Services Administration
HHS	Department of Health and Human Services
HSA	Health Services Administration
HUD	Department of Housing and Urban Development
IAEA	International Atomic Energy Agency
ICC	Interstate Commerce Commission
IFC	International Finance Corporation
IMF	International Monetary Fund
INS	Immigration and Naturalization Service
INTERPOL	International Criminal Police Organization
IRS	Internal Revenue Service
JAG	Judge Advocate General
JCS	Joint Chiefs of Staff
JOBS	Job Opportunities in the Business Sector
LEAA	Law Enforcement Assistance Administration
MBDA	Minority Business Development Agency
MSHA	Mine Safety and Health Administration
MSPB	Merit Systems Protection Board
NARS	National Archives and Records Service
NASA	National Aeronautics and Space Administration
NATO	North Atlantic Treaty Organization
NBS	National Bureau of Standards
NCI	National Cancer Institute
NFIP	National Flood Insurance Program
NHTSA	National Highway Transportation Safety Administration
NLRB	National Labor Relations Board
NRC	Nuclear Regulatory Commission
NSC	National Security Council
NSF	National Science Foundation
NTSB	National Transportation Safety Board
OAS	Organization of American States
OCSE	Office of Child Support Enforcement
OFR	Office of the Federal Register
OJARS	Office of Justice Assistance, Research and Statistics
OMB	Office of Management and Budget
OOG	Office of Oil and Gas
OSHA	Occupational Safety and Health Administration

PAHO	Pan American Health Organization
PHS	Public Health Service
PRC	Postal Rate Commission
PTO	Patent and Trademark Office
RRB	Railroad Retirement Board
RSVP	Retired Senior Volunteer Program
SALT	Strategic Arms Limitation Talks
SBA	Small Business Administration
SCORE	Service Corps of Retired Executives
SCS	Soil Conservation Service
SEA	Science and Education Administration
SEATO	Southeast Asia Treaty Organization
SEC	Securities and Exchange Commission
SLS	Saint Lawrence Seaway Development Corporation
SSA	Social Security Administration
SSS	Selective Service System
TVA	Tennessee Valley Authority
UCPP	Urban Crime Prevention Program
UIS	Unemployment Insurance Service
UMTA	Urban Mass Transportation Administration
UN	United Nations
UNESCO	United Nations Educational, Scientific and Cultural Organization
UNICEF	United Nations Children's Fund
USDA	United States Department of Agriculture
USPS	United States Postal Service
VA	Veterans Administration
VISTA	Volunteers in Service to America
VOA	Voice of America
WHO	World Health Organization

Appendix E
Opinion & Sample Case Brief

OPINION FOR SAMPLE CASE BRIEF

Mills v. Wyman

Supreme Judicial Court of Massachusetts, 1825.
3 Pick. 207.

This was an action of assumpsit brought to recover a compensation for the board, nursing, etc. of Levi Wyman, son of the defendant, from the 5th to the 20th of February, 1821. The plaintiff then lived at Hartford, in Connecticut; the defendant at Shrewsbury, in this state. Levi Wyman, at the time when the services were rendered, was about 25 years of age, and had long ceased to be a member of his father's family. He was on his return from a voyage at sea, and being suddenly taken sick at Hartford, and being poor and in distress, was relieved by the plaintiff in the manner and to the extent above stated. On the 24th of February, after all the expenses had been incurred, the defendant wrote a letter to the plaintiff, promising to pay him such expenses. There was no consideration for this promise, except what grew out of the relation which subsisted between Levi Wyman and the defendant, and Howe, J., before whom the case was tried in the Court of Common Pleas, thinking this not sufficient to support the action, directed a nonsuit. To this direction the plaintiff filed exceptions.

PARKER, C.J. General rules of law established for the protection and security of honest and fair-minded men, who may inconsiderately make promises without any equivalent, will sometimes screen men of a different character from engagements which they are bound *in foro conscientiae* to perform. This is a defect inherent in all human systems of legislation. The rule that a mere verbal promise, without any consideration, cannot be enforced by action, is universal in its application, and cannot be departed from to suit particular cases in which a refusal to perform such a promise may be disgraceful.

The promise declared on in this case appears to have been made without any legal consideration. The kindness and services towards the sick son of the defendant were not bestowed at his request. The son was in no respect under the care of the defendant. He was twenty-five years old, and had long left his father's family. On his return from a foreign country, he fell sick among strangers, and the plaintiff acted the part of the good Samaritan, giving him shelter and comfort until he died. The defendant, his father, on being informed of this event, influenced by a transient feeling of gratitude, promised in writing to pay the plaintiff for the expenses he had incurred. But he has determined to break this promise, and is willing to have his case appear on record as a strong example of particular injustice sometimes necessarily resulting from the operation of general rules.

It is said a moral obligation is a sufficient consideration to support an express promise; and some authorities lay down the rule thus broadly; but upon examination of the cases we are satisfied that the universality of the rule cannot be supported, and that there must have been some pre-existing obligation, which has become inoperative by positive law, to form a basis for an effective promise. The cases of debts barred by the statute of limitations, of debts incurred by infants, of debts of bankrupts, are generally put for illustration of the rule. Express promises founded on such pre-existing equitable obligations may be enforced; there is a good consideration for them; they merely remove an impediment created by law to the recovery of debts honestly due, but which public policy protects the debtors from being compelled to pay. In all these cases there was originally a *quid pro quo*, and according to the principles of natural justice the party receiving ought to pay; but the legislature has said he shall not be coerced; then comes the promise to pay the debt that is barred, the promise of the man to pay the debt of the infant, of the discharged bankrupt to restore to his creditor what by the law he had lost. In all these cases there is a moral obligation founded upon an antecedent valuable consideration. These promises, therefore, have a sound legal basis. They are not promises to pay something for nothing; not naked pacts, but the voluntary revival or creation of obligatons which before existed in natural law, but which had been dispensed with, not for the benefit of the party obliged solely, but principally for the public convenience. If moral obligation, in its fullest sense, is a good substratum for an express promise, it is not easy to perceive why it is not equally good to support an implied promise. What a man ought to do, generally he ought to be made to do whether he promise or refuse. But the law of society has left most of such obligations to the interior forum, as the tribunal of conscience has been aptly called. . . .

Without doubt there are great interests of society which justify withholding the coercive arm of the law from these duties of imperfect obligation, as they are called; imperfect, not because they are less binding upon the conscience than those which are called perfect, but because the wisdom of the social law does not impose sanctions upon them.

A deliberate promise in writing, made freely and without any mistake, one which may lead the party to whom it is made into contracts and expenses, cannot be broken without a violation of moral duty. But if there was nothing, paid or promised for it, the law, perhaps wisely, leaves the execution of it to the conscience of him who makes it. It is only when the party making the promise gains something, or he to whom it is made loses something, that the law gives the promise validity. And in the case of the promise of the adult to pay the debt of the infant, or the debtor discharged by the statute of limitations or bankruptcy, the principle is preserved by looking back to the origin of that transaction, where an equivalent is to be found. . . .

For the foregoing reasons we are all of opinion that the nonsuit directed by the Court of Common Pleas was right, and that judgment be entered thereon for costs for the defendant.

SAMPLE CASE BRIEF

Mills v. Wyman
(Mass. 1825)

Facts:	P voluntarily nursed and cared for D's adult son, who was ill and destitute, until son's death. When D found out, he sent P a letter promising to pay expenses; but later changed his mind. P sues in assumpsit.
Trial Ct:	Judgment for D (nonsuit against P). No consideration given for D's promise to pay.
Issue:	Is moral obligation enough to render promise enforceable?
R:	No. Judgment affirmed.
Reason:	If courts were to enforce purely moral obligations, they would be called on to force people to do all sorts of things they "ought" to do, whether they had promised (as here) or not. Indeed, a promise might be implied in every case from the fact that it "ought" to be done. Distinguish promises to pay valid debt now barred by statute of limitations, infancy or bankruptcy. ***Preexisting legal*** obligation in such cases. New promise merely removes bar to enforcement. Also distinguish cases where promise caused promisee to rely to his detriment (n/a here because promise made ***after*** services rendered).

Appendix F
Common Legal Abbreviations/Law School Shorthand

acq.	acquiescing
adm'r	administrator
a.k.a., a/k/a	also known as
aff'd	affirmed
aff'g	affirming
A.L.J.	administrative law judge
amend.	amendment
art.	article
ass'n	association
BFP	bona fide purchaser
B.T.A.	Board of Tax Appeals
cert.	certiorari
ch.	chapter
cir.	circuit
C.J.	chief justice
C/L	common law
comm'n	commission
comm'r	commissioner
Cong.	Congress
Const.	Constitution
corp.	corporation
ct.	court
D, △	defendant
d.b.a., d/b/a	doing business as
dep't	department
dist.	district
e.g.	for example
Eq.	equity
evid.	evidence
ex'r	executor
fed.	federal
fed'n	federation
gov't	government
guar.	guaranty
H	husband
HDC	holder in due course
H.R.	House of Representatives
i.e.	that is
ins.	insurance
int'l	international
I.R.C.	Internal Revenue Code

J.	judge, justice
JJ.	judges, justices
JNOV	judgment notwithstanding the verdict
juv.	juvenile
K	contract
ltd.	limited
mfg.	manufacturing
mfr.	manufacturer
mgmt.	management
mkt.	market
mun.	municipal
n/a	not applicable
nat'l	national
negl.	negligence
n.k.a., n/k/a	now known as
P, π	plaintiff
P.L.	Public Law
R.	rule
RAP	Rule Against Perpetuities
RE	real estate
ref	referee
reh'g	rehearing
rem'd	remanded
rem'g	remanding
rev'd	reversed
rev'g	reversing
R.R.	railroad
Ry.	railway
S. Ct.	U.S. Supreme Court
S/F	Statute of Frauds
S/L	statute of limitations
S & L	savings & loan association
soc'y	society
sup. ct.	state supreme court
super. ct.	superior court
T.C.	Tax Court
UCC	Uniform Commercial Code
UPA	Uniform Partnership Act
UPC	Uniform Probate Code
U.S.C.	United States Code
v.	versus
W	wife

Appendix G
Common Latin & French Terms in Law

ab initio—from the beginning; from the first act
actus reus—a guilty mind
ad valorem—according to value
a fortiori—with stronger reason; much more
amicus curiae—friend of the court
a priori—from what goes before; from the cause to the effect
arguendo—in arguing

bona fide—in good faith

causa mortis—in contemplation of approaching death
caveat emptor—let the buyer beware
certiorari—to be informed of
contra—against; on the contrary
corpus delicti—the body of a crime
cy pres—as near as possible

de facto—in fact; actually
de jure—of right; lawful
de minimus—of small things; trifles
de novo—anew; a second time
dicta—statements, remarks. Abbreviated form of obiter dictum, "a remark by the way."

en banc—in the bench; full bench
ex parte—by or for one party
ex post facto—after the fact
ex rel.—abbreviation of ex relatione: upon relation or information

forum non conveniens—not convenient forum

guardian ad litem—guardian for suit (of incompetent or infant)

habeas corpus—you have the body

in camera—in chambers; in private
in forma pauperis—in the manner of a pauper
infra—below; within; during
in loco parentis—in place of a parent
in pari delicto—in equal fault
in pari materia—upon the same subject or matter
in personam—against the person
in re—in the affair
in rem—against the thing
inter alia—among other things
inter partes—between parties
inter vivos—between the living
ipso facto—by the fact itself

jus—law; right

lex loci—law of the place

malum in se—a wrong in itself
malum prohibitum—a wrong prohibited
mandamus—we command
mens rea—a guilty mind
modus operandi—method of operating (M.O.)

nexus—a connection to
nisi prius—courts of first impression
non obstante verdicto—notwithstanding the verdict
nunc pro tunc—now for then

pendente lite—pending the suit
per capita—by the head
per curiam—by the court
per se—by itself
per stirpes—by representation
prima facie—at first sight; on the face of it
profit á prendre—right of common
pro se—for himself
pro tanto—for so much; as far as it goes
pur autre vie—during the life of another

quantum meruit—as much as he deserves
quasi—as if; almost as it were
quid pro quo—something for something

res gestae—things done
res ipsa loquitur—the thing speaks for itself
res judicata—a thing settled by judgment
respondeat superior—let the master answer

stare decisis—to abide by decided cases
supra—above; upon

ultra vires—acts beyond the scope of powers

voir dire—to speak the truth

gilbert
LAW SUMMARIES

Current Price List (Prices subject to change without notice)

TITLE	AUTHOR/	PRICE
Administrative Law	Asimow	$10.95
Agency and Partnership	Conviser	9.95
Antitrust	Jorde & Mnookin	9.95
Business Law	Upp	9.95
Calif. Bar Perf. Test Skills	Honisberg	10.95
Civil Procedure	Carrington & Hazard	12.95
Commercial Paper	Whaley	9.95
Community Property	Reppy	9.95
Conflict of Laws	Kay	10.95
Constitutional Law	Choper	14.95
Contracts	Eisenberg	12.95
Corporations	Choper & Eisenberg	11.95
Criminal Law	Dix	10.95
Criminal Procedure	Marcus & Whitebread	10.50
Estate and Gift	McCord	10.95
Evidence	Kaplan & Waltz	12.95
Future Interests	Dukeminier	9.95
Income Tax 1 (Individual)	Asimow	12.95
Income Tax 2 (Corporate)	Asimow	9.95
Labor Law	Gelhaus & Oldham	10.95
Legal Ethics	Morgan	10.95
Legal Research	Honigsberg	9.95
Multistate	Conviser	9.95
Personal Property		6.95
Property	Dukeminier	14.95
Remedies	Bauman & York	10.95
Sales		9.95
Secured Transactions	Whaley	9.50
Securities Regulation	Barber	11.95
Torts	Franklin	12.95
Trusts	Halback, Jr.	10.95
Wills		8.50